DAVID E. LAVIN   DAVID HYLLEGARD

Changing the Odds

Open Admissions and the Life Chances
of the Disadvantaged

Yale University Press   New Haven and London

Designed by Sonia L. Scanlon.

Set in Bembo type by Keystone Typesetting, Inc.

Printed in the United States of America by Vail-Ballou Press,
Binghamton, New York.

Lavin, David E.

    Changing the odds : open admissions and the life
chances of the disadvantaged / David E. Lavin, David
Hyllegard.

       p. cm.

    Includes bibliographical references (p.   ) and index.

    ISBN 0-300-06328-8 (cloth : alk. paper)

      1. City University of New York—Open admission—
Case studies.   I. Hyllegard, David.   II. Title.

LD3835.L375   1996   95-31948

378.1—dc208   CIP

A catalogue record for this book is available from the British
Library.

The paper in this book meets the guidelines for permanence
and durability of the Committee on Production Guidelines
for Book Longevity of the Council on Library Resources.

10 9 8 7 6 5 4 3 2 1

CONTENTS

Many social programs designed to promote equity in American society were put in place during the 1960s and early 1970s. In colleges and universities, one of the most important efforts took place at the City University of New York (CUNY), which initiated an open-admissions policy in fall 1970. Because it aimed to create an unusually high level of educational opportunity, especially for low-income minority youth, and because of the sheer size of the university—it is the third-largest university system in the United States and the nation's largest urban institution—open admissions can be thought of as higher education's most ambitious effort to improve life chances among disadvantaged students.

A broad attack on liberal programs has swept the nation in the 1990s. CUNY's policy, controversial from its beginning, has been a prominent target. Indeed, criticism of open admissions has greatly intensified. According to opponents, the policy has so degraded academic standards that CUNY's diplomas have lost their value, both in the job market and as passports for admission to postgraduate study. Open admissions is frequently seen as yet another failed entitlement program, attempting to educate the ineducable and, in the process, wasting huge amounts of public funds.

Using a data set that contains extensive information on students' achievements—covering the period from high school through college entry to a point more than a decade later—this book examines many of the most significant long-term results and consequences of the open-admissions policy. It assesses students' undergraduate educational attainments and also their postgraduate accomplishments. It describes how educational achievements influenced men's and women's occupational success, including the amount of money they made and whether the jobs they held provided challenging and interesting work. It allows us to assess the difference the program made for the many minority students who otherwise would not have had a chance for college. Our analyses provide estimates of the contribution that open admissions made to the larger economy of New York City. An examination of these outcomes provides a basis for understanding what actually happened under open admissions.

We are indebted to a number of organizations and individuals whose support enabled us to complete this work. After completing initial studies of the first five years (1970–75) of the open-admissions program (reported in a number of publications, including Lavin, Alba, and Silberstein, *Right Versus Privilege: The Open Admissions Experiment at the City University of New York,* 1981), we undertook the follow-up study reported in this volume. Substantial support was provided by a grant to Lavin from the Spencer Foundation. A dissertation fellowship award to Hyllegard from the Spencer Foundation also supported his participation in the research and allowed him to complete his dissertation, a part of which appears as Chapter 5. A grant from the Ford Foundation greatly facilitated the later stages of our data analyses.

A large number of individuals helped us, often in ways that were critical to the project's completion. CUNY Deputy Chancellor Larry Mucciolo facilitated the work in a number of respects, especially by providing Lavin with released time from teaching duties. Barry Kaufman, Jim Murtha, and Audrey Blumberg, successive directors of CUNY's Office of Institutional Research, provided essential technical and physical support that sustained the study. Murtha deserves special thanks for his enthusiastic participation in the intellectual development of the project. We benefited from many stimulating discussions with him about educational and labor-market attainments. Blumberg's concern for our work went beyond her official responsibilities. She went out of her way to provide a supportive environment for our work, and she offered helpful suggestions for some of the chapters in the volume.

Fran Barrett did superb work in integrating a variety of files into one comprehensive data set that we used for most of our analyses. A substantial amount of programming work for some of our earlier research papers was done by the late Nina Fortin. Before she lost a courageous five-year battle with cancer, she was planning to become the data manager for the project and to use the data set for a dissertation on gender aspects of the open-admissions policy. Hazon Na did statistical programming in connection with our effort to address response bias in the data.

Other friends and colleagues provided good advice, and sometimes emotional support when that was needed. Mary Clare Lennon, our friend and the statistical consultant to the project, provided especially valuable counsel in helping us set up some of our most important statistical analyses. As much as she helped, her suggestions were not always followed, and she is not responsible for any remaining technical shortcomings in our work. Richard Alba helped us develop a strategy to address sampling and response bias in our data; we benefited also from his commentary on several chapters. Frank Furstenberg gave us a number of useful comments on Chapter 6. Nava Lerer provided technical assistance on Chapter 9. Elliot Weininger also gave helpful suggestions on portions of the manuscript.

We benefited from discussions with Cathy Aison, Kevin Dougherty, Jerry Karabel, Molly McNees, Rolf and Mary Lea Meyersohn, David Crook, and Paul Attewell. On the home stretch of the project, Catherine Kohler Riessman gave insightful support that improved the quality of the manuscript. We appreciate the patience of Gladys Topkis, our editor at Yale University Press, in waiting so long for the manuscript. Her strategic suggestions for revision helped to improve its quality. We thank Dan Heaton, whose editing made the manuscript more readable.

Changing the Odds

CHAPTER ONE

Perspectives on Open–Access Higher Education

As we approach the end of the century, uncertainty clouds the direction and form of opportunity policies for higher education in the United States. These policies have their roots in a national preoccupation with equality of opportunity that began to take shape at midcentury. Education was one of the most volatile topics of debate during the struggle to broaden opportunity for the members of disadvantaged minority groups. The Supreme Court desegregation decision of 1954 was a fundamental step toward reducing inequalities in schooling. By the early 1960s the focus on higher education had become sharper, as the federal government intervened in the South to begin the racial integration of universities. Throughout the 1960s and during the early 1970s, a variety of public and private efforts were undertaken to lower the barriers to college. Although the specific influence of individual policies cannot be precisely gauged, federal and state grant and loan programs, proliferation of postsecondary institutions, and special admissions programs targeted to minorities all stimulated the increase of enrollment—especially minority enrollment—in higher education. Indeed, the racial gap in the college enrollment of high school graduates practically disappeared: the rate of college enrollment by black graduates, which was 77 percent of the white rate in 1960, reached 98 percent of that rate by 1975 (U.S. Bureau of the Census 1987a, table 233), though, to be sure, this trend was less impressive than it appears because the high school graduation rate of blacks remained below that of whites.

In the latter half of the 1970s, these gains began to erode, and by 1985 the rate of college enrollment for black high school graduates had fallen back to 76 percent of the white rate—just where it had been in 1960 (U.S. Bureau of the Census 1987a, table 233). Although the relative weights of different factors influencing the resurgent gap in college participation are uncertain, one source undoubtedly was the decline in federal support for higher education under the Reagan administration. Part of the decline in black enrollment can be attributed to cuts in student financial aid and to shifts in the types of aid available—away from grants and toward loans. Presumably these changes in financial aid disproportionately affected minorities, who were far more likely than whites to come from low-income families (College Board 1985).[1]

Coincident with federal reductions in support for higher education was a change in the climate of debate about educational policy. Through the 1960s and early 1970s, a liberal perspective, based on a belief that educational attainment has a major influence on an individual's life chances, had been ascendant. This belief was the foundation of various policy efforts to narrow inequality of educational opportunity. After the mid-1970s, a conservative reaction to liberal programs gathered momentum. A spate of reform proposals blamed higher education for an alleged decline in academic standards and for encouraging a pluralism that led to "cultural dilution" of college curricula.[2] Moreover, higher education was sometimes perceived as responsible, at least in part, for diminishing educational quality at lower levels of schooling. In one of the most important reports, the National Commission on Excellence in Education (1983) claimed that the economic position of the United States was at risk because its educational institutions were "being engulfed by a rising tide of mediocrity that threatens our very future as a Nation." Asserting that educational decline was a source of U.S. global economic decline, the report's authors warned that the nation had, in effect, "been committing an act of unthinking, unilateral educational disarmament." Among its many recommendations for reform, the commission called for more stringent requirements for both high school graduation and admission to four-year colleges and universities. In response to the perception of a decline in standards, some states—Florida, for example—instituted standardized testing procedures in an

[1]Possibly in reaction to the aid cuts, minority high school graduates, as Hauser (1988) has suggested, may have increased their rates of enlistment in military service as a means of acquiring entitlements for higher education, thus contributing to the decline in minority enrollments.

[2]An analysis of the major proposals appears in Dougherty and Hammack (1990a, chapter 10). See also a discussion by Hammack (1985). A leading example of the conservative attack on higher education is Bloom (1987), probably the best-selling book about education ever written by an academician. Critics claimed that higher education had abandoned the traditional curriculum and called for a renewed commitment to the idea that "the core of the American college curriculum—its heart and soul—should be the civilization of the West" (Bennett 1984, 30). This camp demanded a focus on works by classical philosophers, European writers, American literature and historical documents, which "virtually define the development of the Western mind" (Bennett 1984, 10). For a good analysis of the pleas for a renewed commitment to the teaching of the "canon," see Aronowitz and Giroux (1988).

effort to ensure that college students were meeting minimum criteria of academic competence.[3] The conservative trend may have disproportionately discouraged college enrollment and depressed educational attainment among minority students, who were more likely than whites to have serious weaknesses in their high school academic preparation.

Neither the climate of debate nor the changes in policy were informed by any systematic evidence about the results of higher education opportunity programs begun in the 1960s and early 1970s. Indeed, when the conservative reaction was gaining ascendancy, the results of these programs were not in. Indeed, one detailed review of the major reform proposals concluded that they were based on weak arguments and poor data (Stedman and Smith 1983); the authors asserted as well that the reformist agenda exhibited a shift away from concern for equal educational opportunity. Though data cannot definitively resolve the policy disputes between liberals and conservatives, they can help to clarify some of the issues in the debate about "equity versus excellence." Given the changing policies and shifts in value priorities over the past three decades, this seems an appropriate time to take stock of college access policies.

One way to assess equity issues in higher education is to examine an institution that made an unusual effort to create educational opportunity. We shall do this for the seventeen-campus, two hundred thousand–student system of the City University of New York (CUNY), the nation's third-largest higher education system and its largest urban university. In 1970 CUNY initiated its open-admissions policy, arguably the nation's most ambitious attempt to expand college access for minorities.

Although the program was limited to a single university system, its outcomes have more general implications for higher education policy. The university is located in a city that contains large concentrations of lower-class blacks and Hispanics, two of the most disadvantaged minority groups in the nation, and typically the main foci of opportunity programs in higher education. Moreover, the CUNY open-admissions policy was designed to create more educational opportunity than other open-access models, and thus it may be regarded empirically as a limiting case from among a range of possible opportunity programs: its results provide an indication of the outcomes possible under the most favorable conditions.

[3]Minimum competency assessment at different educational levels is reviewed in Dougherty and Hammack (1990a, chapter 10).

The City University of New York and Its Open-Admissions Program

The open-admissions policy at CUNY evolved from a complex historical context. The university has its origins in the founding in 1847 of the City College of New York (CCNY), the best-known school in today's multi-campus system of nine four-year (senior) colleges and eight two-year community colleges. Founded through a public referendum, CCNY had a populist mission from the outset. In the words of its first head, Horace Webster, at the inaugural ceremonies, "The experiment is to be tried, whether the highest education can be given to the masses; whether the children of the whole people can be educated; and whether an institution of learning, of the highest grade, can be successfully controlled by the popular will, not by the privileged few, but by the privileged many" (Rudy 1949, 29).

These words were more rhetoric than reality in the college's early years, for the student body consisted mainly of the sons of prosperous merchants and professionals. But by the end of the nineteenth century and the beginning of the twentieth, the college began to play a significant role in the lives of impoverished immigrants, especially Jewish families arriving from eastern Europe. In the 1930s CCNY students were regarded as among the most able in the nation, and the college came to be known as the "proletarian Harvard." Its graduates' achievements in diverse walks of life contributed to a faith in the college as a path out of poverty.

Partly as a result of growing demand, new institutions were added to the municipal college system. Hunter College had been founded in 1870 as a teacher-training school for women, and in the 1920s and 1930s three more four-year schools were established in Brooklyn, Queens, and the Bronx.[4] In spite of these expansions, the colleges could not accommodate all who wanted to attend, especially after World War II. Even the addition of three community colleges in the 1950s failed to provide enough seats.

Although the increasing demand for college was not based on a precise understanding of the stunning economic changes in the United States and especially in New York since the turn of the century, rising educational aspirations were no doubt partly attuned to economic aspirations. Broadly speaking, the transition from an agricultural to an industrial system that began in the 1800s was essentially completed by the first half of this century, and a

[4]In 1917 a branch of CCNY was established in Brooklyn. An independent Brooklyn College was founded in 1930. A branch of Hunter College was established in the Bronx in 1929; it became Herbert H. Lehman College in 1968. Queens College opened its doors in 1937.

new transition was gaining momentum: a shift from a goods-producing economy to a service-rendering one, typically referred to as the emergence of postindustrial society.

Trends in the American occupational profile clearly reflect these developments. The decline in agricultural employment has been spectacular: in 1900 more than a third of all workers were in farming; by midcentury only about 10 percent were so employed, and by the 1980s fewer than four in one hundred were.[5] Decline is also apparent within the lower levels of the blue-collar work force: in 1900 about one in eight workers was an unskilled laborer; by midcentury the figure was one in fifteen. Since midcentury the proportion of semiskilled workers has also fallen, probably as a consequence of the vulnerability of this tier of the labor force to automated production (Featherman and Hauser 1978, chapter 2). Shrinkage in the agricultural and blue-collar sectors of the labor force has been offset by explosive growth in the share of jobs in the white-collar sector: between 1900 and the 1980s, clerical and sales jobs more than tripled (from 7.5 percent to 25 percent), while the share of the top tier of the white-collar category—professional, technical, and managerial workers—expanded from about 10 percent to almost 30 percent of the work force.[6]

As Bell (1973) and others (Featherman and Hauser 1978) have suggested, perhaps the fundamental characteristic of this transformed economy is its implied demand for a college-educated work force. Although scholars may disagree about the mechanisms that link education and the economy and about whether economic changes have brought about an overall upgrade in the skill levels of occupations, educational requirements have risen coincident with change in the occupational structure.[7] Rumberger (1981), for example,

[5]These figures were compiled from U.S. Bureau of the Census (1975, series D, 182–232, p. 139) and U.S. Bureau of the Census (1983a; no. 693, p. 417).

[6]Undoubtedly the proportion of managers and officials has grown even more than these figures indicate, because proprietors, who also are included in this category, have been a shrinking part of the work force.

[7]Broadly speaking, "functionalists" may be contrasted with a variety of critical theorists regarding the relation between education and the economy. The former, exemplified by Bell (1973), Featherman and Hauser (1978), Treiman (1970), and Parsons (1959), hold that the transition from industrial to postindustrial society leads to growth in more complex jobs that require a more highly educated population. Others, like Randall Collins (1979), disagree that educational requirements have increased because work has become more complicated. Some, most notably Braverman (1974), have argued that technology has played a key role in deskilling of

estimates that based on changes in the skill levels of jobs between 1940 and 1970, the percentage requiring four or more years of college increased from 8 to 22 percent, while those requiring less than a high school degree declined from 29 percent to 15 percent.

The national trend from goods production to service has been even more evident in New York. After World War II the city's manufacturing sector began a sharp decline. Accounting for thirty percent of jobs in 1950, manufacturing provided only 20 percent in 1970 and little more than 10 percent by the mid-1980s (Mollenkopf 1988).[8] By contrast, the service sector—including education, the arts and culture, business and financial services, government, health, and social welfare—experienced enormous growth. In 1950 these services accounted for a third of all jobs in the city; by 1970 they provided almost half the jobs. In the 1980s nearly 60 percent of the city's workers were employed in such positions. The pace of change in New York makes it a leading example of a postindustrial city.[9]

These changes in the New York labor market were associated with rising educational requirements for entry-level jobs. Partly because the demand for seats in the city's municipal colleges outstripped available places during the 1950s, entrance requirements rose throughout that decade. Indeed, between 1952 and 1961 the number of new admissions to baccalaureate programs actually declined from 8,859, or 17 percent of high school graduates in the city, to 8,563, or 13 percent (Holy 1962, 91). Because admission to the municipal colleges was becoming more difficult as demand was increasing, questions were being raised about the appropriateness of such a policy in a publicly supported university (Holy 1962, 68–69, 73, 127–28).

In the 1960s requirements stiffened even further: a high school average in the mid- to upper 80s was generally required for admission to CUNY's four-

---

jobs. Whatever the effects of economic change on the quality of work, the proportion of high-status jobs has risen, and so have educational requirements. For a broad review of the literature on this debate, see Spenner (1985).

[8]This trend reflects a decline not only in manufacturing's relative share of the labor market but also in the absolute number of jobs in the sector.

[9]The city's place at the forefront of the national trend is based upon a comparison of New York data (Mollenkopf 1988, table 9.1, p. 226; table 9.2, p. 228) with national data (Singelmann 1978, table A.1, pp. 145–46). National figures are calculated from the sum of percentages employed in production, social, and personal services. New York figures are calculated from the sum of the percentages employed in financial and related services and in government. From a reading of Singelmann, the New York categories appear to match the national ones.

year colleges, and some years an average in the 90s was needed at certain schools. Gaining a seat at many of these institutions was virtually as difficult as in selective private colleges. Even for admission to a community college, students needed at least a 75 average.

The combination of a changing labor market and the growing selectivity of New York's public colleges coincided with a major demographic transition that began in New York during the 1950s. In that decade nearly seven hundred thousand blacks and Hispanics came to New York City, in effect replacing a similar number of whites who left during that time in the postwar exodus to the suburbs.[10] The newcomers typically had little education and few job skills. Unlike earlier periods when much work was available for immigrants with few skills, the changing labor market provided fewer employment opportunities for the new arrivals. As a result they were often unemployed or underemployed, and when they found work it was typically in positions at the bottom rungs of the occupational ladder. Welfare rolls swelled accordingly.

Adding to the difficulties of blacks and Hispanics was their severe disadvantage in the public education system of the city. They typically attended segregated schools where grades generally were quite low; they were much more likely than whites to attend vocational high schools or to be placed in nonacademic tracks within general high schools. Consequently, they were far less likely than white students to receive college preparatory diplomas. These factors limited the number who could qualify for traditional college programs. By the time minority students finished high school, they were poorly positioned in the increasingly rigorous competition for places in the City University. Limited access to college at a time when educational requirements of the labor market were rising foretold a gloomy outlook for life chances in New York's minority communities.

A look at the historical experience of various groups in the university suggests that by the 1960s CUNY was serving different groups in very unequal ways. Around the turn of the century, the student body had been composed largely of the sons and daughters of Jewish immigrants of eastern European origin. They remained the numerically dominant group through the first half of the century. After the Second World War enrollments became

[10]In that decade about 90 percent of the Hispanic immigrants were from Puerto Rico. The estimates of the numbers of blacks and Puerto Ricans are made from figures provided by Glazer and Moynihan (1970, pp. 25–29, 91–94, and table 3).

ethnically more diverse in some respects: students of Irish and Italian ancestry in particular began to attend the university in increasing numbers, and by the late 1960s members of these ethnic groups accounted for a third of entering classes.[11] But what the university had done for these earlier groups arriving from Europe it had failed to do for the new arrivals from the American South and from the Caribbean. Because of the disadvantages to which they were subject in the city's public education system, the latter were largely excluded from CUNY's senior colleges and underrepresented at the two-year level.

Framed by the national preoccupation of the 1960s with issues of equal opportunity in American society, the question of minority access to CUNY grew in importance in that decade. One of the driving forces was the increasing militancy of the civil rights movement. Across the country, civil disobedience, strident demonstrations, and riots had riveted national attention on various issues of racial inequality. A developing sense of urgency about equal opportunity was expressed in the enactment of such "great society" programs as Head Start and the "war on poverty." These programs reflected a belief by the liberal establishment that social policy could and should be used to advance equity.

New York City echoed the tenor of the times, both in the racial tensions that arose with minority efforts to gain greater control over the public schools in their communities, and in efforts to establish a civilian review board to investigate complaints of police brutality toward minority individuals.[12] It was in this broad context that the question of minority representation at CUNY took center stage.

Movement toward a policy of open admissions developed on two fronts.[13] One was institutional. In 1963 Albert H. Bowker left his post as dean of the

---

[11]Irish and Italian Catholics had earlier been less likely to attend the municipal colleges in part because the church discouraged attendance at secular institutions. Moreover, numerous Catholic colleges in the New York metropolitan area attracted a large share of Catholic youth. A more detailed discussion of this topic may be found in Lavin et al. (1981, chapter 1). The rise in the enrollment of these groups in CUNY is consistent with their generally increased educational attainment, especially among the generations that completed their education after World War II. A more extensive consideration of this point is given in Alba (1990, chapter 1). See also Steinberg (1974).

[12]Disputes over school decentralization and a civilian review board are discussed in Berube and Gittell (1969) and Glazer and Moynihan (1970).

[13]A more detailed description of events leading to the open admissions initiative may be seen in chapter 1, Lavin et al. (1981).

Stanford University graduate school to become chancellor of the CUNY system.[14] Paradoxically, one of the main reasons that the university's trustees had hired Bowker was to spur the development of a centralized program of doctoral studies in all of the major academic areas, which he accomplished. But soon after his arrival, he was struck by CUNY's unresponsiveness to the burgeoning college-age population and to the demographic changes in the city. He perceived that political support for the university might erode if it maintained its highly selective admissions policies. He believed that the long-term interests of CUNY required a major expansion of access—one that involved substantial revision of admissions standards.

The transition from the exclusive admissions practices of the early 1960s to the open-admissions policy of 1970 began modestly. In an initial effort in 1964 to increase minority enrollment, Bowker obtained funds from the state to set up in the community colleges an experimental program known as College Discovery. Two years later he gained state support for a special minority admissions program in the four-year colleges. Known by the acronym SEEK (Search for Education, Elevation and Knowledge), it began in fall 1966 and immediately became the major avenue of minority entry to CUNY's senior colleges.

The establishment of these programs added momentum to the drive for broader access to the university. By 1968, Bowker had persuaded the CUNY trustees to approve a 100 percent admissions plan, beginning in 1975. To meet the broad demand for college and to provide further opportunity for minority students, a stratified admissions scheme was proposed in the university's 1968 master plan:

1. the top 25 percent of high school graduates would be offered admission to a senior college baccalaureate program;

2. the top two-thirds of graduates would qualify for community colleges (the top 50 percent of this group would be eligible for transfer programs, while the rest would qualify for career programs);

3. about 6 percent would be admitted to senior colleges through the SEEK program—and thus outside of the regular admissions proce-

---

[14]Until 1961 the municipal colleges were semiautonomous entities that were related to one another through their ties to a New York City Board of Higher Education. In 1961 they were established as a more closely linked set of institutions that were designated the City University of New York. The chancellorship was established at the same time to formulate and coordinate university-wide academic and fiscal policies.

dure—and about 4 percent would be admitted to community colleges via the College Discovery program;

4. all others could enroll in educational skills centers, which would provide job-oriented technical training. These centers also would provide "college adapter" courses designed to identify students with potential for community college–career programs (Board of Higher Education 1968).

Though highly stratified, this plan represented a significant step forward in broadening access to the university. In light of what was coming, however, it seemed quite modest. Indeed, Bowker's foreword to the master plan was prophetic: "Change, however well anticipated, has a way of making the most forward looking plans obsolete. This plan is not likely to be an exception" (Board of Higher Education 1968, vii).

CUNY proposals in this period were sometimes couched in rhetoric about proportions of minority students in the university and whether their representation was in line with their proportions among high school graduates in the city. Such rhetoric helped to crystallize a growing concern among whites, particularly those who formed the traditional Jewish constituency of CUNY: during a period when admission was highly selective, were places being allocated to students who did not meet traditional criteria—at the expense of other qualified students? References to "proportion" in trustee meetings irritated a particularly sensitive nerve in the Jewish community: the noxious concept of the quota, which had once been used against them by private colleges (Steinberg 1974; Wechsler 1977).

At the same time that whites were worried that merit in the admissions process was being eroded by a competing principle of quotas—and hence, that some seats of deserving students would be taken by other less academically able ones—minorities were increasingly dissatisfied, feeling that not enough was being done to advance educational opportunity. Their perception of the university was epitomized by City College, sitting high on a hill in the middle of Harlem, historically the most important and most famous of New York City's black communities. Black and Hispanic students had been criticizing the college on a variety of counts for not doing enough to expand minority enrollment. Even with the SEEK program, blacks and Hispanics in 1968 constituted only about 10 percent of the CCNY student body although they comprised close to a quarter of the New York City high school graduating class (City University of New York 1968–70). In February 1969 a minority student organization called upon the administration to alleviate "conditions that deny the very existence of the Black and Puerto Rican community" (*Observation Post* 1969). The students issued five demands and insisted that the CCNY president, Buell Gallagher, "utilize whatever means necessary" to meet them. In the confrontation to come, these demands formed the agenda for negotiations (*Observation Post* 1969):

1. a separate school of black and Puerto Rican studies;

2. a separate orientation program for black and Puerto Rican freshmen;

3. a voice for students in setting guidelines for the SEEK program, including the hiring and firing of personnel;

4. assurance that the racial composition of all entering classes would reflect the black and Puerto Rican population of the New York City high schools;

5. the requirement of black and Puerto Rican history and the Spanish language for all education majors.

President Gallagher met with the students, but no specific agreements were reached. The group then occupied a part of the administration building for several hours in an effort to demonstrate that it could shut down the college if it so chose (Penzer 1969).

A developing budget crisis at the university intruded upon events at CCNY. The university faced a substantial reduction in the budget for the following year, and Bowker stated that without more funding, there would be no freshman class in the fall. This served to galvanize various student and community groups into action, the most significant manifestation of which was a rally of thirteen thousand CUNY students at the state capitol in Albany in March. Although some progress was made on the budgetary crisis, minority students, apparently fearing that a dollar shortfall would result in "virtually no Black or Puerto Rican students in the University," called for a strike in support of the five demands that had been made earlier (*Campus* 1969). Shortly thereafter, some two hundred minority students, joined later by some whites, occupied campus buildings and announced that the "University of Harlem" would remain closed until the college administration met the five demands (Ackerman 1969).

The propriety of closing the college became an issue in the upcoming mayoral primary, in which John V. Lindsay sought renomination. His base of support included blacks, Puerto Ricans to a lesser extent, and a substantial number of high-status Jews and Protestants, along with a sprinkling of affluent Catholics. Lindsay supported the closing of the college and conciliatory efforts. His main rival, Mario Procaccino, a CCNY alumnus, attracted working-class and lower-middle-class Irish, Italians, and Jews who resided largely in the boroughs outside Manhattan. He and other politicians saw the shutting down of the college as "appeasement." The controversy reflected a larger issue in the city: whether Lindsay had done too much to help minorities, at the expense of whites from the working and lower-middle classes (Glazer and Moynihan 1970, xxvi–xxix).

Shortly thereafter, Procaccino and Mario Biaggi, a Bronx congressman representing a white working-class constituency, along with the militant Jewish Defense League, obtained show-cause orders against the college for shutting down and a court order that set a date for reopening. Congressman Adam Clayton Powell of Harlem urged the insurgents to defy the injunction. By early May the students did vacate the buildings, but matters then became chaotic, with daily incidents of violence that culminated in the burning of the auditorium in the college's main student center (*New York Times* 1969). Such incidents brought an end to the negotiations which had been taking place and Gallagher resigned.

Subsequently, negotiations resumed between the dissidents and the college administration, which now was headed by an acting president designated by the CUNY trustees. The fruit of these sessions was a proposal for what was in effect an ethnically based dual admissions plan, whereby 50 percent of the CCNY freshman class in fall 1970 would be drawn from poverty areas or designated ghetto high schools, while the other half would be selected under the traditional competitive admissions criteria, high school grades and Scholastic Aptitude Test scores (Board of Higher Education 1969a).

The proposal was sent to the college faculty senate for approval, but scathing public reaction preempted faculty discussion. All of the mayoral candidates attacked the proposal. Procaccino threatened to initiate legal action to prevent its implementation, claiming that it was "unfair and discriminatory" and would exclude "intelligent, qualified, and ambitious students" from CUNY (Fox 1969a; McNamara 1969). Mayor Lindsay, initially noncommittal, later asserted that "if this is a quota system, I am against it" (Fox 1969a; Greenspan 1969; McNamara 1969).

Eventually, the faculty senate voted to reject the dual admissions plan and recommended instead the admission over the next two semesters of a few hundred additional students from poverty areas, who were not to take the place of any students who qualified for admission under the competitive criteria (Fox 1969b, 1969c). But the senate, in sending this proposal to the university's Board of Higher Education, also stated that "a large disadvantaged segment of the City population, for social, economic and educational reasons, has been unable to receive these benefits [of higher education]. The most equitable way to attain this stated goal is by a system of 'open enrollment' financially supported by the City, State, and Federal Governments" (Faculty Senate 1969).

In June the spotlight shifted to Bowker and the CUNY trustees. Public hearings underscored the conflicts inherent in any plan that used ethnicity as a principle for admissions. The perceived conflict between merit and quotas seemed irreconcilable. Ultimately, a way out of the quandary was found in a proposal put forth by the powerful New York City Central Labor Council, a coalition of major unions. Representatives of this group argued that many members of white ethnic groups—particularly Catholics of Irish and Italian ancestry—would be shut out of any plan that gave special preference to minorities and imposed stringent admissions criteria for everyone else. The Labor Council proposed that the only proper plan was one that would guarantee admissions to all (Board of Higher Education 1969b). Only this idea seemed to put to rest the fear that increased representation of some groups would come at the expense of others. Both within and outside the university, a consensus seemed to form around the approach of letting everyone in.

By early July, Bowker and his staff had decided that an open-admissions program was the solution to the impasse over the expansion of access to the university and that the plan of 100 percent admissions by 1975 should be moved up to fall 1970. The proposal to guarantee to every graduate of a New York City high school a place in the university beginning in the fall of 1970 was approved by the trustees not only for City College but across all the colleges of the university (Board of Higher Education 1969c). In effect, Bowker's early drive for expanded access, which he promoted not only as a matter of equity but also as one of institutional self-interest, coalesced with the concerns voiced in the student uprising. Together, both institutional and student interests formed a mechanism for a huge expansion of the university.

The funding for this expansion was by no means assured at the time the open-admissions resolution was passed, but Bowker was ultimately able to obtain the support of Mayor Lindsay and—grudgingly—Governor Nelson Rockefeller (Gordon 1975).

The CUNY board's open-admissions decision left a major question unanswered: what should be the mechanism for allocating students to the various CUNY colleges? The process of hammering out an actual admissions model engendered further controversy. A special commission had been appointed and charged with the task of developing a set of admissions criteria. The members of the commission represented important constituencies of the university, including groups that were traditional beneficiaries of CUNY education as well as advocates for minority group aspirations. These groups had different conceptions of a proper admissions plan. A key issue was not merely access to the university but access to *senior colleges.* Minority members of the admissions commission perceived the four-year schools as far more valuable in the struggle to overcome disadvantaged status (University Commission on Admissions, 1969, 62):

> Less than fifty percent of Black and Puerto Rican students who enter high school graduate; the majority of the survivors fall in the bottom halves of their classes, with large numbers graduating with averages below seventy (70). What, one must ask, will be their earning capacities and ability to provide for their families twenty years hence, in competition with their white contemporaries who will have gone to the senior colleges and graduate schools? What will be their relative earning capacities even if they finish two-year career programs in community colleges and go on to become X-ray technicians and low-level managers in factories? In short, we see unending societal clash unless this vicious educational cycle is smashed. We propose to do this by giving *all* high school graduates a fair and equal chance to achieve a B.A. degree.

On the other side, traditional constituents of the university continued to be concerned that the effort to broaden access would undermine admissions criteria based on academic merit. Some feared that increased opportunity for minority students might come at the expense of seats for previously qualified students (Board of Higher Education 1969d). There was, in short, a perceived conflict between equity and excellence in the admissions process.

Ultimately, the university formulated an admissions model that addressed both concerns. The plan created two admissions pools, one for the senior colleges and the other for the two-year schools. Students who graduated from high school with at least an 80 average (in academic, college preparatory courses) *or* who ranked in the top 50 percent of their high school graduating class were guaranteed a place in a senior college if that was their preference (Board of Higher Education 1969e).[15] The two criteria combined a traditional admissions standard with one intended to provide greater access. The high school–average criterion meant that students who would have qualified for a senior college before open admissions would continue to do so; the primary aim of the class-rank criterion was to increase minority representation in the senior colleges by creating a pathway for students from ghetto high schools where averages tended to be low. Students who fell short of the senior college criteria were placed in the community college pool.[16]

In September 1970 a freshman class of almost 35,000 students took their seats at CUNY—a 75 percent increase over the previous year's entering class. The open-admissions era began under a glare of media publicity, both national and local. That the national spotlight focused on CUNY may seem curious, for open-access higher education is hardly a new idea in American higher education. Indeed, its roots go back to the middle of the nineteenth century, when the land-grant colleges were established under the first Morrill Act of 1862. These colleges, most located in the Midwest, offered admission to all high school graduates; in the 1930s the general college of the University of Minnesota was open to any student with a high school diploma (Wechsler 1977, 241–42). After World War II, California had established its so-called differential access version of open admissions, wherein any high school graduate could attend one of the levels of the state's public higher education system.

[15]High school average and class rank were calculated for all applicants, regardless of the type of high school they attended. Among graduates of vocational high schools or among those from nonacademic tracks in comprehensive schools, for example, average and rank were based just on the academic courses taken. In effect, CUNY's program made the type of high school or curriculum track irrelevant to the admissions process.

[16]In spite of what its name seems to imply, the open-admissions policy did not guarantee that every applicant could attend the college he or she preferred. Within the two pools, admission to a particular college was competitive. If there were more students who picked a certain college than there were places available at that school, the available seats went to those with the higher averages. Those who were not admitted to the college of their first choice in this competition would then be placed with the candidates for the college of their second choice, and the competitive process would begin again if the demand for places exceeded the supply.

Part of the reason for the attention given to CUNY was that the events leading to open admissions embodied so clearly the political and racial conflict that characterized American society in the 1960s. Also striking was the sheer abruptness of change: no major educational institution had ever moved so quickly from a highly selective admission standard to a policy of guaranteed access for all high school graduates.

CUNY's program incorporated other unique features. One was the admissions model itself. At least on paper, the plan was less stratified than the three-tiered California model, in which the university level accepts only the top 12.5 percent of high school graduates, the state colleges admit the top third, and the two-year community colleges accept all others. The CUNY system formally distinguished only two- and four-year colleges, thus constituting a two-tiered system. Its open-admissions model was designed to generate a less rigid sorting of students between senior and community colleges than the California system allowed. In effect, the CUNY effort was more senior college–oriented and was especially intended to increase minority enrollment in these institutions.

A second feature of the university's effort to increase educational opportunity concerned mobility between its two- and four-year colleges. To further enhance their chances of earning a baccalaureate degree, all graduates of the community colleges were guaranteed admission to a senior college with full credit. According to the plan, the community colleges would not be dead-end institutions whose primary function was to provide terminal vocational education.

A third unique aspect of open admissions was CUNY's concept of educational opportunity, which embraced not only access but also outcome. In its decision to commit the university to a policy of open admissions, its board of trustees stated that opportunity would be merely an illusion if access were followed by a high rate of student failure. Accordingly, the university developed extensive programs of remediation, counseling, and related services that were designed to enhance students' academic chances. In addition, the board decided that students should not be dismissed for academic reasons during the grace period of the freshman year. In effect, the responsibility for academic success lay not only with the students but also with the institution.

Overarching the open-admissions program was a financial-aid policy that had been in place since CCNY's founding in the nineteenth century: free tuition. CUNY's colleges were tuition free for all matriculated students, including those who were attending part-time.

OPEN ADMISSIONS AND ACADEMIC STANDARDS

CUNY's program was in the forefront of the egalitarian efforts of the time, arguably the most ambitious effort to create educational opportunity ever attempted in American higher education. Its far-reaching nature produced great concern in many quarters. One source of anxiety was the university's rapid transformation from one of the nation's more selective institutions into its most accessible. Some questioned whether the open-admissions policy could reverse the effects of prior economic and educational disadvantage, which were especially severe among New York City's minority youth. Given their handicaps, there was concern that academic standards would be swept away in a deluge of incompetent students. Ultimately, the degradation of CUNY diplomas might, it was feared, undercut graduates' chances of landing good jobs and acceptance for postgraduate study. Vice President Spiro Agnew, for example, denounced the CUNY plan as a giveaway of "100,000 devalued diplomas" (1971, 81). Others saw in open admissions a threat that ultimately would erode even the standards of the professions:

> Though I know many brilliant people I would not care to have as my doctor or my children's teacher, it is undoubtedly true that a unidimensional measure of academic excellence can be used to set a special, higher floor for many occupations and professions. The ardently egalitarian . . . are fundamentally unconvincing: one can dismiss them with the curse that they should cross the river on a bridge designed by an engineer from an engineering school where students were admitted by lottery; and that their injuries should then be treated by a doctor from a medical school where students were admitted by lottery; and that their heirs' malpractice suit should then be tried by a lawyer from a law school where students were admitted by lottery. (Mayer 1973, 47)

Others anticipated that the program would cruelly thwart the aspirations of students whose appetites for educational attainment would be whetted only to be frustrated as they flunked out in droves. From a deluge of entrants would emerge a trickle of graduates. In the way this public debate was framed, CUNY had launched a no-win policy: if many of the new students graduated, standards had gone down the drain. If they flunked out, open admissions had failed because it could not eradicate the effects of severe disadvantages that students brought with them to college.

Overview of the Issues

In assessing what actually happened under the open-admissions policy, we shall examine a number of questions that pertain to outcomes of the program. The open-admissions blueprint was designed to broaden access to the university for minority students—mostly blacks and Hispanics—who had been largely shut out beforehand.[17] How well did the program succeed in attracting students who could not have gotten into CUNY otherwise? Other higher education systems have attempted to enhance educational opportunity by expanding their community college tier. CUNY's effort focused more on providing access to baccalaureate programs, especially for minority students. To what extent were entering students actually placed in senior rather than community colleges? Whatever their initial level of placement, how much success did students experience in their college careers, and how well did minority students do compared with whites? We shall address this question by examining graduation rates for both associate's and bachelor's degrees. More broadly, we shall examine educational attainments over the long term, more than a decade after college entry. This investigation will give a sense of how far students ultimately were able to go in higher education; what proportion went away empty-handed, starting college but never earning a degree; what proportion earned an undergraduate degree; and what proportion were able to use the opportunity provided by open admissions to complete postgraduate programs, not only at CUNY but the broader system of higher education. These critical questions form the substance of the next chapter.

The open-admissions policy was an intervention that aimed to boost the life chances of educationally and economically disadvantaged students who would otherwise have had no opportunity for college. To what extent did the program actually foster success in the labor market? That is, how did the educational attainments reviewed in Chapter 2 translate into socioeconomic attainments? Did the program do as much for black and Hispanic students as it did for whites? What factors other than educational credentials influenced job-market experiences? For example, it is well known that women typically earn less than men. Does that inequity mean that women received less benefit from the open-admissions program, even when their educational attainments

---

[17]At the time the open-admissions program started, few Asian students—less than 1 percent—were enrolled in CUNY. Indeed, because there were so few of them, they were not included as a separate category in the annual ethnic censuses conducted by the university. Because of their small numbers, it was not possible to include them in the statistical analyses of this study.

were comparable to men's? Another consideration is the effect of employment sector: do individuals in the public and private spheres differ in how well they do in their careers and how rapidly they move ahead? By examining such variables as gender and employment sector we can evaluate the importance of educational attainments relative to other influences. Such an examination can provide a sense of both the potentialities and the limits of educational policy in a larger social context. In addressing these questions and issues, we shall look at different types of job rewards. In Chapter 3 we will examine both the status of the jobs that individuals held and how much money they were earning. In Chapter 4 we will look further at these aspects of jobs, using them to describe how the work careers of former students developed. Although status and earnings are fundamental aspects of work, they are not the only important features. Other significant considerations include whether a job is challenging and interesting, whether it requires judgment and responsibility, and whether it includes authority over the work of others. In Chapter 5 we will consider access to such jobs, and the difference that open admissions made in helping individuals secure such employment.

The ramifications of the open-admissions policy extend beyond the results for its immediate beneficiaries, the students who were admitted to CUNY under the provisions of the program, beginning in 1970. The large majority of the students who took advantage of open admissions represented the first generation in their families to attend college. By extending a collegiate opportunity to them, the program aimed, implicitly at least, to set in motion an educational momentum that would carry over to their children. The gains to individual students might thus be transmitted across the generations, so that a self-sustaining class of college-educated men and women would begin to develop in heretofore educationally disadvantaged communities. To what extent might this have happened among the offspring of the students who came to CUNY in the early 1970s? To address this question we shall examine the familial and educational environments of children of former CUNY students. What proportion were living in households in which both parents were present, and what proportion were with a single parent? It is arguable that the household configuration producing the most favorable life chances for children is a two-parent family in which the spouses have high levels of educational attainment (a B.A. or more), while single parents without college credentials provide less favorable chances for their offspring. What were the various family and educational configurations in which the children of our respondents were living, and were minority children distributed differently across these configurations than were white children? In addressing such questions, we will assess in Chapter 6 the extent to which open admissions may have helped to consolidate intergenerational gains among whites, blacks, and Hispanics.

Beyond the leverage that college provides in obtaining more–highly rewarded jobs, it is also thought to produce nonmaterial benefits. For example, evidence suggests that college enhances such critical thinking skills as the ability to identify and question the assumptions made in arguments. It also appears that college encourages commitment to civic participation, increases interest in cultural activities, helps to produce a positive sense of self-esteem, and contributes to feelings of satisfaction with life. If such nonmaterial outcomes are desirable and if education enhances the likelihood of attaining them, then access to those outcomes constitutes an equity issue much like those that concern job status and income. In effect, we shall examine whether the open-admissions policy, by contributing to greater educational attainments, increased students' chances of realizing some of the nonmaterial benefits of college. Such assessments are the focus of Chapter 7.

THE STAGES OF OPEN ADMISSIONS

The questions and issues that we have described to this point will be assessed with data collected on students who entered CUNY in the initial few years of the original open-admissions policy (1970–72). As we observed earlier, that policy appears, at least on paper, to have produced a noteworthy degree of educational opportunity, embodied in its focus on access to baccalaureate study, in its provision of various supportive features designed to enhance students' chances for academic success, and in the provision of free tuition. These features of open admissions were in effect during the period from 1970 through the 1975–76 academic year—an interval during which one might say that the form of the policy remained pure. Our analyses of this initial stage of the program are designed to assess what it could do when, in effect, it provided more favorable conditions to facilitate students' academic progress.

By the mid-1970s a grave fiscal crisis had overtaken New York. As the city entered an era of scarcity, CUNY received a severe buffeting. The university was thrown into crisis as it struggled over ways to deal with sharp and sudden budget reductions and an even bleaker future. The open-admissions program was undercut as important changes in academic and fiscal policies were instituted. Beginning in fall 1976, CUNY's century-old tradition of free tuition was swept away, criteria for admission to its four-year colleges became more stringent, and in other important ways the academic climate at the university became more difficult. Did these changes influence students' educational chances? Was their academic progress affected—was there a change, for example, in the rate at which they earned credits? As indexed by the grades they earned, did the quality of their academic performance change? Ultimately, were graduation rates diminished? Were the academic chances of disadvantaged minority students affected more than others'? To explore such questions, as we do in Chapter 9, we shall compare the academic careers of freshmen who entered CUNY in 1970 (before the fiscal crisis) with the class that entered in 1980 (after the crisis). Looking at academic careers in two decades separated by major policy changes in the university will provide a context for assessing the long-range significance of the open-admissions experiment. In effect, we will look at what happened to student academic outcomes as CUNY shifted from its liberal open-admissions policy to a more conservative approach to access and academic requirements.

Sociological Perspectives on Open Admissions

The questions that we have been discussing resonate with a long-standing controversy among social scientists about the effect of education on socioeconomic life chances. The debate revolves around the interpretation of a central conclusion that emerges from research: educational attainment is the single most important influence on occupational success, overshadowing by far the direct effects of family background.[18] According to one perspective, sometimes referred to as the "functional" view, this preeminence of education indicates that high status in American society can no longer be directly inherited but must be gained in accordance with universalistic achievement criteria, the most important of which are educational attainments.[19] Those who earn the more valuable credentials—bachelor's and postgraduate degrees—do

[18]According to results reported in Blau and Duncan (1967), about 14 percent of the variance in a son's occupational status is explained by the occupational status of his father, whereas the son's educational attainment explains about 30 percent. (The measure of occupational status is son's first job.)

[19]Of course, educational attainment is not the only basis for increased universalism in occupational attainment. Antinepotism rules and legislation against ethnic and gender discrimination in employment have helped to create broader employment opportunity.

so by displaying competence in an educational system that selects and sorts on the basis of academic performance. According to this perspective, the processes of educational sorting and selection are based mostly—though not exclusively—on merit, and therefore individuals can go as far in education as their talents will take them. From this vantage point, then, individuals from low-status origins can find in the educational system an opportunity for social and economic mobility. Education serves to loosen the linkages between social origins and social destinations.[20] According to this line of thinking, such policies as open admissions, which enhance educational opportunity, would be expected to facilitate access to good jobs.

Not all scholars share such optimism about education's egalitarian function. Although they accept the findings about the important influence of educational attainment on labor-market rewards, many are unconvinced that family background has waned as a determinant of socioeconomic success. As Karabel and Halsey (1977b, 19) have stated, social inheritance has taken on a new but no less important form:

> If . . . the inheritance of status in modern societies takes place through the transmission of "cultural capital," then the distinction between ascription and achievement becomes a misleading one. . . . The privileged no longer reproduce their positions solely through property but also through the acquisition of superior education for their children. Rather than describing this process as heightened universalism it would seem more accurate to view it as a new mechanism performing the old function of social reproduction. Social inheritance, whether through the transmission of property or through the transmission of cultural capital, is still social inheritance.

In this critical perspective on education then, schools are less agents for social mobility than institutions that serve to reproduce inequality from generation

---

[20]A considerable literature reflects this point of view. Some of the best examples are Bell's exposition of the development of postindustrial society (1973), the classic analysis of status attainment and social mobility by Blau and Duncan (1967), and Clark's work on the "expert" society (1962). One of the most important theoretical statements is that presented by Talcott Parsons (1959). A good summary of this position, often referred to as the "functional perspective" is to be found in Hurn (1993, see especially chapter 2). Parsons explicitly notes that family background factors play a role in educational attainment, but he is very clear in asserting that in the main, universalistic standards of achievement are the primary bases for evaluating students' school performance. For a discussion of the mobility function versus the social reproduction effects of schools in the context of research on status attainment, see Bielby (1981).

to generation. Although the various critics differ about how schools contribute to the reproduction of inequality, they share a skepticism that the selection and sorting functions of schools are fundamentally meritocratic. They see in the curriculum and assessment procedures of schools a playing field on which students from advantaged social backgrounds are better positioned for the academic competition than are those from lower social classes and minority ethnic status.[21] Because children from higher-status families typically have better-educated, more affluent parents, they tend to bring with them to school more of the characteristics that schools reward. Because schools prefer some forms of language usage to others, for example, students from higher-status families may be advantaged because their linguistic socialization enables them to read, write, and speak in ways that more closely match school expectations than do the language styles of lower-status children.[22] More broadly, the cultural capital held in higher status families—predispositions including tastes in music, literature, cinema, and theater; periodicals and newspapers read; uses of leisure; types of vacations taken, styles of dress, styles of social interaction, and so on—gives their children more familiarity with the content of the school curriculum and probably facilitates interaction with teachers.[23]

Part of the academic edge provided by parents who have high levels of cultural capital is that, because of their greater educational attainments, they typically are better able to help their children with schoolwork. Moreover, as Lareau (1989) has shown, high-status parents more frequently interact with teachers on behalf of their children. All in all, the advantages that accrue to

[21]Critiques of the functionalist position are expressed in the work of a number of scholars. One of the best known is the neo-Marxist study of Bowles and Gintis (1976), who see schools as a major institution for reproducing the hierarchical social and economic relations of capitalism. Another position is represented by the work of Collins (1979), who argues that, for the most part, educational credentials are unnecessary for effective job performance. Rather, credentials represent a cultural "currency" that provides their holders with eligibility for the better-rewarded jobs. In the race for credentials, individuals from high-status groups are better able to compete, thus maintaining their advantage vis-à-vis other aspiring groups (i.e., minorities, lower social class groups).

[22]This perspective on language as been developed most notably in the work of Basil Bernstein (1977). See also his article (1973) in Karabel and Halsey (1977a). Whereas Bernstein focuses on social class differences in linguistic usage, the work of Labov (1972) addresses race differences through analysis of black dialectical usage.

[23]The concept of cultural capital has been developed most notably in the work of Pierre Bourdieu. See, for example, his article (1977) in Karabel and Halsey (1977a), as well as Bourdieu and Passeron (1970). A good overview of Bourdieu's work is provided by Swartz (1990).

higher-status children are reflected in their greater likelihood of placement in high-ability classroom groups. Ability grouping in turn tends to enhance further their academic performance. Students in low-ability groups tend to learn less, most likely as a consequence of lower teacher expectations and less demanding curriculum content. Of course, all of this works to the advantage of higher-status children, thus ratifying their status as strong students.

These disparities in elementary school performance have a continuing influence on academic careers; students who were in the upper-ability groups, for example, might be expected to outperform lower-group children on standardized achievement tests, which often play an important role in high school curriculum placement. Low test scores may lead to placement in lower, non-academic tracks. Because of track differences in curriculum content and, possibly, more negative teacher attitudes toward lower-track students, these youngsters do not do as well in high school and are less likely to enter college than those in academic tracks.[24] If they continue their schooling, they are more likely to enter community colleges. These two-year schools are far less valuable than four-year ones; students who begin college in the former are significantly less likely ever to earn a bachelor's degree, even if they aspire to one, and if they receive a two-year associate's degree, its leverage in the labor market is typically very modest relative to that of the B.A.[25]

In the end, then, proponents of the critical perspective believe that the educational system serves to transmit inequality from generation to generation while at the same time preserving an illusion of equality. Standardized tests and the seemingly hard currency of grades give the schools a patina of objectivity and fairness that make their function of social reproduction less visible. Ultimately, a stratified system of education—in which ability grouping at the primary school level is linked with curriculum tracking in high school,

[24]There is an extensive literature on tracking which in its broad outlines indicates that track placement is partly determined by socioeconomic status, that track influences how much is learned, and that tracking adds to, rather then diminishes, preexisting academic inequalities. Nonetheless, the consequences of tracking appear to be more complex than has been portrayed by some reproduction theorists. Some important analyses of tracking may be found in Oakes (1985), Gamoran (1992), Gamoran and Mare (1989), Gamoran and Berends (1987).

[25]Over the past three decades a large literature has accumulated in response to controversy about the functions of community colleges and the socioeconomic value of the associate's degree. Some of the more important examples are Clark (1960), Karabel (1972), Brint and Karabel (1889), Dougherty (1987, 1994), and Cohen (1990). Other citations regarding the issue of community colleges will be made, as appropriate, in succeeding chapters.

which is connected in turn to four-year and two-year tiers in higher education—provides niches into which students are sorted, with significant consequences for their respective life chances.

The two views of education that we have summarized here may not be as diametrically opposed as they appear. As one writer has pointed out (Bielby 1981), there are no studies that show schooling to be independent of social origins, nor are there any showing that schooling is completely determined by the circumstances into which one is born. Differences between perspectives are mainly ones of emphasis. Nonetheless, each perspective generates contrasting expectations about the results of a policy such as open admissions. Compared with the functional view, the critical perspective leads to much less optimistic expectations that the policy could make a deep dent in class or ethnically based inequalities. But taken together, these perspectives provide a broad theoretical context that can be useful in interpreting the outcomes of the open-admissions program.

Assessing the Outcomes of Open Admissions

Three data sets have been used to analyze the questions and issues that we have been describing. The first, an anonymous annual census conducted by the university, allows us to distinguish blacks and Hispanics from non-Hispanic whites in order to examine (in Chapter 2) important changes that took place in the ethnic composition of CUNY's four-year and two-year colleges after the open-admissions policy was initiated.

For all of the other analyses in Chapters 2 through 7, we have assembled a large longitudinal data set. Its origins go back to the fall of 1970, when CUNY's seventeen senior and community colleges initiated the open-admissions policy. As part of the study, large samples of the first three freshman classes to enter after the program began—the 1970, 1971, and 1972 entrants—were surveyed by questionnaire, generally either at registration or in required freshman courses. The numbers of students in the sample surveys for each year and the size of their corresponding populations were as follows: 1970, 13,525, or 43 percent of the 31,596 entrants; 1971, 8,527, or 24 percent of 35,639; 1972, 12,725, or 36 percent of 35,545.[26] The survey data include information

[26]The number of entrants does not include students who were admitted under special admissions programs instituted in the 1960s. These programs involved minority students almost exclusively. Because special program students received services, including stipends, at levels not

on socioeconomic background, including race and ethnic group membership, gender, age, family income on entry to CUNY, parental educational attainments, educational aspirations, reasons for attending college, and self ratings of academic ability.

Subsequently, these survey data were integrated with students' official academic records, including: (1) high school background information, such as high school average and the number of college preparatory courses taken; (2) information on placement in CUNY, including the level of college (senior or community) at which students began their studies and, for two-year entrants, their initial curricular placement (liberal arts vs. career or vocational programs); and (3) academic performance information covering the period from fall 1970 through spring 1975, including grade point averages, credits earned, whether students took remedial courses and how many they took, whether they dropped out or "stopped out" (temporarily suspended their college education), whether they transferred from a community to a senior college, and what CUNY degrees they earned.

These samples provide good representations of the populations and have been the basis for a number of studies analyzing various outcomes of the open-admissions policy over its first five years, including academic performance processes and graduation rates (Lavin et al. 1979, 1981; Alba and Lavin 1981).[27] This five-year interval was adequate to delineate many of the important results of the program and to analyze ethnic differences in academic success. Nonetheless, at the end of that time, the record seemed incomplete for some key bottom-line educational results, like graduation. By spring 1975 large proportions of students had neither graduated nor dropped out—they were persisting in college. Others, who appeared in our records as dropouts, may have temporarily interrupted their studies because of the need to work full-time, or for other reasons; still others may have transferred out of CUNY and ultimately graduated from other colleges (the initial studies were able to

generally received by students entering under the open-admissions program, including them in our analyses would have further complicated an already complex study.

[27]Detailed comparisons of the samples with the populations have been presented in Lavin et al. (1981). The samples contain a slightly higher proportion of able students than the populations. This bias is small with respect to high school grades, transfer, and college grades, larger but still modest with respect to graduation rates. Across all samples the graduation rate is less than 5 percentage points higher than the rate in the population. Overall, we concluded that the samples provided good representations of the populations, and there seemed little reason to suspect that findings based on the samples were invalid.

report only what happened within the university). Obviously, an unfolding of the full graduation and dropout picture required more time.

To complete that picture we conducted a follow-up survey in 1984 for a subsample of approximately 5,000 respondents who were members of the samples from the original 1970–72 cohorts. The new survey expanded the time frame of the data set, adding information on educational attainments as of 1984. It included all degrees earned (ranging from high school diploma through advanced postgraduate and professional degrees), not only from CUNY but also from the wider higher education system. The survey also provided information on labor-market experiences, including employment status as an undergraduate, year of first full-time job and job title, number of years employed since 1970, employment status in 1978 and 1984, job title in 1978 and 1984, salary for the 1978 and 1984 jobs, and the type of organization for which the respondent worked in these years. Information was also collected on marital status (including, among those who were married, employment status and salary of spouse), number of dependent children living with the respondent, attitudes about work, self-image, and satisfaction with various aspects of life.

The new survey data were merged with the original 1970, 1971, and 1972 freshmen cohort files, which were then combined to form a single file. This integrated data set is used for almost all of the analyses in Chapters 2 through 7. It contains information on the lives of respondents from the time they were in high school and in their teens, to a time twelve or more years after they had begun college, when typically they were in their early to mid-thirties. This file allows us to explore what happened to them and what their experiences during and subsequent to formal education tell us about the success of the open-admissions policy.

Because this data set contains about 5,000 respondents from the combined original or "mother" sample of about 34,700 cases, we wanted to assess how well the characteristics of the former matched those of the latter. To do so we compared the two, using a large number of variables common to both. The details of this procedure are presented in the appendix. In some respects the subsample differs from the mother sample. Most notably, CUNY graduation rates as of 1975 are higher among the members of the follow-up sample, implying that subsequent educational attainments in this subsample would exceed those in the mother sample. To adjust for nonresponse bias, we developed a weighting procedure, which is described in the appendix. It adjusted the values for variables in the subsample so that they closely matched those in the mother sample. Although we obviously do not have measures in the latter sample for every variable measured in the former, the adjustments produced by our weighting model add to our confidence in the validity of the conclusions that we have drawn from our subsample.

As we said earlier, the open-admissions policy was undercut by the severe fiscal crisis that hit New York City in the mid-seventies. To assess the impact of changes in the program on educational opportunity at CUNY and on students' college careers, we have used a third data source: a longitudinal file that tracked the academic progress of students who entered CUNY in 1980, after the policy changes. The academic success of these entrants will be compared with that compiled by the students who entered in 1970 under the original open-admissions policy. This 1970 data set was, of course, put together for the initial studies of open admissions. Our comparison of academic outcomes in the 1970 and 1980 cohorts will help to deepen our understanding of the long-term success of open admissions.

CHAPTER TWO

How Far Did They Go?
Expanded Access and Ultimate Educational Attainments

From 1960 through the mid-1970s undergraduate enrollment in U.S. colleges more than doubled, from three and a quarter million to more than eight million (U.S. Bureau of the Census 1983a, table 257). In addition to the growth in sheer numbers, a new socioeconomic and academic student profile emerged. Lower-income students, racial and ethnic minorities, women, and older students accounted for a larger share of total enrollments. These newer recruits were more likely than traditional students to enter college with academic deficiencies. One result was the emergence of remedial programs, in senior as well as community colleges. According to one national survey (Rouche and Snow 1977), by the mid-seventies remedial courses were in place at the great majority of four- and two-year colleges, including some of the nation's more selective institutions.

The City University of New York provides perhaps the most dramatic example of the sea change that took place over this period, as it moved abruptly from a selective to an open-access institution. By virtue of its open-admissions blueprint, which was designed to provide a seat in college for all high school graduates, to smooth the pathway to four-year colleges, and to ensure that students' academic chances would be enhanced by large-scale programs of remediation and other support services, the university—which already had a tradition of free tuition—aimed to create educational opportunity for large numbers of students who otherwise would have had no chance for college.

In examining the educational results of the open-admissions policy, this chapter addresses two broad questions. First, how much opportunity did the program actually create? There are various ways of assessing opportunity. One is to focus on group differences in high school graduates' rates of college entry as an indicator of disparities in opportunity. Earlier we cited such differences

An early version of this chapter was published with David B. Crook in *The American Journal of Education* (Lavin and Crook 1990).

in summarizing the progress of blacks through the mid-seventies and the subsequent erosion of these gains. But a measure of mere college entry conceals as much as it reveals, because it fails to take account of stratification in higher education. Although there are different ways of describing its tiers, an important distinction is between four-year colleges and the two-year or community colleges. The latter grew dramatically during the period under consideration, enrolling 14 percent of all undergraduates in 1960, 24 percent in 1970, and more than 30 percent by 1975 (U.S. Bureau of the Census 1983a, table 257). Considerable evidence (Brint and Karabel 1989; Dougherty 1987, 1992, 1994) suggests that these collegiate tiers are associated with very different chances for the attainment of bachelor's degrees—and, partly as a result, with different chances for entering the more-rewarded positions in the labor market. Thus, ethnic disparities of initial positioning in higher education imply subsequent inequalities of life chances. In assessing educational opportunity under open admissions at CUNY, we shall consider placement in senior and community colleges.

Within community colleges, curriculum placement is another facet of opportunity. Broadly speaking, these institutions have two curricular tracks. One, the liberal arts, is commonly regarded as leading to transfer to four-year schools and the B.A degree; the other, comprises a variety of technical-vocational programs—X-ray technology and secretarial studies, for example—that are typically considered to be terminal, that is, not linked with further educational advancement.[1] Differences in curriculum placement carry obvious implications for life chances, and so ethnic differences in such placement may be thought of as an aspect of educational opportunity.

The second broad question we shall address concerns educational outcomes.

To what extent did opportunity translate into educational attainment? Using their initial positioning in the university as the base, how far were students able to climb the educational ladder? How many entered college but left without earning a degree? What proportions of four-year entrants eventually earned B.A. degrees and how likely were community college entrants to receive A.A. degrees?[2] How successful were community college students in

[1]According to Cohen and Brawer (1982), by the late 1970s these vocational curricula began leading more often to senior college transfer.

[2]The bachelor of arts degree, of course, is not the only baccalaureate degree. Others include bachelor of science, bachelor of fine arts, and the like. Similarly, associate's degrees may be granted

eventually earning a B.A.? How often did students complete graduate education, receiving an advanced degree that added to their chances of entering more rewarded professional positions?

These questions are examined from a perspective in which ultimate educational attainments are seen as being influenced by contingencies occurring at earlier points in educational careers. We assess, for example, how high school experience, other background factors, and initial positioning in CUNY influence the chances of earning a B.A. degree and the time it takes to complete it. Then we examine how the length of time to earn a degree in turn affects the chances of completing a postgraduate degree.

In assessing educational outcomes, our principal focus is on open-admissions students—the ones whose entry to each level of CUNY was made possible by the policy—and how well they did by comparison with students whose entry to CUNY was not dependent on the policy. Because open admissions was explicitly designed to extend access for minority students, the analyses also focus on ethnic differences in educational attainments and upon explanations of disparities between minority students and others. Our analyses distinguish three groups: whites, blacks, and Hispanics.[3] When we speak of "minority students," it is the two latter groups to which we refer.

Placement in the University

The influence of open admissions in creating college opportunity can be seen in a variety of ways. One focuses on rates of college attendance in New York City. In fall 1969, the last year before the open-admissions policy was inaugurated, 57 percent of the previous spring's New York City high school graduates enrolled in college; a year later the college-going rate jumped to 76 percent (Birnbaum and Goldman 1971), substantially exceeding the national

---

in arts and in science. To smooth exposition we use B.A. to denote all bachelor's degrees and A.A. to denote all associate's degrees.

[3]In this book, when we speak of ethnic groups or of ethnic differences, our use of the term *ethnicity* refers to common racial or national ancestry. In regard to white ethnicity, our original studies (Lavin et al. 1979, 1981) distinguished two ethnic groups based on religion in the 1970 and 1971 entering classes: Jewish and Catholic students (the latter comprising mainly those of Irish and Italian ancestry). For 1972 entrants, however, we were unable to include an item on religion in the social background survey. Because we have combined all three entering classes in this follow-up study, we have aggregated those of varying white ethnicities into the category *white*.

rate of 61 percent for the high school class of 1970 (U.S. Bureau of the Census 1983a, table 250, p. 158). Whites in New York were more likely to enroll than minorities: their college-going rate was 78 percent, compared with 67 percent for blacks and Hispanics.

That this leap in college enrollments was largely a consequence of the open-admissions program is shown by the dramatic increases in the size of freshman classes entering the CUNY system during the initial years of the program (table 2.1). Over the 1970–72 period the number of entrants averaged more than 34,000, almost double the size of the 1969 class, the last to enter before the program began.[4] The number of blacks and Hispanics enrolling also leapt upward under open admissions. Minorities constituted about 9 percent of the 1969 freshmen, but accounted for nearly one quarter of the students who entered between 1970 and 1972. The number of minority freshmen nearly quintupled after 1969, from fewer than 1,700 to more than 8,000 annually. Although there had been apprehension that an increased minority presence in CUNY might come at the cost of places for whites who had qualified under the stiff pre–open admissions criteria, the number of whites actually increased substantially, from fewer than 16,000 in 1969 to an average of almost 26,000 between 1970 and 1972.

How did open admissions influence the placement of students in CUNY's two- and four-year institutions? The policy did not merely funnel minority students into the community colleges. It paved the way for many students to enter CUNY's four-year institutions: after open admissions the number of minority freshmen in senior colleges increased almost sevenfold, while their numbers quadrupled at community colleges. As a consequence of their relatively larger increase at the four-year schools, the ratio of community to senior

---

[4]This number does not include students admitted under the two special admissions programs targeted to minorities which were begun in the mid-1960s, before open admissions started. One program, SEEK (Search for Education, Elevation and Knowledge) brought students into senior colleges; the other, College Discovery, brought them into community colleges. Minority individuals comprised about 90 percent of the students in these programs. Before open admissions, these programs were by far the predominant path of entry to CUNY for minority students. After open admissions, the contribution of these older programs to the minority presence in the university declined markedly as the new policy brought a large number of minority students into the university. SEEK and College Discovery students are not included in this study because of their small numbers in our survey data. This is not a disadvantage, for it would be inappropriate to include them in analyses of academic outcomes; they received services and financial stipends at a level not offered to open-admissions students.

What Do Women Want?

I want a red dress.
I want it flimsy and cheap,
I want it too tight, I want to wear it
until someone tears it off me.
I want it sleeveless and backless,
this dress, so no one has to guess
what's underneath. I want to walk down
the street past Thrifty's and the hardware store
with all those keys glittering in the window,
past Mr. and Mrs. Wong selling day-old
donuts in their café, past the Guerra brothers
slinging pigs from the truck and onto the dolly,
hoisting the slick snouts over their shoulders.
I want to walk like I'm the only
woman on earth and I can have my pick.
I want that red dress bad.
I want it to confirm
your worst fears about me,
to show you how little I care about you
or anything except what
I want. When I find it, I'll pull that garment
from its hanger like I'm choosing a body
to carry me into this world, through
the birth-cries and the love-cries too,
and I'll wear it like bones, like skin,
it'll be the goddamned
dress they bury me in.

Kim Addonizio

Table 2.1 Freshman Enrollments, by Level of College and Minority Status Before and After Open Admissions

	Entrants			Percentage Minority
	Total	White	Minority	
Senior colleges				
1969	10,058	9,646	412	4
1970–72[a]	18,105	15,230	2,875	16
Community colleges				
1969	7,587	6,329	1,258	17
1970–72[a]	16,155	10,753	5,402	33
University totals				
1969	17,645	15,975	1,670	9
1970–72[a]	34,260	25,983	8,277	24

Source: CUNY Annual Censuses.

Note: Enrollments do not include freshmen admitted through the special admissions programs, SEEK and College Discovery. Black and Hispanic students are combined to form the category *minority.*

[a] Figures are averages computed for the three entering classes in 1970, 1971, and 1972.

college minority freshmen fell from more than three to one to less than two to one. Though minority freshmen were more likely to be found in community colleges, they were more equally distributed across the levels of the university after open admissions began than before.

Just how important open admissions was for minority access to the university may be seen in table 2.2, which shows the proportions of whites, blacks, and Hispanics whose entry to each level of the university was made possible by the program. In reading the table one should keep our use of the term *open-admissions student* in mind: in senior colleges open-admissions students were those who entered with a high school average of less than 80, the minimum generally required for entry to that level of college before the program took effect; in community colleges open-admissions students were those who entered with a high school average below 75. Before the policy took effect students whose average was less than 75 typically would not have been admitted to either level of the university. Open admissions was especially critical for the senior college chances of blacks: it paved the way for three of

every four black senior college freshmen. Hispanics were also substantial beneficiaries: half of Hispanic four-year entrants would not have qualified before
open admissions. And although the policy was designed to create senior college access for minorities, whites also benefited: nearly a third of white senior
college freshmen were open-admissions students. Large majorities of every
group would not have been admitted to the community colleges but for the
open-admissions program. Overall, the policy made possible the entry of
nearly seven in ten blacks and more than four in ten Hispanic students to some
level of the university.

One noteworthy aspect of the benefits to whites under open admissions
has not generally been recognized: although the proportion of whites admitted under the program was the lowest among the three groups, whites nevertheless greatly outnumbered open-admissions blacks and Hispanics at both
levels of the CUNY system. Even though very large *proportions* of the black
and Hispanic students at the university entered via the program, most of the
open-admissions students were white. So although the public generally perceived open admissions as a minority program, its benefits were widely dis-
persed throughout New York City's ethnic communities.

As we said earlier, level of college is not the only aspect of placement with
implications for opportunity. Curriculum is also important, especially for
those who begin in a community college. Essentially, these institutions offer
two curricula, the liberal arts and the technical-vocational. The former is
oriented to transfer to a four-year college, while the latter is generally considered terminal, though at CUNY, some technical-vocational programs dove-
tail with similar programs in the four-year colleges. There is, nonetheless, a
clear distinction between the two: liberal arts students are expected to transfer;
for those in the technical programs, transfer is simply an option.

At CUNY's community colleges under open admissions, minority students were less likely than whites to be found in the liberal arts curriculum.
Overall, about half of whites were so placed, compared with a little more than
a third of blacks and a quarter of Hispanic students. Among whites the likelihood of placement in liberal arts was not dependent upon their admissions
status. Among minority students, by contrast, open-admissions students were
more likely to be found in liberal arts. In other words, contrary to conventional wisdom, which suggests that the better students will be found in liberal
arts, weaker students were more often found in that track. An earlier study
determined that curriculum placement reflects student preference: more than
90 percent of community college students were placed in their preferred

Table 2.2 Placement of Ethnic Groups, by Level of College and Admissions Status

Percentages of Open-Admissions Students

Ethnicity	Senior Colleges	Community Colleges	All CUNY[a]
White	30 (2,133)[b]	57 (1,323)	28 (3,456)
Black	74 (227)	79 (482)	68 (709)
Hispanic	49 (171)	64 (284)	44 (455)
All students[c]	35 (2,531)	62 (2,089)	34 (4,620)

Source: Follow-up survey.

Note: Here and in subsequent tables, the 1970, 1971, and 1972 cohorts have been aggregated.

[a]Students who entered with a high school average of less than 75.

[b]Percentages have been computed from weighted data; unweighted frequencies are reported here in parentheses and will not be repeated in subsequent tables.

[c]Here and in the tables to follow, totals exclude Asian students and other nonwhites, as well as students for whom data are missing on any of the variables in question.

curriculum (Lavin et al. 1979, 1981). Student preference is explained to a large degree by high school background. Those who graduated from non-academic curriculum tracks in high school were more likely to prefer a vocational curriculum in community college, in particular the better students, who had clearer occupational goals. On the other hand, for many weaker students the liberal arts curriculum appears to have been a residual choice made in the absence of any clear occupational or academic goals.

In summary, the influence of the open-admissions policy was reflected in a sharp rise in rates of college enrollment among high school graduates. By opening its doors wide, the university greatly expanded educational opportunity, not only for minority students but also for whites. The number of blacks and Hispanics at the university grew dramatically, and consistent with the policy's focus on increasing access to baccalaureate education, inequalities in the distribution of ethnic groups across the levels of CUNY narrowed. Nonetheless, disparities were not eliminated: even in the wake of open admissions, minority students were more likely to begin at a community college and to pursue a vocational curriculum. To the extent that community college entry and pursuit of a vocational curriculum depress the likelihood of earning a B.A., minority students, despite their gains, would continue to be hampered by their initial placement at the university. This is an issue to which we will return later in the chapter.

Open Admissions and the Students It Brought In

Who were the students whose entry to CUNY was made possible by open admissions, and how different were they from "regular" students, the ones who would have been admitted even if there had never been an open-admissions program? Compared with regular enrollees (in senior colleges these were students with high school averages of 80 or higher; in community colleges they were the ones with averages of at least 75), were the open-admissions students more impoverished? Did they differ in other aspects of social background, such as their parents' education? Beyond their lower high school averages, how different were they in other academic respects, such as exposure to college preparatory courses in high school and such basic academic skills as reading and math? How far did they intend to go in higher education, and what did they hope to get out of college? An exploration of such questions will help to give a sense of who the open-admissions students were, and of what their characteristics portended for their chances of collegiate success.

In looking at the characteristics of open-admissions and regular students, we shall control for their placement in a senior or community college and for their ethnic origins (table 2.3). We have already seen that open-admissions students were drawn disproportionately from minority groups. Because ethnicity is typically correlated with other important characteristics such as income, the ethnic consequences of the policy could be associated with other respects in which regular and open-admissions students differed.

DIFFERENCES IN SOCIOECONOMIC BACKGROUND

Open admissions brought in large numbers of economically disadvantaged students. The ethnic disparities in income generally are much larger than differences associated with admissions status. In senior colleges at least half and often more than 60 percent of black and Hispanic students came from families with incomes below $10,000, whereas among whites the percentages generally are far lower. In the community colleges three-quarters or more of minority students came from such low-income families—at least twice the proportion of low-income whites. Indeed, economic differences between whites and minorities are even wider than they appear, because the latter generally belonged to larger families. Many black and Hispanic entrants came from unusually harsh circumstances. Twenty percent of Hispanic community college students and nearly 15 percent in the senior college open-admissions category were from families with incomes below $4,000; less than 5 percent of whites had incomes this low. In effect, then, though open-admissions entrants were not so different economically from their regular classmates, CUNY's policy brought about a substantial enlargement of the pool of low-income college students. Because the economic resources of minority students typically were very meager, the program was especially critical for their college chances.

Although much of the influence of family income on educational attainment undoubtedly is felt in events occurring well before college—in the ability of families to afford such cultural resources as books, magazines, interesting vacations, and extra help for school, such as tutoring, all of which can make a difference in the quality of early school performance—its effects might continue to be seen in college—by affecting the chances, for example, that a student would need to work full time while going to school. Even though CUNY was a free-tuition university when open admissions began, many students worked at full-time jobs during their college years, presumably to pay living expenses and to help their families. In the four-year colleges, open-admissions students more often held such jobs than regular students, but ethnicity also made a difference: minority students worked full-time more frequently than whites. Among community college students, where holding a full-time job was more common, ethnic disparities were considerably wider; a third and more of minority students were so employed, compared with about a fifth of whites. Overall, across the university, about 30 percent of minority students and 13 percent of whites worked full-time. Students who did so could be expected to find that work took away from study time, perhaps diminishing their chances for academic success. Moreover, full-time work could force students to attend college on a part-time basis, thus extending the time they needed to earn a degree.

Parental educational background is another potential influence on attainment in higher education. As with income its effects begin much earlier in the educational sequence. Parents with at least some college education, for example, may generally be better able to help with homework, to interact more effectively with teachers, and to transmit to their children those forms of

Table 2.3 Socioeconomic and Academic Characteristics of Freshmen in Senior and Community Colleges, by Admissions Status and Ethnicity

	Level of College														
	Senior						Community						All CUNY		
	Regular Admissions			Open Admissions			Regular Admissions			Open Admissions					
	W	B	H	W	B	H	W	B	H	W	B	H	W	B	H
% male	48	29	43	60	40	55	34	22	32	59	45	42	51	39	42
Mean age	17.8	18.8	18.1	18.3	19.0	18.8	18.5	22.6	19.2	18.9	20.1	21.0	18.3	20.1	19.6
% age 20 or older	1	6	4	4	11	7	4	44	18	10	24	39	4	23	21
Father's education															
% some college or more	37	30	18	27	22	21	26	6	8	25	22	12	31	20	14
Mother's education															
% some college or more	25	29	15	20	25	7	12	9	6	18	18	9	20	19	9
% first-generation college attender	55	58	72	63	60	77	68	85	88	67	69	82	61	68	80
% income <$10,000	35	51	61	41	75	66	34	79	85	39	77	84	36	75	76
Mean high school average	86	83	85	76	73	76	80	79	79	70	69	70	80	72	76
Mean college preparatory credits	14.9	13.9	13.5	13.4	11.6	12.1	13.0	10.5	10.9	10.9	9.4	8.8	13.4	10.4	10.9

% rate self academically above average	43	21	16	17	8	10	27	11	13	16	11	10	30	11	12
% rate getting a general education as important	91	87	95	87	86	88	85	84	88	81	83	94	87	84	91
Degree intentions															
A.A. or less	1	0	4	1	3	2	24	21	31	18	15	16	8	12	14
B.A.	24	33	28	34	36	39	23	24	23	24	22	18	26	26	25
More than B.A.	61	53	54	49	50	44	25	26	16	24	30	21	45	36	31
Not sure	14	14	14	16	11	15	30	29	30	34	33	45	21	26	30
Test results															
% need language skill help	12	22	49	41	68	68	39	91	77	61	85	91	29	72	70
% need math remediation	14	51	44	46	67	67	46	92	81	69	91	98	33	79	70
% taking remedial courses	25	60	50	53	77	65	33	55	54	54	65	64	38	66	59
Mean remedial courses taken[a]	1.4	2.1	2.0	2.0	2.4	2.5	1.5	1.9	1.8	1.6	2.0	2.4	1.6	2.1	2.2
% employed full-time as undergraduates	6	12	14	14	23	23	18	43	30	21	33	37	13	31	28
Freshman grade average	2.8	2.4	2.4	2.1	1.8	1.9	2.6	2.5	2.6	2.0	1.8	1.9	2.5	2.0	2.2
Mean credits per semester	13.4	11.9	11.0	10.5	8.3	8.1	10.9	9.0	9.4	8.3	6.9	6.2	11.3	7.9	8.2
Number of cases (unweighted)	1621	74	103	512	153	68	690	126	127	633	356	157	3456	709	455

Source: Follow-up survey.

Note: W = white; B = black; H = Hispanic.

[a]Calculated for those who took remediation.

cultural capital that add to the chances of school success.[5] Some of the differences rooted in family culture might continue to exert a direct influence on collegiate attainments.

The open-admissions policy was expected to extend the higher education franchise to many students who would represent the first generation in their families to attend college. Clear majorities of open-admissions students in both four- and two-year schools were indeed first-generation collegians (community college students were more likely to be so than senior college entrants). Hispanic students were the most likely to be new recruits to higher education: three-quarters and more were the first in their families to attend; blacks were a bit more likely than whites to be in the first college generation. Overall, however, what stands out most clearly is the share of CUNY students in general, both open admissions and regular, who were first-generation college entrants. In an institution such as CUNY, with a tradition of serving poor and immigrant groups, perhaps this similarity between regular and open-admissions students is not so surprising.

One way in which open-admissions and regular students clearly differed was in gender representation. Although the open-admissions policy had no specific gender focus, it played a somewhat different role for men than it did for women. Although the program helped make college possible for both men and women, it appears to have been more important in opening the door to men. Without exception—for all ethnic groups and at both senior and community colleges—men accounted for a greater percentage of open-admissions students than of regular students. Indeed, 80 percent of all black males enrolled in senior colleges and 90 percent in community colleges were open-admissions students (corresponding figures for Hispanic men were 55 and 70 percent). White men were less dependent on the program, especially for gaining entry to CUNY's senior colleges. Open admissions clearly boosted the collegiate representation of young minority males, sometimes described as an "endangered species" because they were more likely to be deceased, in prison, or unemployed than in college.

Open-admissions students typically were older than their regular classmates when they started college, and entrants to the two-year schools were older than senior college freshmen. Age differences are clearly associated with ethnicity: relative to whites, minority freshmen, especially in community colleges, were far more likely to have been twenty or older. In effect, many of

[5]A good analysis of parent-school interaction may be found in Lareau (1989).

the minority students were beginning college at an age when students traditionally were completing their studies. In part this reflects the fact that a
disproportionate number of minority students were above the modal age for
their grade when they completed high school (National Center for Education
Statistics 1990, 1:18–21; 2:16–17), and in part it may be that a greater proportion of minority students than whites were entering college after a hiatus of a
year or more, during which they encountered disappointment in the job
market.

These age differences might have created further disadvantages. Students
who are older than the conventional age of seventeen or eighteen—especially
those who are in their twenties when they start college—may, by the time they
complete it, be subject to accumulating constraints of the life cycle, such as
marriage and children. Such events, in turn, diminish the likelihood of continuing on into graduate education and earning the degrees that generally
provide entrée to the better-rewarded jobs.

HIGH SCHOOL BACKGROUND AND ACADEMIC SKILLS

Open-admissions students had weaker high school records than did their
regular classmates. Their high school grades were obviously lower, for grades
were the basis for defining admissions status. Typically, the average grades of
open-admissions students were ten points below those of regular students.
Differences between white and minority students are minimal within the
same category of admissions status. Taking into account that most minority
students were in the open-admissions category and most whites were regular
students, however, ethnic differences are larger. Overall, for example, the high
school average of all senior college whites was 83, while for blacks it was 76
and for Hispanics 80. These disparities would lead one to expect differences in
collegiate success, because one of the literature's best-documented findings is
that high school average is the single most important influence on success in
college, whether measured by grade point average, rate of progress toward a
degree, or graduation (Astin 1993; Lavin 1965).

Another way in which the high school experience of open-admissions
and regular students differed is in the extent of academic preparation for
college. Over their four years of high school, students in college-bound high
school curricula typically take more college preparatory courses in such fields
as English, social studies, math, and science than do students in vocational
tracks or more diluted academic ones. Open-admissions students entered

CUNY with less exposure to college preparatory work. Typically, they were about 1.5–2 academic credits behind regular students. Students usually take four such credits per year in high school, so open-admissions students, in effect, often entered college with a semester's less academic preparation than regular students.

Minority students were more likely than whites to have graduated from nonacademic high school tracks. They had taken fewer college preparatory courses than whites, even within the same category of admissions status. Across admissions categories differences in preparation between whites and minorities were quite wide. In senior colleges, for example, open-admissions blacks started at CUNY more than three-quarters of a year behind white regular students; Hispanics were almost as far behind. There was a similar gap in the community colleges.

Because the open-admissions policy was designed to create a clear pathway to baccalaureate studies for students who began in community colleges, it makes sense to look at the range of academic preparation found across a diverse multicampus educational system such as CUNY's. In terms of college preparatory course work taken in high school, open-admissions students in community colleges were a year or more behind regular students in senior colleges. To cite the widest disparity, black and Hispanic open-admissions students in community colleges received the equivalent of about a year and a half less high school academic preparation than did regular white students in senior colleges. Such an ethnic inequality is especially noteworthy given that, in spite of the influence of open admissions in expanding the enrollment of minority students in four-year institutions, the modal placement for blacks and Hispanics was as open-admissions students in community colleges, while the modal placement for whites was as regular students in senior colleges.

Partly as a consequence of these differences in high school experience, open-admissions students were more likely than regular students to begin their college careers with academic deficiencies. According to the results of university-wide basic skills tests administered to freshmen in 1970 and 1971, open-admissions students entering senior colleges were far more likely than regular students to need remedial work in language skills and in math. In community colleges white open-admissions students were more in need of help than regular ones; among minority students, very high percentages showed deficiencies, irrespective of admissions status.

Minority students were much worse off than whites even within the same admissions category. Among senior college open-admissions students, for example, 68 percent of blacks and Hispanics but only 41 percent of whites needed additional work in language skills. In the two-year colleges there were vast disparities between whites and minorities in both admissions categories; the minority enrollee who didn't need remedial work was clearly an exception.

As one would expect, differences in academic skills were associated with actual placement in remedial courses: at both senior and community college levels open-admissions students were more likely than regulars to find themselves taking remedial work. Ethnicity also made a difference: minority students were far more likely than whites to be placed in remedial courses. Even among students of the same admissions status, higher percentages of black and Hispanic students were so placed. Often, the differences were quite substantial. Overall, about six in ten minority students took remedial courses, compared with less than four in ten among whites.

The remedial load students took was often quite heavy. For example, a quarter of open-admissions students in senior colleges took three or more remedial courses. The proportion taking such heavy remediation was particularly high among minority students—48 percent among blacks and 41 percent among Hispanics. Whatever the benefits of CUNY's efforts to bolster the academic skills of entering freshmen, there was a cost to students: remedial work typically carried little or no credit, and thus placement in such courses slowed initial progress toward graduation.

ATTITUDES AND ASPIRATIONS

Differences in students' high school records appear to have been associated with their academic self-confidence. Upon entering college students were asked to estimate their academic abilities in comparison with that of their college classmates. Open-admissions students were less likely than regulars to see themselves as academically above average. Ethnic disparities were also apparent: across the university about three in ten whites but only about one in ten minority students saw themselves as above average. Level of academic confidence might have influenced the likelihood of persevering in college if students encountered difficulties in their studies.

Notwithstanding the academic disadvantages that open-admissions entrants typically brought with them, they were quite ambitious in their educational aspirations, if a bit less so than regular students. Half of white and black students and more than 40 percent of Hispanics in the four-year schools said that they wanted to go beyond the B.A. into postgraduate education. The aspirations of community college entrants were lower relative to senior college students, with quite a few planning to complete their education at the A.A. level. Nonetheless, many two-year students—both white and minority—set their sights high, intending to go on to a B.A. or higher degree. For large numbers of students, then, community college was perceived as a stepping stone to further educational achievements.

Alongside those entrants who were able to specify their aspirations were others who were uncertain about their educational goals. Among community college students, 30 percent or more were not sure of their degree intentions when they started college, considerably more than the percentage of senior college students who felt undecided when they started. Open-admissions students in the two-year schools were more unsure than others. For these students, weaker high school records and a shakier sense of academic confidence may have made firmer educational plans contingent upon the outcomes of academic and other experiences in college.

Overall, across the entire university system, students were quite ambitious in their educational goals. Although the aspirations of minority students were not as high as those of whites (mainly because the proportion of minority students in two-year schools, where aspirations were lower, was greater than the proportion of whites), more than half of blacks and Hispanics wanted at least a B.A. As we said earlier, open admissions was, both in its entrance criteria and in its policy of encouraging transfers from community to senior college, a baccalaureate-oriented program. Student aspirations were in tune with this emphasis.

The differences between open-admissions and regular students and between whites and minorities—in social and educational background, personal characteristics, and college contexts—lead to different expectations about their subsequent academic success. Open-admissions students were older, were more likely to be male, and had weaker high school records, in terms of both exposure to college preparatory courses and performance in those courses. They had less academic self-confidence, and after entering college they took more remedial work. Because of these differences open-admissions students could be expected to earn lower college grades, make slower progress in earning degree credits, and ultimately be less likely to graduate. Minority students typically were more subject to these disadvantages than whites. Moreover, they carried additional burdens of economic disadvantage and a greater likelihood of having to work full-time while in school. In terms of their initial placement in CUNY, they more often started out in community colleges, and, once there, in vocational programs. Thus, in their efforts to capitalize on the opportunities created by open admissions, minority students shouldered more burdens than their white classmates. In the following sections, we shall examine how these differences in background characteristics, educational histories, and college contexts influenced educational attainments.

Undergraduate Degree Attainment

The critical question about the opportunity that open admissions created is to what extent students were able to take advantage of it. Using their initial positioning in the university as the base, how successful were students in earning undergraduate degrees? By 1984, twelve or more years after these students had begun college, their graduation record seemed largely complete. More than 70 percent of those who had started at one of CUNY's four-year institutions earned bachelor's degrees (table 2.4).[6] Regular students were far more likely to have earned B.A.'s than were open-admissions students. More than 80 percent of the former but only 56 percent of the latter had B.A.'s by 1984. A small proportion of entrants (4 percent) earned associate's degrees.

Ethnic membership made a difference for baccalaureate chances. Overall, more than three-quarters of whites but only 56 percent of blacks and less than half of Hispanics who started in CUNY's senior colleges earned B.A. degrees. These disparities are partly due to the typically weaker high school background of minority students, which made them more dependent on open admissions than whites for entry to the university. But even among students of the same admissions status, ethnic differences stand out. For example, among open-admissions students, the graduation rate for whites (61 percent) surpassed that for blacks (49 percent). Hispanics (39 percent) lagged substantially

[6]Eighty-seven percent of these degrees were granted by CUNY colleges and 13 percent were awarded by other institutions in the wider higher education system. Of the students who had not received any college diploma by this time, 13 percent were enrolled in college in 1983 or 1984, though we do not know whether they were actually working for a degree or simply taking courses for career advancement or other reasons. While some of these persisters undoubtedly earned a degree after 1984, and others who were not then enrolled may have returned to school to complete their undergraduate work, ultimate rates of graduation seem unlikely to have increased in any dramatic way. For example, if all of the nongraduates who were enrolled in 1983 and 1984 eventually earned a degree, the overall graduation rate would have been raised by less than four percent.

Table 2.4 B.A. Attainment Rates Twelve or More Years After Entry, by Admissions Status and Ethnicity: Senior College Entrants

Percentages

| | Admission Status | | |
Ethnicity	Regular	Open	Total
White	84	61	77
Black	74	49	56
Hispanic	59	39	49
All senior college entrants	82	56	73

Source: Follow-up survey.

Note: Because the 1970, 1971, and 1972 cohorts have been aggregated, results are after fourteen years for the 1970 cohort, thirteen years for 1971, and twelve years for 1972.

behind, although their greater likelihood of earning an associate degree helped to ensure that at least half had something to show for their efforts.

These ethnic differences in long-term graduation rates raise questions about a policy that aimed not only to bring minority students into college but also to enhance their chances of academic success. Why did blacks and Hispanics graduate at lower rates than whites? As we said earlier, minority students tended to be disadvantaged in terms of a number of characteristics that research has found to be associated with B.A. attainment. Relative to whites, they more often came from low-income families and their parents had less educational attainment. Perhaps open admissions was unable to overcome the influences of such disadvantages. In addition to their lower high school averages, minority students were also more likely than whites to have come to CUNY from nonacademic high school tracks. Though the university established extensive compensatory programs, perhaps they were not sufficient to overcome weak preparation for college. Indeed, because minority students took more noncredit remedial work than other students, perhaps they more often became discouraged over slow progress toward a degree. In spite of the fact that CUNY had free tuition until 1975, minority students, more often than whites, needed to work full-time in order to meet their living expenses while going to college. This may well have interfered with the amount of time they could devote to their studies, thus lowering their chances of earning the bachelor's degree.

To explore these potential effects, we conducted a regression analysis of baccalaureate attainment among senior college entrants; to avoid overburdening the text we will summarize the results without presenting the table. The analysis confirms that virtually all of the 21-percentage-point difference in the B.A. attainment rates of whites and blacks shown in table 2.4 and about half of the 28-point gap between whites and Hispanics can be explained by several— but not all—of the variables for which we have controlled.[7] Ethnic differences are not accounted for by disparities of social background: though white students came from families with higher incomes and their parents had more education, these inequalities did not directly influence the chances of earning a B.A. degree. On the other hand, high school grades were very important: those with higher averages had a better chance of graduating college. High school track also played a role: students from nonacademic tracks or from a more diluted academic curriculum that offered fewer college preparatory courses were less likely than others to earn a bachelor's degree. Further, our analyses indicate that, at least for the early years of open admissions, the CUNY compensatory effort did not offset the influence of high school back-

---

[7]We regressed B.A. attainment on the following variables: gender, ethnicity, age at matriculation, family income, father's education, mother's education, high school average in college preparatory courses, and total units of academic course work in high school. In addition, we controlled for academic self-rating and the importance accorded to getting a broad, general education as a reason for deciding to go to college. We also controlled for degree aspirations, full-time work while in college, and the number of remedial courses taken.

Because the dependent variable in this regression, B.A. attainment, is a dichotomy, logistic regression is arguably more appropriate than Ordinary Least Squares regression. The split on the dependent variable is not extreme, however, a situation in which OLS and logistic regression tend to produce similar estimates (Cleary and Angel 1984; Hanushek and Jackson 1977). Even when the split is extreme, estimates from the two procedures may be close to one another (Cleary and Angel 1984). When we ran a logistic version of this regression, we obtained estimates close to the OLS coefficients that we have opted to present here. Throughout the book the great majority of regression analyses involve a continuous dependent variable. For consistency of presentation, we have used OLS regression in the relatively few cases where a dependent variable is dichotomous.

A brief word is in order for readers unfamiliar with OLS regression analysis. Put simply, it is a statistical technique that estimates the influence of each of several variables on an outcome—that is, on a dependent variable—while the other variables are controlled. In effect, one can assess the net effect of any given variable with the others held constant. A straightforward explanation of how to read the results of regression analysis has been written by Richard D. Alba (see Lavin et al. 1981, 318–26). For an extensive treatment, see Cohen and Cohen (1983).

ground: students who needed remedial work and received it had no better chance to earn a B.A. than comparable students who did not receive such services.[8] Graduation chances were diminished by full-time employment, which depressed the grades that students earned. Thus the greater tendency of minority students to work full-time did indeed lower their chances for graduation.

As we mentioned, deficits on the variables associated with graduation do not completely account for the lower B.A. attainment rates of Hispanics. Even when the full set of determinants is controlled, the gap between the graduation rates of whites and Hispanics remains substantial—about 16 percentage points. The persistence of this differential suggests that uncontrolled factors associated with Hispanic ethnicity—including the fact that for many English was not their primary language—hindered academic progress in the senior colleges.

All in all, then, the open-admissions policy did not erase the influences of earlier disadvantage, which continued to make themselves felt as senior college entrants moved through their college careers. Nonetheless, disadvantages did not predestine students to failure. Substantial numbers of open-admissions students succeeded in earning bachelor's degrees. Indeed, nearly 60 percent of the B.A.'s awarded to blacks and almost a third of those to Hispanics were earned by students admitted through open admissions (among whites the figure was less than 20 percent). So in spite of the lower rates of graduation for blacks and Hispanics, the program had a substantial effect in increasing the numbers of minority students who earned B.A. degrees.

RESULTS FOR COMMUNITY COLLEGE STUDENTS

As we said in Chapter 1, a central feature of CUNY's open-admissions policy was a guarantee of transfer to a four-year college for those who completed an A.A. degree. Among the students who started in community colleges, about half received this degree (table 2.5). Admissions status was associated with graduation chances—regular students were more successful in completing an

---

[8]Lavin et al. (1981, 247–49) have pointed out that not all students who needed remediation received it, thus providing an approximation to a natural experiment in which to assess CUNY's remedial programs. However, there is reason to believe that some remedial students differed from nonremedial ones in ways not measured in the research—for example in academic motivation. Such a possibility confounds a natural experiment and may have produced an overly negative picture of remediation's impact.

Table 2.5 A.A. Attainment Rates Twelve or More Years After Entry, by Admissions Status and Ethnicity: Community College Entrants

Percentages

	Admissions Status		
Ethnicity	Regular	Open	Total
White	57	44	50
Black	63	43	47
Hispanic	55	47	50
All community college entrants	58	44	49

Source: Follow-up survey.

A.A. than were those in the open-admissions contingent. In contrast to the earlier studies of open admissions (Lavin et al. 1979, 1981), however, where after five years substantial differences separated whites from blacks and Hispanics, ethnic differences over the longer term narrowed: in both regular and open-admissions categories, black and Hispanic students were at least as likely as whites to earn an A.A.

How successful were community college entrants in transferring to four-year colleges? In examining this question we have chosen to consider all students, regardless of their degree intentions at the time they entered college. We have done so because aspirations at that point could change later on.[9] Some students may have scaled down initially high aspirations as a consequence of academic disappointments. Others may have raised their sights as a result of positive educational experiences, and still others, initially unsure of how far they wanted to go in higher education, may have formed a clearer sense of direction as their college careers unfolded.

In the aggregate, half of community college entrants eventually transferred to a four-year college (table 2.6). This is about double the rate found in the initial studies after five years (Lavin et al. 1981), indicating that many students

[9]Many studies (for example, Velez 1985; Astin et al. 1982; Anderson 1981) limit their samples to those who initially held B.A. aspirations or who enrolled in academic programs—the ones that are more closely geared to transfer. Such designs foreclose the possibility of change in degree intentions.

Table 2.6 Transfer Rates Twelve or More Years After Entry, by A.A. Degree Attainment, Curriculum, Admissions Status, and Ethnicity

Percentages

	Admissions Status		
	Regular	Open	Total
	Community College Entrants Who Earned an A.A.		
Liberal arts	83	76	79
Vocational	57	56	56
All curricula	66	65	66
	Community College Entrants Who Did Not Earn an A.A.		
Liberal arts	50	42	45
Vocational	26	23	24
All curricula	38	32	33
	All Community College Entrants		
White	55	47	50
Black	56	46	48
Hispanic	49	44	46
All students	54	47	50

Source: Follow-up survey.

made this move well after their initial enrollment. Open admissions students were only slightly less likely to transfer than regular students, and minority students were about as likely as whites.

Students took different pathways to senior colleges. As one might expect, those who completed an A.A. in the liberal arts curriculum were by far the most likely to take the next step into the senior colleges; about eight in ten of these students took advantage of CUNY's guarantee of admission for A.A. recipients. Open-admissions graduates were only slightly less likely to transfer than regular graduates. Even the graduates of career programs, the ones conventionally thought of as terminal, were fairly mobile: more than half made it to a senior college. Having an A.A. degree was not a prerequisite for transfer: quite a few liberal arts students—half of regular students and about 40 percent of open-admissions students—leapfrogged to a four-year school without a degree. Transfer rates were lowest among career program students who never earned A.A.'s. Nonetheless, a quarter of these students managed a move to a four-year school, suggesting that over time some of those who entered vocational programs without initially aspiring to a bachelor's degree raised their sights.

Questions about the role of community colleges in providing opportunity for higher education are not answered conclusively by identifying who transfers and who does not. Transfer, if it is to be meaningful, must be accompanied by a reasonable chance to earn a B.A. Among the transfers, more than 60 percent succeeded in earning bachelor's degrees. Admissions status made a difference for degree chances: almost 70 percent of regular transfers received diplomas, compared with almost 60 percent for the open-admissions contingent. Though minority students had been about as likely as white students to earn associate's degrees and to transfer to a four-year college, they fell well behind whites in rates of baccalaureate attainment. Almost 70 percent of white transfers received bachelor's degrees, but less than half of minority transfers did.

In summary, among the total group of minority students who began their studies at community colleges, rates of B.A. attainment were below those of white entrants. Thirty-five percent of the latter had completed bachelor's degrees by 1984, compared with 23 percent of blacks and 21 percent of Hispanics—gaps in graduation that were smaller than among senior college entrants, but substantial nevertheless.[10]

[10]When we regressed an indicator of B.A. attainment on a large number of independent variables for all entrants to community colleges, we found that these deficits of 12 percentage points for blacks and 14 points for Hispanics are largely explained by differences in high school background, community college curriculum, and freshman grades. Adjusted differences between whites and both minority groups were about 5 percentage points, not statistically significant gaps.

UNIVERSITY-WIDE RATES OF B.A. ATTAINMENT

A consideration of educational attainments across the entire CUNY system provides the broadest perspective for addressing a critical question: to what extent were minority students, the intended beneficiaries of the open-admissions policy, able to capitalize on the new educational opportunities by earning B.A.'s? By 1984, minority students at CUNY had completed B.A.'s at about half the rate of whites: 60 percent of whites had graduated, compared with about a third of minority students (table 2.7). No doubt minority students earned B.A.'s at lower rates in part because they were disadvantaged in terms of high school grades, high school track, and having to work full-time while in college. Yet there may be an additional source of disadvantage to minority students: B.A. attainment rates for community college entrants were vastly lower than for those who began at four-year schools. In the aggregate, 74 percent of the latter earned a bachelor's degree, but only 31 percent of two-year entrants did. We have already seen that although open admissions substantially increased minority representation at the senior colleges, blacks and Hispanics nevertheless were much more likely than whites to have entered a community college, rendering them most vulnerable to any negative effect of the community colleges on prospects for obtaining a B.A.

Previous research on the sources of the low B.A. attainment rates of community college entrants has implicated attributes of the institutional environment of two-year colleges, as well as their articulation with four-year institutions. This community college effect has been found to persist even when differences in the characteristics of the students who attend the two types of institution have been controlled—such characteristics as degree aspirations, high school preparation, and employment while in college. Why does attending a community college tend to depress the chances of completing a B.A.? Norms supporting terminal study, counseling that seeks to align educational aspirations with early academic performance, problems in transferring credits to the upper level, and inadequate academic preparation in the two-year colleges are among the many factors that have been cited (for reviews see Dougherty 1987,1994; Lee and Frank 1990; Lee et al. 1993). Earlier research confirmed the existence of such an effect at CUNY, when student academic careers had been tracked for five years (Alba and Lavin 1981). But whether community college entry still exerts a negative influence after twelve or more years, when two-year entrants have had much more time to complete their bachelor's degrees, is a question we now explore.

Table 2.7 B.A. Attainment Rates, by Level of Entry and Ethnicity

Percentages

	Level of Entry			
Ethnicity	Senior College	Community College	Difference	All CUNY
White	76	35	41	60
Black	55	23	32	33
Hispanic	49	21	28	32
All students	74	31	43	54

Source: Follow-up survey.

To examine whether a community college effect partly accounts for the comparatively low rates of bachelor's degree attainment among minority students, and to disentangle such an effect from individual characteristics that may also affect B.A. attainment rates, we carried out a regression analysis of baccalaureate attainment, including entrants to both tiers of CUNY (results are shown in Appendix B, table B.1). The analysis has two stages. Included in the first are measures of social background (ethnicity, gender, father's education, mother's education, family income, age at entry) and high school preparation (grade average in academic courses, number of academic courses taken). Also controlled are educational aspirations on entry to college, the amount of confidence the student had in his or her academic abilities, and an indicator of whether the student was attending primarily for vocational or for general educational reasons. Also included is the level of college entered (senior or community), employment status in college, the number of remedial courses taken, and curriculum pursued. In a second stage of the analysis we have added college grade point average during the first year to these predictors.[11]

[11]As we said in note 6, we have opted to use OLS regression here, rather than logistic regression. Again, the split on the dependent variable, B.A. attainment, is not extreme, and a logistic regression produced results similar to the OLS estimates. The pooled standardized coefficients shown for ethnicity, family income, and for degree aspirations are "sheaf" coefficients, described by Heise (1972).

Several individual characteristics clearly influence the likelihood of earning a B.A. Such aspects of social origins as family income and parents' education appear to have little direct influence on B.A. attainment; their effects are transmitted indirectly through their effect on performance in high school. The latter, including the amount of college preparatory course work taken and grades, are important determinants of B.A. completion: each college preparatory course improved B.A. chances by about 1 percentage point. More important was the quality of the work done in those courses. All else equal, students who had earned good grades in high school were more likely than weaker students to complete B.A.'s. Although women were a bit more likely to receive B.A.'s than men, this difference disappears once disparities in high school background are taken into account. Members of minority-groups, most of whom were open-admissions students, were disadvantaged because of relatively poor high school averages. High school grades influence graduation in large part through their effect on college grades.

In addition to high school background, other characteristics contributed to the lower graduation rates of minority students. Majoring in liberal arts increased prospects of completing a B.A. by about 7 percentage points, but minority students were less likely than whites to choose this major. Having to work full-time, as a larger proportion of minority students did, lowered degree chances by 5 percent, mainly because work had a negative effect on college grades. Grades themselves had a powerful impact: a difference of one letter grade in the first year (such as the difference between a B and a C average) was associated with a 13 percent difference in graduation chances. Blacks and Hispanics earned lower grades on average than others, hurting their chances of finishing. Students with stronger academic self-confidence were more likely to complete a B.A., and minority students were generally less confident than whites. Degree intentions had an important influence on B.A. attainment, but blacks, Hispanics, and whites did not differ much in these aspirations. Because community college students generally had lower aspirations than senior college entrants, however, this factor partly explains why the former were less likely to earn B.A.'s.

Even with these characteristics of individuals controlled, community college entry is one of the most powerful predictors of B.A. attainment. With controls, the large unadjusted difference between senior and community college B.A. rates (43 percentage points) narrows considerably, but community college entry continues to have a substantial negative influence: two-year entrants were 19 percentage points less likely to earn a baccalaureate than comparable students who started college in a four-year school. Minority students, then, are further disadvantaged by their overrepresentation in the community college tier.

In summary, this analysis explains most of the wide differential in B.A. attainment that separated whites from minorities under open admissions. The 27-percentage-point difference in B.A. attainment rates between whites and blacks and the 28-point white-Hispanic gap are reduced to 3 and 8 percentage points, respectively. Relative to whites, the high school preparation of black and Hispanic students was weaker, and they more often held full-time jobs. Partly as a result of these disadvantages, they compiled lower grade point averages. But minority students were also more likely to start college in a two-year school, and this additional constraint on baccalaureate attainment fell more heavily upon them than on whites.

Our analyses necessarily lead to a mixed judgment about students' success in earning undergraduate degrees. Many students whose entry to CUNY was made possible by open admissions were able to use this opportunity to good advantage. The chance for college that the policy provided was especially important for minority students who started in four-year schools: 53 percent of the B.A.'s awarded to them went to open-admissions students. In community colleges minority students were, over the long haul, as successful as whites in earning associate's degrees. Among those who went on to earn a B.A., open admissions provided a very substantial opportunity: 75 percent of the baccalaureates to black two-year college entrants were received by the open-admissions contingent, as were 57 percent of those to Hispanics; open-admissions whites also benefited, receiving half of the bachelor's degrees. In spite of these successes, the achievements of open-admissions students did not equal those of regular students, and minority students were well behind whites in B.A. attainment. Nonetheless, social origins, educational background, and experiences once in college did not predestine students to success or failure. When the doors of CUNY were opened wide, the opportunity that the university provided was one that a great many students used well.

These results provide little support for the fears that accompanied the birth of open admissions. Although a substantial number of open-admissions students graduated, the data hardly sustain the apprehension that CUNY would turn into a diploma mill under the program. Neither do the results support the concern of some that the university would turn into a revolving door, whetting the appetites of open-admissions students for education and then frustrating them as they flunked out in droves. Using the actual achievements of students as the measure, the truth does not lie near either of these extremes.

Academic Timetables

In considering degree attainments under the open-admissions policy, our focus is upon how far students were able to climb the rungs of the educational ladder, including the attainment of postgraduate degrees. Not only is the bachelor's degree a prerequisite for going further, but the amount of time it takes can make a difference as well. We expect that additional time needed to finish a B.A. will have a negative impact on the likelihood of postgraduate study, in part because long-term study imposes costs not incurred by students who finish within the traditional time frame. Chief among these costs are earnings forgone. The greater the forgone earnings, the greater the incentive to capitalize immediately on the bachelor's degree instead of pursuing postgraduate studies. Students who work full-time are not exempt from this cost. Indeed, they find themselves in the paradoxical position of needing to work to support themselves as they attend school, while the time this may add to their academic career delays the benefits (such as higher earnings) from the degree.

In addition, students' ages at the time they complete their B.A. may be negatively related to earning a postgraduate degree. Older bachelor's recipients may be more likely than younger ones to have assumed family and other obligations that compete with the demands of advanced study.

Although social scientists have for decades been aware of the need for long time periods to assess educational attainments (Kerckhoff 1980; Thomas 1981), the role of time in undergraduate careers remains poorly understood. Evidence indicates that the conventional yardstick used for judging academic success—the four- or five-year graduation rate—is increasingly out of alignment with the changing realities of student academic careers (Eckland 1964; California State Colleges 1969; Campbell 1980; California Postsecondary Education Commission 1987; Levin and Levin 1991). The extended time frame used in this study allows us not only to estimate ultimate B.A. rates more accurately but also to examine the determinants of time to B.A. and its consequences for postgraduate degree attainment.

Our follow-up data reveal dramatically that student progress toward graduation can extend over many years and thus that the story of CUNY's open-admissions policy requires a long time in the telling. In the senior colleges the academic careers of large proportions of graduates stretched far beyond the four-year interval. Nearly half needed more than four years to complete their bachelor's degree, 16 percent needed more than five years, 8 percent took more than seven years, and 5 percent went beyond nine years (table 2.8). Time played a critical role for the open-admissions graduates. About 60 percent went beyond four years to finish their studies; more than 25 percent needed longer than five years (compared with 13 percent of regular graduates), and 16 percent needed more than seven years (6 percent of regulars went beyond seven years).

As these findings imply, different time perspectives provide much different impressions of the graduation picture. If we assess graduation rates after four years, regular-admissions students were nearly two and one-half times as likely as open-admissions students to have completed a B.A. After an additional year, however, the graduation rate for regulars was only 1.8 times that of open-admissions students, and by the end point of our data, the ratio had dropped to 1.5 to 1. In short, over time there was a narrowing of the disparity between the two categories of students.

Ethnic differences in the length of time to graduate are striking. Among the senior college entrants, only 15 percent of whites but almost 40 percent of blacks and a third of Hispanic graduates needed more than five years. Just how large time looms in the undergraduate careers of minority students is revealed by the percentages who took more than nine years to finish their bachelor's degrees: 15 percent took that long, compared with 4 percent among whites. Among open-admission students, the proportions are even higher: one-quarter of Hispanic degree holders and almost a fifth of blacks went beyond nine years, compared with 7 percent of white open-admission graduates.

Graduation takes even longer among the community college contingent. Less than a quarter were able to make it from community college to a bachelor's degree in four years. Nearly a third needed more than seven years, and a fifth went beyond nine years. Open-admissions graduates were slower than regulars, and in both admissions categories, minority graduates took longer than whites: overall a quarter of blacks and nearly a third of Hispanic graduates needed more than nine years (less than 20 percent of whites took this much time). In sum, not only were B.A. rates low for community college entrants, but graduates took a long time to finish. On average they needed 6.7 years, compared with 5.1 years for those who started college in four-year schools.

When we look at the time it takes to complete a B.A. on a university-wide basis—that is, without controlling for the level of college initially entered—ethnic disparities are dramatic (table 2.9). If a longitudinal study tracked

Table 2.8 Time Required to Attain B.A., by Level of Entry, Admissions Status, and Ethnicity

Admission Status	% Still Working Toward B.A. After:			
	4 Yrs.	5 Yrs.	7 Yrs.	9 Yrs.
	Senior College Entrants			
Regular	39	13	6	4
White	38	12	6	4
Black	60	30	12	5
Hispanic	54	27	17	10
Open	62	27	16	9
White	61	25	14	7
Black	71	42	25	19
Hispanic	62	43	30	25
All students	45	16	8	5
White	43	15	7	4
Black	67	38	20	15
Hispanic	57	33	22	16
	Community College Entrants			
Regular	69	42	25	17
White	64	36	21	13
Black	97	81	52	33
Hispanic	88	63	42	25
Open	85	62	35	19
White	79	55	28	17
Black	91	77	50	23
Hispanic	94	72	44	33
All students	77	53	30	20
White	74	47	26	18
Black	91	78	48	26
Hispanic	90	70	45	30

Source: Follow-up survey.

Table 2.9 Time to B.A. Degree, by Ethnicity

| | Percentages | | |
| | Ethnicity | | |
Years	White	Black	Hispanic
4	50	21	29
5	28	20	23
6	8	12	8
7 or more	14	48	41

Source: Follow-up survey.

students for only six years, it would fail to report 14 percent of the B.A.'s eventually earned by whites, more than 40 percent of those received by Hispanics, and almost half of those earned by blacks.

In order to gain more insight into the factors that influence the length of undergraduate careers and to distinguish them from the determinants of ultimately earning a B.A., we conducted a regression analysis of the number of years it took degree holders to complete the B.A. Included in the analysis are the same variables for which we controlled in the analysis of B.A. attainment: ethnicity, social origins, gender, high school preparation and performance, level of college entered, degree aspirations, academic self-confidence, general versus vocational orientation to college, employment status in college, remediation, and final grade point average (which we substituted for first-year GPA).

Before taking account of these factors, black graduates averaged 1.7 years more than whites and Hispanics 1.5 more years. When the additional variables are taken into account (Appendix B, table B.2), full-time employment while in college emerges as the most important determinant of time to B.A., adding 2.4 years to the course of study. Grade point average also played a substantial role: a difference equivalent to one letter grade translated into a difference of a year; that is, a student with a B average graduated a year ahead of one with a C average who was comparable in other respects. Taking remedial courses slowed progress toward the B.A.: each course delayed graduation by almost a fifth of a year. Community college entry had a strong effect, delaying the degree by four-fifths of a year.

In the aggregate, these variables explain most of the differences in the time that whites and minority students require to earn a B.A. Minority graduates took longer to finish partly because they were more likely to work full-time, they took more remedial courses, they compiled lower grade point averages, and they were more likely to have begun at a community college. But even after these factors are accounted for, minority graduates still took longer: blacks used about four-tenths of a year more than whites, and Hispanics remained nearly a half-year behind.

This analysis of the course of undergraduate careers shows that persistence toward the bachelor's degree over long periods of time—often more than twice the normatively prescribed four- or five-year period—characterized the efforts of substantial proportions of students, especially those of minority background. Such persistence has mixed implications for a policy of open admissions. On the one hand, the tenacity with which many used educational opportunity testifies to the energy and ambition that many were able to draw upon in overcoming obstacles on the way to completion of a degree. On the other hand, the greater amount of time used by open-admissions students and particularly minority ones constitutes another form of disadvantage: prolonged study delays the time when educational credentials can begin to produce their yield in the labor market, and may (as we shall consider in the next section) reduce the chances of earning an advanced degree. If additional time is a disadvantage, it is one rooted in earlier handicaps. To earn a B.A., minority students more than others had to overcome disadvantages associated with weak high school preparation, community college entry, and full-time work while in college. Many were unable to clear these hurdles. But for the many who did succeed, there often were new costs in the form of extended time to degree completion.

Postgraduate Degree Attainment

Over several decades, manufacturing jobs have been on a sharp downward slope in cities such as New York, while those in the service sector—in financial services, legal services, research and information processing, education and culture, for example—have grown dramatically (U.S. Department of Labor 1988). It is precisely in these expanding sectors that educational requirements are typically highest.[12]

---

[12]New York has been experiencing a cyclical employment contraction in the service sector.

In such a changing labor market, a major innovation such as CUNY's open-admissions policy must be assessed not only in terms of the extent to which the new students it attracted to college were able to convert opportunity into A.A. and B.A. degrees but also by the extent to which the policy added to students' chances for the attainment of even more advanced degrees —the ones requisite for entry to the more rewarded positions in American society. Indeed, opportunity for graduate and professional training is one of the more important equity issues in higher education (Thomas 1987).

Under open admissions, progress beyond the bachelor's degree to the attainment of master's and advanced professional degrees was not a rare occurrence, though the great majority of the students who earned postgraduate degrees did so at the M.A. level (table 2.10).[13] As one would expect, the level at which students entered CUNY was associated with the chances of earning a postgraduate degree: senior college entrants were far more likely to do so than were those who started in community colleges. Regular students were much more successful than their open-admissions classmates, especially in the senior colleges. Still, quite a few in the open-admissions contingent were able to take the opportunity that the policy gave them and climbed to the highest rungs of the educational ladder: a fifth of whites and blacks and more than 10 percent of Hispanics earned postgraduate degrees.

When we look at postgraduate degree attainment across both of CUNY's tiers—that is, university-wide—differences between whites and minorities are quite substantial: the former were about two and a half times more likely to earn some kind of postgraduate credential (25 percent of whites but about 10 percent of minority students completed a graduate program). A portion of this difference seems due to the winnowing process that took place during the undergraduate years. As we saw earlier, about 60 percent of whites but only about one-third of minority students earned B.A.'s. Among the baccalaureate holders, ethnic differences in rates of postgraduate degree attainment narrow considerably, but whites remain well ahead: around 30 percent of black and

---

Nonetheless, there is no reason to believe that over the long term, these jobs will not continue as dominant components of the area's economy.

[13]Master's degrees were earned in diverse fields: about 20 percent were in health and social services (nursing, M.S.W., M.P.A.), about 35 percent were in education, 15 percent were in business, and 15 percent were in arts, humanities, or social science.

We believe that the count of postgraduate degrees was largely complete as of 1984. For those who had completed the B.A., we looked at the number who reported being enrolled in education in that year. Only a handful said that they were still in school.

Table 2.10 Postgraduate Degree Attainment, by Level of College Entered, Admissions Status, and Ethnicity

Percentages

Level of College

	Senior		Community		
Educational Attainment	Regular Admissions	Open Admissions	Regular Admissions	Open Admissions	All CUNY
All Entrants					
M.A.					
White	29	17	10	5	18
Black	30	18	3	4	9
Hispanic	17	10	6	3	8
Advanced degree[a]					
White	13	3	3	1	7
Black	7	2	2	1	2
Hispanic	3	2	1	1	1
Any postgraduate degree[b]					
White	42	20	13	6	25
Black	37	20	5	5	11
Hispanic	20	12	7	4	9
B. A. Recipients					
Any postgraduate degree[b]					
White	50	33	31	21	42
Black	48	41	17	21	31
Hispanic	33	31	27	22	29

Source: Follow-up survey.

[a]Professional and doctoral degrees.

[b]Includes master's, professional, and doctoral degrees.

Hispanic B.A.'s went on to complete postgraduate study; more than 40 percent of white B.A.'s did.

To gain a better understanding of ethnic differences in completion of a postgraduate degree, we assessed the influence of a number of factors, including the number of years it took to complete the B.A., whether students had started college at a four-year or a two-year school, whether a student worked full-time as an undergraduate, college grades, and how old a student was at receipt of the B.A. (the table is not presented).[14] The single most important influence on postgraduate degree attainment is how long it took to earn the B.A. A student who completed a B.A. in five years was 10 percent more likely to receive a postgraduate degree than a student who was comparable in other ways but took seven years. Students who took longer were older when they received the B.A., suggesting that age norms and competing obligations associated with age—marriage, parenthood and the necessity of working—diminish graduate school chances. Not unexpectedly, college grade point average had an effect: a difference of a letter grade made a 9 percentage point difference in the chance of earning a graduate degree. The results also suggest that starting in a community college diminishes graduate school chances because of the additional time it takes to get a B.A. via that route.

Overall, this analysis explains the ethnic disparities in postgraduate degrees. Minority students' lower grades in college, and, of most importance, the fact that they took substantially longer than whites to complete their B.A.'s lowered their chances of receiving a postgraduate degree. Further hindering their chances is the fact that minority students were typically older than whites when they started college.

These findings on graduate degrees help to clarify one of the more heated controversies surrounding open admissions. As we noted in the first chapter, many had feared that lowering the access barriers would lead to a decline in academic standards at the university and, ultimately, to a serious erosion in the value of CUNY baccalaureates. One symptom of devaluation would be a tendency of graduate school admissions offices to downgrade the CUNY diploma as an entry credential. We do not have all of the data necessary to know whether this happened. We do not know, for example, how many students applied to graduate schools outside of CUNY, how many were

---

[14]Other independent variables in the regression were ethnicity, high school average, and degree aspirations on entry to college. The regression was conducted for B.A. recipients only, and the dependent variable, postgraduate degree attainment, combined M.A.'s and advanced degrees.

admitted, and how acceptance rates compared with those for comparable students in the pre—open admissions era. However, we do know that of all graduate degrees earned, 65 percent of the M.A.'s and 94 percent of the advanced and professional degrees were granted by universities outside of CUNY. The fact that substantial numbers of students were admitted to graduate studies and met the standards set by other universities at least suggests that the CUNY diploma retained considerable value after open admissions.

A Note on Gender and Educational Attainments

Although the open-admissions policy had no specific gender focus, it is important to take note of differences between men and women in educational attainment, especially because gender emerges as an important consideration in subsequent chapters that analyze the association between educational credentials and labor-market outcomes. Although their edge was not great, women generally surpassed men in educational achievement. They were less likely to leave college without a diploma of some kind. For example, among minority students about half of men but less than 40 percent of women failed to earn any degree (among whites about 30 percent of men but less than a quarter of women came away empty-handed). Among degree holders, women were more likely than men to earn A.A.'s, and they were generally equal in B.A. attainment; they led men—though not by much—in completing postgraduate degrees (especially at the M.A. level): their postgraduate attainment rates were 27 percent among whites (compared with 24 percent for men), 12 percent among blacks (men's rate was 7 percent) and 11 percent for Hispanics (men were at 8 percent). As we said earlier, women were less likely than men to be open-admissions students. Their stronger high school backgrounds largely explain their superiority in educational attainment.

The Impact of Open Admissions

There is no easy bottom-line statement to be made about the impact of open admissions on the educational attainments that we have been reviewing. Minority students did less well at every step (table 2.11). They were far more likely to drop out of college without any degree (reflected in the table as holding a high school diploma for the highest degree earned). Indeed, among black and Hispanic open-admissions students in community colleges—the modal category of entry for minority students—half never earned any college

Table 2.11 Highest Degree Earned, by Level of College Entered, Admissions Status, and Ethnicity

| | Percentages | | | | |
| | Senior | | Community | | |
Educational Attainment	Regular Admissions	Open Admissions	Regular Admissions	Open Admissions	All CUNY
High school diploma					
White	13	33	30	45	27
Black	19	44	32	51	44
Hispanic	35	48	40	50	43
A.A.					
White	3	6	29	25	13
Black	5	7	39	26	23
Hispanic	6	13	36	31	25
B.A.					
White	42	41	28	24	35
Black	40	29	25	18	23
Hispanic	39	27	18	15	23
M.A.					
White	29	17	10	5	18
Black	30	18	3	4	9
Hispanic	17	10	6	3	8
Advanced degree[a]					
White	13	3	3	1	7
Black	7	2	2	1	2
Hispanic	3	2	1	1	1

Source: Follow-up survey.

[a]Includes professional and doctoral degrees.

credential. Minority entrants who did receive a diploma were more likely to be found with an associate's degree than were whites. Overall, two-thirds of blacks and Hispanics never went beyond the associate level, compared with only 40 percent of whites. Whatever the undergraduate degree, typically it look minority students longer to earn it. Subsequently, they were less likely to be found among the ranks of master's or advanced degree holders.

These disparities between white and minority students in educational attainment derive partly from differences in high school experience. Blacks and Hispanics more often came from nonacademic high school tracks, and in the academic course work that they did take, they tended to receive lower grades. These inequalities of high school background bred new disadvantages in college: they influenced students to apply to community colleges and to choose placement in vocational curricula. These placements lowered the probability of earning a bachelor's degree. But whatever the level of entry to college, the weaker high school preparation and performance of minority students also diminished their baccalaureate chances. The minority students who completed bachelor's degrees took longer to do so than whites, partly because the full-time jobs that they more often held while attending college added substantially to the time they needed to finish. Also extending the time to degree were the poorer college grades earned by minority students: undoubtedly, they more often found themselves repeating courses or taking additional ones to make up for credits lost. Moreover, community college placement added to the length of the baccalaureate process: all else equal, initial placement in a two-year institution added almost a year. This disadvantage fell most heavily upon minority students. At both two- and four-year schools, weak preparation increased the likelihood of placement in remedial courses, adding to the time needed for degree completion. The greater difficulties experienced by minority students in completing a bachelor's degree and the longer time period they needed to finish lowered, in turn, their chances of earning a postgraduate degree.

In following students from the inception of open admissions through their eventual educational attainments to 1984, we have seen a process of cumulative disadvantage unfold. Inequalities of economic status and high school background created new disadvantages in college. These new burdens further diminished minority chances of achieving the top credentials in the higher education system. In effect, a chain of contingencies that originated in events before college hindered minority students' eventual attainments in higher education. Even such an ambitious intervention as open-admissions, coming after important inequalities had already been produced by a variety of social processes, was unable to eliminate disparities in attainments.

It is hard to find in these results much basis for the fears that open admissions would cause CUNY's academic integrity to unravel. Using graduation as the test, it hardly appears that CUNY was giving away diplomas to undeserving students after opening its doors to all high school graduates. That weaker students did much less well than those with stronger academic backgrounds is consistent with what would be expected in an institution where academic processes were operating. Moreover, many graduates continued to be accepted for postgraduate study in non-CUNY institutions and to meet the requirements of those places successfully.

Notwithstanding the policy's limitations, open admissions produced substantial benefits. In order to convey the magnitude of its effects, we have developed (from table 2.11) a set of projections to the populations involved. In the years 1970–72, about 100,000 black, Hispanic, and white students entered the university as first-time freshmen. More than 52,000 of these students entered senior colleges, among them about 18,000 open-admissions students. More than 47,000 students entered community colleges—almost 30,000 as open-admissions students. For both levels of college and both admissions statuses within each level and each ethnic group, we have estimated the numbers in the population who earned each type of degree. The projections are shown in table 2.12.

More than 68,000 students who began as freshmen during the first three years of open admissions eventually graduated from the various levels of the higher education system. More than 27,000 of these graduates, or 40 percent, were open-admissions students. More than 21,000 completed a graduate program, 5,200 of them coming from the open-admissions ranks.

In order to portray the amount of opportunity created by the program, we have constructed an index consisting of the ratio of total degrees produced to the number of degrees earned by regular-admissions students (the number of degrees that would have been earned in the absence of an open-admissions program). Thus, a ratio of 3 would mean that open admissions tripled the number of degrees earned. These ratios are presented in table 2.12.

Though all groups benefited from the opportunity flowing from open admissions, benefits to minority students, especially black students, were dramatic. While open admissions increased the number of bachelor's degrees earned by white senior college entrants 1.4 times, for example, it tripled the number of B.A.'s earned by senior college blacks and increased Hispanic B.A.'s 1.7 times. Among community college entrants, though open admissions doubled the number of white B.A.'s, it more than tripled those going to blacks and increased those to Hispanics two and one-half times. Overall, across CUNY's

Table 2.12 Estimated Number of Degrees Earned by All First-Time Freshmen Who Entered CUNY, 1970–72, by Level of College Entered, Admissions Status, and Ethnicity

Ethnicity	Level of College							
	Senior			Community			All CUNY	Ratio[a]
	Regular Admissions	Open Admissions	Ratio[a]	Regular Admissions	Open Admissions	Ratio[a]		
All Entrants								
White	31,460	13,676		13,265	17,801		76,202	
Black	1,033	2,878		2,117	7,867		13,895	
Hispanic	1,773	1,703		2,182	3,828		9,486	
All students	34,266	18,257		17,564	29,496		99,583	
A.A. Recipients								
White	944	821	1.9	3,847	4,450	2.2	10,062	2.1
Black	52	201	4.9	826	2,045	3.5	3,124	3.6
Hispanic	106	221	3.1	786	1,187	2.5	2,300	2.6

B. A. Recipients

White	13,213	5,607	1.4	3,714	4,272	2.2	26,806	1.6
Black	413	835	3.0	529	1,416	3.7	3,193	3.4
Hispanic	691	460	1.7	393	574	2.5	2,118	2.0

M.A. Recipients

White	9,123	2,325	1.3	1,327	890	1.7	13,665	1.3
Black	310	518	2.7	64	315	5.9	1,207	3.2
Hispanic	301	170	1.6	131	115	1.9	717	1.7

Advanced Degree Recipients[b]

White	4,090	424	1.1	371	249	1.7	5,134	1.2
Black	72	58	1.8	42	63	2.5	235	2.1
Hispanic	46	32	1.7	13	46	4.5	137	2.3
All students	29,361	11,672	1.4	12,043	15,622	2.3	68,698	1.7

Source: Follow-up survey and CUNY censuses.

[a]T/R, where T = total degrees, R = degrees earned by regular students.
[b]Includes professional and doctoral degrees.

tiers, if we combine open-admissions students at both levels, the program more than tripled the number of black baccalaureates and doubled Hispanic ones.

The open-admissions policy added substantially to the numbers receiving postgraduate degrees, as well. Across the university, it increased white master's degrees 1.3 times, more than tripled those going to blacks, and increased Hispanics' by more than one and two-thirds. It more than doubled the number of blacks and Hispanics who earned doctorates or advanced professional degrees. Overall, more than 1,300 blacks and Hispanics who earned a graduate degree had been admitted as open-admissions students.

In contemplating these outcomes of open admissions, we should keep in mind that though the program attracted students from a broad spectrum of groups, it was especially critical in helping to enlarge the pool of college-educated and professional minority men and women. Whites who entered CUNY under open admissions generally had more economic resources than minorities and had somewhat better high school preparation. If CUNY had not been open to them, many would have gone elsewhere to college. Minority students, because of their generally more impoverished circumstances and weaker educational backgrounds, typically did not have such options.

This review of open admissions and long-term educational attainments reveals, then, a mixed picture. The policy created opportunities that were well used by many and CUNY was especially crucial for the chances of minorities. Notwithstanding the achievements that we have documented, wide disparities separated the attainments of whites and minorities. In part the gap reflects educational and other disadvantages that are pervasive in society and that a social intervention such as open admissions, coming at a relatively late stage in students' lives, could not entirely overcome.

CHAPTER THREE

How They Did at Work

The Difference That Education Made

It is an article of faith in the United States that a college education provides the key to the better-rewarded occupations—the ones that offer high income, status, and interesting work. Indeed, seven of every ten U.S. citizens believe that a college-educated person will earn much more money than one who hasn't gone to college (Kluegel and Smith 1986, 45–46).[1] Though the expectation of material reward is not the only reason that students attend college, nearly 75 percent of freshmen rate getting a better job and making more money as important—higher than the proportion endorsing any other reason for going to college (Astin et al. 1987). Occupational reasons received similarly high ratings when our sample of former CUNY students first started college.

Belief in the material benefits of college has deep roots in the folklore of the City University. Over the years the many CUNY alumni from humble origins who went on to surpass their parents' standing nourished a faith in the university as a pathway out of poverty.[2] The open-admissions policy aimed to reaffirm that faith. It was based on the premise that the creation of educational opportunity would ultimately boost socioeconomic life chances among the many low-income and minority students that it brought into college, thereby helping to narrow inequalities of status and income that separated minority and white communities.

Public faith in the economic value of college is consistent with a substantial body of social science research that confirms the impact of education on job status and earnings (Blau and Duncan 1967; Featherman and Hauser 1978; Jencks et al. 1979). Indeed, there is a consensus that education has

---

[1]But as Kluegel and Smith demonstrate (1986, table 3.2), Americans also perceive that with more and more people going to college, the value of a college education is declining.

[2]Gorelick (1981, chapter 6) points out that the student body at City College, overwhelmingly Jewish by the early 1900s, represented only a tiny proportion of the Jewish population in the first decades of the century. Nonetheless, she concludes that the achievements of this small group came to take on an enormous symbolic importance.

become the single most important influence on occupational status and economic rewards, though, to be sure, there is considerable disagreement about why this is so. According to one viewpoint, which we referred to in Chapter 1 as the "functional" perspective, education has come to be far more important than social origins in influencing success in the labor market. The increased importance of education is best understood as a response to the transition from industrial to postindustrial society, bringing with it growth in more complex occupations that require a more highly educated population (Bell 1973; Featherman and Hauser 1978; Treiman 1970). According to this perspective, education plays a key role in identifying talented individuals and training them for the more rewarded positions in the occupational system (Parsons 1959). Because the processes of selection and allocation are viewed as fundamentally meritocratic, education is seen as playing a central role in loosening the linkages between social origins and social destinations.

As we pointed out in Chapter 1, this view has been sharply challenged by various critical theorists who argue that schools serve to reproduce social inequality while preserving an illusion of meritocracy. One of the best known of these critiques is the neo-Marxist argument of Bowles and Gintis (1976), who contend that through a variety of social mechanisms, such as providing different curricula for different social class and ethnic groups, students are differentially socialized by schools.[3] They receive different types of training and they develop different aspirations and cognitive and interpersonal skills. The result is the social reproduction of inequality: largely as a consequence of their schooling experiences, working-class students are most likely to end up in working-class jobs, while those of higher-class origins are destined for the more rewarded positions. In this view the education system is harnessed to the needs of capitalism, attempting to produce workers who accept the relations of domination and subordination that characterize the world of work.

The functional position also has been challenged by a "credentialism" perspective advanced most notably by Randall Collins (1979), who argues that formal schooling serves mainly to certify the acquisition of attitudes,

---

[3]In essence, the Bowles and Gintis argument fits in with the tracking conception that we described in Chapter 1. For them, however, tracking can occur in two broad ways: (1) across schools, where school composition tends to be homogeneous in terms of social class and/or ethnicity; and (2) within schools, where schools are more heterogeneous in their socioeconomic composition. In the first case, lower- or working-class schools typically have a different curriculum than in middle- or upper-middle-class schools. In the second case, social origin is associated with track assignment within the school.

behaviors, and values, rather than providing technical skills necessary for the demands of work. Also, educational requirements rise because they help to enhance the status of certain occupations and serve to control the entry of individuals from lower social origins. In this view, as less privileged groups press their claims for equal educational opportunity, higher status groups have raised the educational requirements for desirable positions in an effort to maintain their advantages. The result is a process of educational inflation in which the educational credentials needed for jobs keep rising.

Although these views differ in important ways, they are not directly opposed, and each has contributed to an understanding of the relation between education and social stratification. But whatever their merits and shortcomings, one fact is compatible with all of them: advanced credentials have more value than less-advanced ones. The high school diploma no longer provides much leverage for obtaining desirable jobs. Its main function now is to create eligibility for college. The cutting edge for access to the more desirable jobs has moved from high school to college. In a city like New York, the importance of college is magnified by job growth in financial and legal services, information processing, education and culture—key service sectors in one of the citadels of the developing global economy (Kasarda 1983; U.S. Department of Labor 1988).

The growing significance of higher education has important implications for a policy of open admissions, especially in light of research findings suggesting that among those who graduated college with a bachelor's degree during the period between the early 1970s and the mid-1980s (when most of our respondents were entering the labor market), there was a loosening of the association between social origins and destinations (Hout 1988). Moreover, research indicates that relative payoffs for a B.A. degree are larger for blacks than they are for whites (Featherman and Hauser 1978, 342; Jencks et al. 1979, 200). These findings suggest that such policies as open admissions could have considerable potential in helping to narrow economic inequalities among ethnic groups.

How did the educational attainments reviewed in Chapter 2 translate into socioeconomic attainments in the labor market, and what was the contribution of open admissions to the economic success of those who came to CUNY after the policy started? What was the job-market fate of minority students relative to whites? How did those who graduated from community colleges with associate's degrees fare by comparison with senior college graduates who held B.A. degrees? What has been the job market success of those who had some college exposure but never earned a diploma? How has the economic success of women compared with that of men? These are some of the bottom-line questions that must be addressed in assessing the consequences of an open-access higher education policy. Their examination forms the substance of this chapter.

In considering the economic fate of those who had entered CUNY after open admissions began, we shall focus on several aspects of labor-market experiences. We shall begin the analysis with a look at employment status in 1984—twelve or more years after initial enrollment in college, describing the proportions who were working full-time and part-time, were unemployed, or who were not in the labor force at all, and examining some of the reasons for these different job-market situations.

Next, among those employed full-time, we shall examine occupational status and annual earnings—two key aspects of work that are major components of an individual's social standing in society. We shall assess how educational attainment, ethnicity, gender, and other factors influenced the success of individuals on these dimensions of work.

In the last section of the chapter, to estimate more precisely the impact of the open-admissions policy upon life chances, we focus upon the open-admissions students—the ones whose entry to CUNY's senior and community colleges was made possible by the program. By comparing the labor-market position of those who earned degrees with the position of those open-admissions students who came away with hardly any college experience and thus without any credential beyond a high school diploma, we shall estimate the policy's contribution to the lives of its beneficiaries—both as individuals and in the aggregate.

Though our main focus is upon ethnic differences in labor-market outcomes, we shall also take account of issues involving gender and the labor market. Differences between men and women in labor-force participation, segregation in the workplace, and earnings inequality suggest that labor-market processes differ according to gender (Jacobs 1989; Reskin and Hartmann 1986; England and McCreary 1987). Although the open-admissions policy had no explicit gender focus, women, as we saw in Chapter 2, comprised more than half of the students who entered CUNY after open admissions, and substantial proportions would not have been admitted without the policy. Consequently, in examining the sources of ethnic differences in labor-market results, and in assessing the influence of the open-admissions policy in boosting life chances, we have carried out separate analyses for men and women.

In focusing on the labor-market results of former students twelve years or more after they had started college, we must keep in mind that we are restricting our attention to the "final" outcomes as of the end point of our data in 1984, when respondents were typically in their early to mid-thirties. Whatever their degree of economic success may have been at that point, the results were arrived at in different ways. Some, for example, who started out rather modestly in jobs of relatively low status and pay, advanced over time to positions of greater responsibility and higher earnings. Others experienced very limited advancement over time; in effect, they found themselves stuck in dead-end jobs. These considerations, having to do with the ways that careers developed, are addressed in Chapter 4.

Labor-Force Participation

In examining the influence of open admissions on socioeconomic attainments, we first consider how individuals were distributed across various labor-force categories (table 3.1). Typically, in federal government statistics, the major distinction is between those who are participants in the labor force and those who are not. Participants include those who are employed, either full- or part-time, and those who are unemployed—that is, out of work but looking for a job. Not considered part of the labor force are full-time students, persons who are tending to family responsibilities on a full-time basis, those who are not working and not looking for a job (sometimes referred to as "discouraged workers"), retirees, and those who are unable to work due to disability.[4] Our data on labor-force distributions include these categories. In addition, among part-time workers, we distinguished those who were looking for a full-time job from those who worked part-time by choice.

Our examination of labor-force participation begins with an assessment of

---

[4]Typically, employment and unemployment rates are calculated using labor-force participants as the base. This procedure has been a source of controversy, because exclusion of discouraged workers lowers the unemployment rate. In our discussion of labor-force status, we shall consider all respondents in calculating rates of employment, unemployment, and the like. Those who are neither working nor looking are such a small portion of our respondents that they could have only a minuscule influence on unemployment rates. For a discussion of the labor force and related concepts, see Hall (1986).

Table 3.1 Labor-Market Participation in 1984, by Gender and Ethnicity

Percentages, Except as Noted

Labor Force Status	Males			Females		
	W	B	H	W	B	H
In labor force						
Employed full-time	92.2	86.7	91.4	62.1	77.5	66.7
Part-time by choice	1.9	3.4	0.4	11.9	5.0	7.5
Part-time, looking for full-time	0.9	0.4	0.9	1.0	3.4	3.6
Unemployed	2.8	5.7	7.0	1.4	4.9	5.1
Not in labor force						
In school	1.2	1.4	0.0	1.5	3.6	4.8
Tending family	0.3	0.0	0.0	21.2	3.4	11.1
Not working, not looking	0.1	0.1	0.4	0.5	0.5	0.7
Disabled	0.7	2.3	0.0	0.5	1.7	0.6
N (unweighted)	(1,585)	(266)	(180)	(1,848)	(477)	(282)

Source: Follow-up survey.

Note: W = white, B = black, H = Hispanic.

unemployment. The policymakers who shaped open admissions hoped that the program would make some dent in the high rates of long-term poverty that were generally believed at that time to be endemic in minority communities.[5] The structural transformation of urban economies that was well under way in the late 1960s, as well as the poor educational prospects of minority youths, were adding to the growing mismatch between educational require-

[5]This belief in widespread long-term spells of poverty gave way to a more optimistic view, based on research at the University of Michigan (Hill 1981; Duncan 1984), which suggested that poverty status tended to be relatively short. According to Wilson (1987, 9–10), however, more recent work indicates that 60 percent of those in poverty at any given moment are in a poverty cycle that will last at least eight years.

ments in the job market and minority educational attainments.[6] One result was swelling rates of joblessness among these youth. CUNY's program was intended, as some CUNY administrators put it, to turn "tax-eaters into tax-payers." Although we have no data on unemployment in the late 1960s and early 1970s among CUNY entrants or their parents that we could compare with respondents' employment status in the 1980s, it is clear that by 1984, twelve or more years after they had started college, few were unemployed. Overall, 2.8 percent were out of work. Among white men, the jobless rate was less than 3 percent. Black men were at 5.7 percent—only about half the New York–area unemployment rate of 11.2 percent for black males in the corresponding age group (U.S. Bureau of the Census 1984a, table 213). Unemployment among Hispanic men was 7 percent—the highest among former CUNY students, but still below the area rate for Hispanic males (8.7 percent). Unemployment among women was below that of men in the same ethnic category, but minority women were more likely to be jobless than were white women.

Even though rates of unemployment were generally low among our respondents, educational attainment was still associated with joblessness, at least to a modest degree. For example, about 4 percent of those who left college without any degree were out of work; among A.A.'s the figure was 3 percent and for those with B.A.'s or higher, it was less than 2 percent.[7]

Ethnic differences in joblessness are due in part to group disparities in educational attainment. Even when whites and minorities have comparable educational attainments, however, there remain small but consistent differences in favor of whites. Among males with bachelor's degrees, for example, 2

[6]Some, notably Waldinger (1986–87) and Bailey and Waldinger (1991) have expressed skepticism about the adequacy of the skills-mismatch concept to explain the economic situation of minorities. They document substantial increases in minority employment in those areas that have been growing in the postindustrial economy. But this is not necessarily inconsistent with a coexisting reality of very high rates of joblessness among minorities, particularly among young blacks and Hispanics.

[7]One should not conclude from the relatively narrow differences in unemployment rates associated with different levels of educational attainment that education is only weakly associated with joblessness. In our data the distribution of educational attainment is truncated, because high school graduation is the minimal level of attainment. Where the full range of educational levels is represented, differences in unemployment are far wider. For example, in 1984 the unemployment rate was 12.1 percent for those with less than four years of high school, whereas it was only 2.7 percent among those with four or more years of college (U.S. Bureau of the Census 1992, table 637). Educational attainment is, of course, not the only influence on unemployment.

percent of whites were out of work; for blacks and Hispanics, the figures were 3 percent and 4 percent, respectively. About 2 percent of white women with A.A. degrees were unemployed; among black and Hispanic women the figure was just over 3 percent.

When we widen our focus from unemployment to the broader profile of labor-force participation, striking gender differences appear. The situation among men seems quite straightforward: the overwhelming majority—more than 90 percent in the aggregate—held full-time jobs. Those men who were not working full-time were more likely to be unemployed than in any other labor-market category. Hardly any men were out of the labor force. Women, however, present a more complex profile. They were far less likely than men to hold full-time paid jobs. About 60 percent of white women and two-thirds of Hispanic women did. Blacks were the most likely among women to work full-time—more than three-quarters were doing so. Women who were not working full-time were distributed among a more diverse set of labor-market situations. Substantial percentages were out of the paid labor force, tending to family responsibilities, or, if they were employed, had chosen to work on a part-time basis. This was especially true among whites—a third were found in these activities, as were about 20 percent of Hispanic women. The picture for black women is different: less than 10 percent were found in homemaking activities or working part-time by choice.

Overall, these gender differences are consistent with what is generally known about labor-force participation: though women's participation has risen throughout the century, men remain well ahead (Reskin and Hartmann 1986, 2–3). The explanation for this disparity is thought to lie in persisting differences in family roles: women are less likely to hold full-time jobs if they are married and engaged in child rearing (for review, see Hall 1986, 191–231). The likelihood of full-time employment is further diminished among women with high-earning spouses (Spitze and Spaeth 1979).

To clarify the influences on women's full-time employment as well as the substantial ethnic differences among them, we examined the role of educational attainment and family context, assessing the effects of the highest degree that respondents earned, their marital status, the number of children they had, and, for those who were married, their spouse's salary.[8] Whether women

---

[8]To clarify better the distinction between holding a full-time job versus tending family full-time or choosing to work only part-time, we defined the dependent variable as 1 for full-time workers, and 0 for those tending family or choosing part-time work. Other labor-market destina-

held full-time jobs seems to be associated more with family factors than educational ones, but there are important ethnic variations in familial effects.

Among whites, marital status had a modest effect, married women being about 5 percent less likely to hold a full-time job, but the effect of parenthood was dramatic: each dependent child reduced the likelihood of full-time work by more than 25 percent. Among married women, the husband's salary also played a role: wives with higher-earning spouses were less likely to work full-time than comparable women whose husbands earned less money. Educational attainment influenced employment only among those with advanced and professional degrees: they were more likely to hold a full-time job; holders of other college credentials were no more likely to be working full-time than those who left college without any diploma, suggesting that the ones who decided initially on graduate training were more career oriented than those who terminated their education earlier.

The pattern among Hispanic women partly resembles that of whites. Having dependent children was important, but not to the same extent as for whites: each child reduced the likelihood of holding a job by around 10 percent. Having a higher-earning spouse also decreased the likelihood of full-time employment. Educational attainment had no influence on full-time work. Among blacks, in contrast to white or Hispanic women, full-time employment is not very predictable; in effect, neither marital status, husband's income, or number of children was associated with holding a full-time job.[9]

These results are consistent with the fact that black women long have had the highest labor-force participation rates among women (though the rate for whites has increased relative to blacks). They also seem consistent with national data suggesting that the labor-force participation of married black women (with husbands present) is considerably greater than that of whites, even with the age of children taken into account (U.S. Bureau of the Census

---

tions were excluded from the analyses. As discussed in Chapter 2, note 6, this is one of the instances of a dichotomous dependent variable, where we opted to use OLS regression. Because there are large ethnic differences among women, we ran separate regressions for each group. We included spouse's salary in the regressions with the other variables, even though it is contingent on being married. To do so we followed the procedure for handling contingent missing data described by Cohen and Cohen (1983). Our analyses here are less precise than we would like because we do not have information about the timing of marriage or of the birth of children.

Parallel analyses for men are not reported. They were not very informative because there is so little variation in their labor-force situations.

[9]The R^2 is 0.03 for blacks, 0.26 for Hispanics, and 0.50 for whites.

1987b, table 655).[10] The proclivity of black women to work regardless of family situations suggests, perhaps, the presence of a distinct cultural pattern rooted in the severe economic handicaps historically faced by black men and women in U.S. society. On the other hand, though there have been important changes in attitudes about women and work, beliefs that women belong at home raising children and tending to the family may still diminish the labor-market participation of white and Hispanic women.

To sum up, educational attainment had a modest influence on labor-force situations, particularly in helping to diminish unemployment. Because the open-admissions policy increased the number of individuals who earned college credentials, unemployment rates were undoubtedly lower among our respondents than they would have been in the absence of the policy. Because a larger proportion of minority students owed their college entry to the program, this benefit was probably greater for them. But the most important findings concern full-time employment. The overwhelming majority of men held full-time jobs. This fact reflects the powerful normative expectation that men, by the time they have reached their late twenties and early thirties and are out of school, should be working. Although women were much less likely to hold full-time jobs because of family and child care commitments, more than 60 percent did. Indeed, if we leave aside those who were out of the labor market because they were tending family and those who chose part-time work—mostly, we think, because of family obligations—then women's employment rates rise to levels that are much closer to those of men.[11] Overall, given our respondents' ages (typically they were in their early thirties when their labor-market situations were assessed) and above-average educational attainments (all respondents were at least high school graduates), high rates of full-time employment are to be expected. Educational influences on job holding are undoubtedly smaller within such a selected group than in a more

[10]We considered whether the effect of children might vary according to the marital status of the mother. Among blacks, mothers who had never been married had almost the same probability of working full-time as married ones.

The same is true for Hispanics. Twenty-two percent of black women were single mothers. The figure for Hispanics is 8 percent. Less than 1 percent of white females were in this category. How these ethnic differences in single-mother status can modulate the effects of the open-admissions policy will be considered in Chapter 6.

[11]If one recalculates women's full-time employment rates after removing those in the categories *tending family* and *part-time by choice,* full-time rates are 93 percent for whites, 85 percent for blacks, and 82 percent for Hispanics.

diverse population that included the full range of schooling outcomes. The significance of education, then, is to be seen not so much in its influence on employment status as in how well that large majority who worked full-time were doing in their jobs. This is the topic to which we now turn.

Success in the Labor Market

A variety of dimensions can be used to describe how successful people are in their work. Jobs vary according to the status or prestige accorded them, their income, how much authority they carry, and the complexity of the activities typically required of their incumbents. In assessing how well former CUNY students were doing in their work, we shall focus upon occupational status and earnings, two of the most important aspects of peoples' jobs, and the ones most often examined by social scientists in studies of job-market inequality. In Chapter 5 we shall consider other dimensions, such as job authority and work complexity.

In examining labor-market success, we focus on individuals who were employed full-time in 1984. We begin with an overview of our respondents' occupational situations in the New York metropolitan area labor market, where about 90 percent were employed.[12] To provide a comparative perspective, we shall look, for both men and women, at how jobs in the nation, the New York area, and among the CUNY group are distributed across the standard occupational categories used by the U.S. Bureau of the Census (table 3.2).

The profile of former CUNY students is clearly unusual, not only by comparison with the distribution of workers nationally but also relative to the profile for the New York–area labor market. Our respondents are set apart primarily by their heavy concentration in the two white-collar sectors that include managerial and professional jobs, as well as technical, sales, and administrative support (including clerical) positions. About 80 percent or more of the CUNY men worked in white-collar jobs, compared with only 50 percent nationally. Women's concentration in white-collar jobs is even greater: more than 90 percent are found there, compared with a national figure closer to 70 percent. The proportion of white-collar job holders in the CUNY group is even greater than that found in the New York–area labor

[12]The New York metropolitan area includes New York City as well as Westchester, Putnam, and Rockland Counties in New York State, and Bergen County in northern New Jersey.

Table 3.2 Occupational Category Representation, by Gender and Ethnicity: National, New York–Area, and CUNY Distributions

Percentages, Except as Noted

	Managerial-Professional	Technical-Sales-Adm.	Manufacturing & Operators[a]	Service
		Males		
National	29.2	21.1	41.7	5.1
New York City	35.1	26.8	28.0	9.8
CUNY survey respondents				
White	57.0	30.0	10.5	1.7
Black	32.3	46.2	14.3	5.7
Hispanic	34.3	42.8	12.1	8.3
		Females		
National	28.4	43.5	13.4	13.9
New York City	34.5	45.3	9.3	10.8
CUNY survey respondents				
White	62.2	35.1	0.7	2.0
Black	37.4	55.6	1.4	5.2
Hispanic	39.0	55.1	2.2	3.2
CUNY respondents' mean SEI score	69.3	51.6	28.1	20.1
CUNY respondents' mean earnings	$30,001	$23,345	$26,228	$17,661

Sources: Follow-up survey for CUNY data. For national figures: U.S. Bureau of the Census (1984a), table 280. Data are presented for the age interval 30–34. New York figures are for the New York SMSA. Data are presented for the age interval 30–34, the interval in which 90 percent of our respondents were found in 1984. For New York data: U.S. Bureau of the Census (1984a), Part 34, New York, table 221.

Note: Rows total less than 100 percent because farming, forestry, and fishing occupations are not included.

[a]Includes precision production, craft, repair, operators, fabricators, and laborers.

market, which, as one of the citadels of the postindustrial economy, contains a larger share of white collar jobs than are found nationally.

As one would expect from their heavy representation in the white-collar tiers, relatively few former CUNY students are found in other sectors of the labor market. Especially in the blue-collar manufacturing sector—typically the province of men in a sex-segregated labor market—their small proportions stand in dramatic contrast to the national picture, where more than 40 percent of males work in manufacturing. The blue-collar representation of CUNY men is small even relative to the New York labor market, where more than a quarter of all men are found in the manufacturing sector. And though only a small fraction of women work in the blue-collar sector in the national and New York labor forces, the tiny portion of CUNY women found there is smaller still.

That such an overwhelming majority of former CUNY students was found in the white-collar echelons of the New York labor market can likely be attributed to the fact that their minimum educational attainments exceeded those in the national and local labor forces. This clustering in white-collar work must, at least in part, be counted as a consequence of the opportunities created by the open-admissions policy.

In spite of the heavy concentration in these tiers, large differences are apparent in the way white and minority workers are distributed. The fundamental distinction is between those holding positions in the professional-managerial sector and those in the lower-level white-collar tier—in technical, sales, and administrative support jobs. Among men, typical top-echelon jobs held by former CUNY students are office manager, teacher, and "elite" professional: lawyer, doctor, or engineer. Among the top-tier women there were also many office managers and teachers, but fewer were found in the top professional positions; a substantial proportion worked as registered nurses. Among men in the lower white-collar tier, former students typically were assistant managers, computer programmers and operators, and technicians in radiology, engineering, and medical laboratories. Women also were frequently employed as assistant managers and technicians, but many also worked as secretaries in business, law, and medicine. Whites were far more likely than blacks and Hispanics to be found in the upper-level professional and managerial positions. Indeed, clear majorities of white men and women held such jobs. Though substantial percentages of minorities did also, their modal employment category was found in the second level. To be sure, minorities were also more likely than whites to have blue-collar manufacturing jobs or to be working in the service sector. But clearly, the major ethnic disparities are found within the realm of white-collar work.

The categories that we have been using to describe sectors of the labor market—for example, managerial-professional, as opposed to manufacturing and service—may be roughly demarcated from one another and ranked according to the average social status or prestige of the occupations contained within each and according to their average annual earnings. As we said earlier, these two dimensions of work, occupational status and earnings, are the ones we shall use to assess further the socioeconomic success of former CUNY students.

For readers unfamiliar with the conception and measurement of occupational status, some explanatory comments are in order. Sociologists view occupational status as a fundamental dimension of the social stratification system in society.[13] Broadly speaking, there have been two approaches to its measurement. In one, the prestige of occupations is assessed by asking people to inspect a list of job titles and to rate the social standing of each (on a scale from *excellent* to *poor.*). These scores are aggregated and occupations can then be ranked according to their prestige. Though people's judgments are influenced by a number of factors, education and earnings appear to be the most important: occupations that require or attract highly educated workers and that pay very well tend to be the most prestigious.

Because information on educational level, income, and occupation is found in census records, researchers have been able to use these data to estimate the status of occupations directly rather than conduct surveys of prestige. The best-known and most widely used of these objective techniques is the socioeconomic index, or SEI, developed by Duncan (1961), which assigns scores to occupations using aggregated educational attainment and earnings data for the incumbents of each job title. Scores are available for virtually all of the job titles listed in the Census Bureau's occupational classification system. We shall use this measure to assess job status.[14] The SEI yields scores for occupations ranging from 0 to a high of 96; physicians, for example, scored

[13]For a discussion of occupational status and its measurement, see Hall (1986, especially chapter 5). One of the classic discussions of occupational status and its use in studies of social stratification, mobility, and the like, is Blau and Duncan (1967).

[14]Duncan constructed this index by using the education and income data for men in each occupation. Subsequent research has found that gender interacts with occupation in status and prestige ratings of occupations (see Hall 1986; Jacobs 1989). Far and away, however, education and income are the most important influences on the prestige accorded to job incumbents.

92.1. bank officers and financial managers 79.5, elementary school teachers 71, bank tellers 52, X-ray technicians 48, clerical supervisors 43.6, home appliance installers and mechanics 27, welders 24, gas station attendants 17.9, and dishwashers 11.

Although job status is a key aspect of success—it is a major factor in defining the public identity of individuals—earnings can be seen as even more compelling, especially in assessing an open-admissions policy that was targeted to groups containing large proportions of individuals from low-income and impoverished family backgrounds. Our use of earnings as a second measure of job success needs to be clarified, however: it may seem redundant on first thought, because we noted above that earnings is a component of the SEI. But it enters into the calculation of the SEI score as the proportion of workers in an occupation who have incomes above a specified level. Our measure is independent of this factor; it simply refers to the annual earnings reported by individual respondents. Even though the incumbents of high-status positions typically earn more than those in lower-status occupations, there is wide variation in earnings within occupations. Indeed, Jencks and his colleagues (1972, 225–26) have pointed out that there is almost as much income inequality within occupations as there is among randomly chosen individuals. Hence, it is important to have earnings data at the level of the individual.

The census occupational categories clearly differ from each other in terms of the occupational status and earnings associated with them (shown in the bottom panel of table 3.2). The mean job status or SEI scores show a distinct ordering: professional and managerial jobs outrank technical, sales, and administrative support positions, while the latter substantially outrank manufacturing and service jobs. A similar, though not identical, ordering is apparent for earnings: those who worked in professional and managerial occupations made considerably more than those employed in the lower white-collar category. The latter earned somewhat less than those in blue-collar manufacturing or operator jobs, but service positions lagged far behind.

The ethnic contrasts noted earlier—whites were far more likely to be found in professional and managerial jobs, while minorities were more likely to work in the lower white-collar tier—translate into inequalities of status and earnings. On average, among both men and women, the status of positions held by whites exceeds the status of those held by minorities (table 3.3). There is about a ten-point difference separating whites from blacks—roughly equivalent, for instance, to the difference between a high school teacher and a medical secretary, or between a computer systems analyst and a health tech-

Table 3.3 Occupational Status and Earnings, by Educational Attainment, Gender, and Ethnicity

Educational Attainment	Males				Females			
	White	Black	Hispanic	Total	White	Black	Hispanic	Total
	Occupational Status Scores							
H.S. diploma[a]	49.2	40.6	41.0	46.9	58.3	43.8	48.7	52.0
Some college[b]	51.1	44.4	50.9	50.0	57.7	50.9	47.2	54.8
A.A.	55.2	51.5	49.6	54.2	53.9	49.6	55.0	52.9
B.A.	62.4	59.6	59.2	62.0	61.6	52.6	59.8	60.2
M.A.	66.1	65.1	59.6	65.8	64.0	60.4	66.9	63.8
Advanced	83.3	—[c]	—[c]	83.3	76.1	—[c]	—[c]	72.5
Mean	61.0	49.9	53.0	59.2	61.1	51.1	54.6	58.6

Mean Earnings

H.S. diploma[a]	$27,201	$21,004	$20,224	$25,358	$21,610	$17,391	$16,270	$19,235
Some college[b]	27,898	22,586	22,839	26,382	23,035	19,486	18,760	21,705
A.A.	27,574	25,634	22,005	26,763	21,741	19,709	21,040	21,055
B.A.	31,790	26,533	27,259	31,121	24,757	20,658	22,726	24,020
M.A.	32,636	27,794	23,741	31,905	24,699	21,032	24,429	24,328
Advanced	41,009	—[c]	—[c]	40,851	30,507	—[c]	—[c]	28,896
Mean	31,154	24,072	23,816	29,801	24,140	19,770	20,455	22,954
N (unweighted)[d]	1,304	206	153	1,663	1,049	332	174	1,555

Source: Follow-up survey.

[a]Respondents dropped out before completing one semester of college (fewer than fifteen credits).

[b]Respondents never earned any college degree but completed one or more semesters.

[c]Insufficient cases.

[d]Number of cases slightly higher for occupational status scores.

nologist. The white-Hispanic gap is a bit narrower—on the order of eight points among males and six among females. Ethnic differences in mean annual earnings are substantial and favor whites.[15] Among males the gap is about $7,000 between whites and the two sets of minority respondents. Disparities among women, though not as wide, are still sizable: on average white women earned about $4,000 more than blacks and about $3,500 more than Hispanics.

Gender disparities have a different cast than ethnic ones. To begin with, men and women held jobs of essentially equal status, but this similarity seems to have been produced by different occupational profiles. Although women were more likely to be in professional-managerial and other white-collar occupations, within the top tier, men tended to hold the higher-status positions (doctors, lawyers, etc.) and women the lesser ones (registered nurses, social workers, teachers). Of course, men also were more likely to be doing blue-collar work, and the substantially lower rank of these jobs seems to have offset the higher status of their positions in the upper white-collar sector. As a result, there are no overall gender differences in occupational status. The most evident feature of the earnings picture is the low salaries of women relative to men: overall, they were more than $6,800 behind, earning 77 cents on the male dollar. In every intraethnic comparison, the salaries of men were higher. Using the earnings of white men as the benchmark, women were far behind. To cite the widest difference, black women trailed by more than $11,000; on average they earned 63 cents on every dollar earned by white men.

In summary, our review of the labor-market situations of CUNY respondents who were full-time workers shows that they were overrepresented in the white-collar sectors relative to the New York–area labor force. This overrepresentation largely resulted from educational attainments that surpassed the average for their age category (30–34). Nonetheless, minorities lagged considerably behind whites in status and earnings. These findings are consistent with research literature showing that whites are more likely than minorities to hold the better-rewarded positions in the U.S. occupational system (for reviews, see Farley 1984; Jaynes and Williams 1989). For women the situation is paradoxical: though on an equal footing with men in terms of status, they are

[15]In order to provide continuity with later analyses where earnings are regressed upon a number of independent variables, we have presented earnings data in table 3.3 using the mean. There is little difference between these results and those produced by using the median. Outliers do not appear in the arrays.

well behind in earnings. This contradiction has been noted also in other studies (England 1979; England and McCreary 1987).

Influences on Status and Earnings

What explains the inequalities in labor market success that we have just reviewed? Because a fundamental assumption of the open-admissions policy was that educational opportunity would ultimately produce benefits in the labor market, we shall begin by examining how educational attainment is associated with occupational status and income. Before taking up this issue, however, we need to clarify one aspect of educational attainment: although open admissions was designed to create educational opportunities that would lead to a degree, substantial proportions of CUNY entrants did not graduate. Some earned fewer than 15 credits and thus failed to complete even a semester of college. Others accumulated a semester's worth of college credits or more.[16] To assess the possibility that students may have profited from even a partial exposure to college, we have distinguished these two groups in table 3.3, designating the early dropouts with the label *high school diploma* and assigning the label *some college* to those who had more extended collegiate experience. This distinction also enables us to compare the value of college experience short of a degree with the value of credentials (A.A., B.A., M.A., etc.).

Among whites as well as minorities and for both men and women, educational attainment made a difference in career chances. Relative to those with only a high school diploma, holding a degree generally conferred an advantage in status and earnings, though the size of increments varies with each step up the educational ladder. The bachelor's degree seems to be the threshold at which there are clear and consistent job rewards. B.A. holders appear far better off in status and earnings than those with high school diplomas, and they are generally ahead of those who completed some college.[17] Proponents of community colleges as an avenue of opportunity for poor and disadvantaged

---

[16]Those whom we are calling high school graduates earned an average of 3.3 credits. Among this group, almost a third earned no credits, and about half accumulated no more than 3 credits (the equivalent of one college course). Those we designate as having had some college earned an average of 40.6 credits. Among them, 65 percent completed up to three semesters (45 credits).

[17]We speak of differences in table 3.3 only when a statistical procedure (t test) indicated significance at the 0.05 level or better.

students do not receive a great deal of encouragement from our data, for the benefits of the A.A. seem ambiguous: relative to high school graduates, those who earned a two-year degree usually held higher-status jobs (white women are an exception), and some groups (black males and females, Hispanic females) had a dollar advantage. But by comparison with those who had some college experience short of a degree, the payoffs to an A.A. appear slim: among Hispanic men, white women, and black women, there was no status benefit to the two-year degree, and it provided no significant earnings advantage to any group. Relative to the B.A., A.A. graduates were generally behind in job status and in salaries. The M.A. degree hardly boosted earnings beyond the B.A. level, partly, perhaps, because of the relatively low salaries going to those working in education, a field in which many of these graduates were found. Overall, despite the inconsistencies we have noted, there is generally a positive relationship between educational achievements and labor-market rewards.

Credentials seem important in helping to narrow ethnic inequalities in job rewards. Among those who earned only a high school diploma, blacks and Hispanics generally lag further behind whites in occupational status than do credentialed minority workers relative to comparably credentialed whites. Among males with only a high school diploma, for example, the status difference between minority and white graduates is about eight points, while the gap among those holding B.A.'s is less than three points. A similar pattern is apparent for women.

Credentials also help to narrow income inequalities: generally speaking, minority workers are more disadvantaged relative to whites at the high school diploma level than they are at other educational levels. Among high school graduates, for example, black men earn only 77 cents on the white male dollar, but they earn 83 cents at the B.A. level (comparable figures for Hispanic men are 74 cents and 86 cents); Hispanic women make 75 cents on the white woman's dollar at the high school level, but 92 cents among B.A.'s; comparable figures for black women are 80 and 83 cents. Notwithstanding such benefits of credentials, ethnic inequalities are not eradicated among those at the same levels of educational attainment: even with education controlled, the status and earnings of whites continue to exceed those of minorities.

The job-market situation of women differs from that of men in a number of respects. The most striking difference is the low earnings of women: almost without exception, male salaries exceed those of women in the same category of educational attainment and ethnic membership. Most startling is that white males with only high school diplomas earn more than women at almost every level of educational credential. Only white women holding advanced or professional degrees earn more. Later in the chapter we shall examine further these gender disparities by looking at differences between men and women in college major fields.

For a policy such as open admissions, which was intended to narrow ethnic inequalities of educational attainment and thereby to reduce socioeconomic ones, these findings are disturbing. Even though the educational opportunities created by the policy translated into labor-market payoffs for many, the program obviously did not erase ethnic disparities, for inequalities between whites and minorities remained, even when their educational credentials were at the same level. This fact merits closer examination. To better define education's role and to provide a broader picture of the sources of socioeconomic inequality, we have considered other potential influences that may help to clarify both the contribution and the limitations of an open-access policy in helping to boost individuals' occupational status and income.

One influence commonly included in research is social origin, which we measured by parents' educational level and income at the time our respondents first entered CUNY in the early 1970s. Although we saw in Chapter 2 that social origins had no direct effect on the attainment of higher education credentials, that factor might still exert an independent influence on occupational standing and earnings. Parents' education might affect aspects of cultural style, including speech patterns and physical appearance, especially dress. Individuals with more highly educated parents might possess more of the qualities preferred by employers when they make hiring or promotion decisions. Moreover, in economically advantaged families, kinship and acquaintance networks more often might include well-placed individuals who can facilitate access to better-paying and higher-status jobs.

In addition to educational credentials, students' rates of progress through college might also have influenced job rewards by affecting the amount of work experience they could have compiled with their highest degree in hand. As we saw in Chapter 2, holding a full-time job in college not only diminished the chances of getting a B.A. but was also the most important factor influencing how long it took to get it; on average, working delayed degree completion by more than two and a third years. Time to B.A., in turn, was the single most important influence on whether students would earn a more advanced degree. So not only did working while in college produce disadvantages in the form of lower educational attainment, it also took away from the time that graduates could have been in the labor market with the leverage of their degrees working for them. Of course, full-time work while in college could have helped to compensate for this disadvantage, since it did add to work experience and thus may have contributed to eventual job rewards. But if the payoff to postdegree work experience is greater than to predegree experience—and research suggests that it is (Griffin 1978)—this imbalance would count as yet another disadvantage of having to work full-time while in college. In effect, the cumulative disadvantage that we observed in the educational attainment process may have continued to develop in affecting fortunes in the labor market. In our further examination of success in work, we shall assess the role of pre- and postdegree work experience.[18]

Job status and earnings are, of course, also influenced by developments outside of education. Such structural features of the labor market as the sector, public or private, in which a job is located may make a difference. Research indicates that occupational upgrading, one of the hallmarks of a postindustrial economy, appears especially pronounced in the private sector. In New York City, for example, the dramatic expansion of private-sector business services—financial, legal, insurance, and the like—has fueled sharp growth in managerial, technical, and professional employment (U.S. Department of Labor 1988; Waldinger 1986–87). Growth in these types of jobs has been greater in the private than in the public or governmental sector in part because private organizations typically introduce advanced production technologies (computer-aided labor processes, for example) more rapidly because of competitive pressure to lower costs. These technologies may increase the number of jobs in the managerial tier (Attewell 1990) so that, relative to the public sector, the private sector may provide more opportunities to obtain high-status, well paying jobs.

To provide a more detailed picture of influences on occupational status and earnings, we have carried out two sets of multiple regression analyses—one for men and one for women—that include the factors we have discussed above. The results for men confirm that academic credentials explain a major part of inequality in occupational status (table 3.4). Indeed, educational attainment is far and away the most important influence. On the other hand, neither the educational level nor the income of parents appears to have had

[18]We measured predegree experience by calculating the number of years intervening between the year of respondent's first full-time job and the year in which the highest degree was conferred. Postdegree experience was calculated as the interval between the year of highest degree and 1984.

any lingering effects on occupational standing and do not explain any of the ethnic differences in job status. But the analysis does shed additional light on why, among men with equal educational credentials, minorities hold jobs of lesser standing than those held by whites: public-sector workers are found in lower-status positions than those in the private sector. Research indicates that minority workers are disproportionately found in public-sector employment, perhaps because increased efforts of governmental agencies to eliminate discriminatory practices (Farley 1984; Kaufman and Daymont 1981; Kaufman 1986) make those jobs more attractive than private-sector positions. Minority workers may also gravitate toward the public sector after meeting with disappointments in hiring or promotion in the private sector. Whatever the reasons, among our respondents, black and Hispanic men were somewhat more likely to work in the public sector than whites (a third of minority men did so, compared with about a quarter of whites), and this disparity explains a portion of the gap in status between white and minority workers. Work experience, whether it was accumulated while in college or after college, did not boost subsequent job status. Overall then, ethnic disparities in job status are primarily a result of differences in educational attainment and in the likelihood of public-sector employment. After taking credentials and job sector into account, remaining ethnic differences in job status are sharply reduced and seem to have little substantive significance.

The earnings picture for men is more complex. Differences in educational attainment between white and minority workers are the most important source of income inequality, but not the only one. There is, for example, a continuing effect of prior disadvantage in socioeconomic origins: those who entered CUNY from lower-income families earned less in 1984, and blacks and Hispanics were the groups most likely to come from low-income backgrounds. Just as with job status, employment sector is an important influence. A dollar penalty is associated with public employment: such workers earned almost $4,000 less than private-sector workers who were comparable in other respects. This disadvantage fell most heavily on minority workers. Work experience influences earnings, but experience compiled after the completion of schooling counts far more heavily than that accumulated before: the economic reward from a year of postdegree experience is nearly three times as great as that conferred by a year of predegree work. Blacks and Hispanics had more predegree experience than whites, but its relatively meager returns did little to offset the disadvantages of lower credential attainment that resulted partly from having to work full-time while in school. Minorities also had a bit

Table 3.4 Determinants of Occupational Status and Earnings: Males

| | Occupational Status Scores | | | | Annual Earnings (Dollars) | | | |
| | Model 1 | | Model 2 | | Model 1 | | Model 2 | |
	Unstandard-ized	Standard-ized	Unstandard-ized	Standard-ized	Unstandard-ized	Standard-ized	Unstandard-ized	Standard-ized
Ethnicity[a]		.192***		.062*		.192***		.093***
Black	−11.06		−3.83		−7,081		−3,126	
Hispanic	−7.97		−2.03		−7,338		−3,861	
Father's ed. (at least some college)			1.71	.038			696	.021
Mother's ed. (at least some college)			−.60	−.011			116	.002
Parents' income[b]				.043				.091**
<$10,000			1.20				−3,335	
$10,000–14,999			2.18				−1,799	

	(1)	(2) b	(2) β	(3)	(4) b	(4) β
Educ. attainment[c]			.503***			.479***
Some college		2.56			2,122	
A.A.		7.59			6,490	
B.A.		14.83			12,023	
M.A.		20.61			16,206	
Advanced		35.97			24,679	
Work exp. before highest degree		−.11	−.019		528	.119***
Work exp. after highest degree		.19	.035		1,453	.371***
Public sector job		−9.30	−.211***		−3,993	−.124***
Constant	60.96	47.52		31,154	10,991	
R^2 adj.	.036	.294	.036		.140	
N (unweighted)	1,745	1,663				

Source: Follow-up survey.

[a]The reference category is whites.

[b]The reference category is $15,000 or above.

[c]The reference category is high school diploma.

*p <0.05

**p <0.01

***p <0.001

more postdegree work experience than did whites, but this experience edge reflected the fact that minority workers generally did not go as far in education. The ethnic disparities in salaries produced by credential differences were far more powerful than those produced by differences in work experience. For example, blacks with an A.A. typically had a year more postdegree employment experience than whites with a B.A., but this experience advantage of around $1,450 is dwarfed by the gap of more than $5,500 that separates B.A. earnings from those at the A.A. level. Blacks who completed some college but did not receive a degree (their modal category of educational attainment) had, on average, three and a half years more work experience than white B.A.'s. In this case blacks' experience advantage of about $5,100 is offset by a credential advantage of almost $10,000 for whites.

This examination of the determinants of earnings suggests that educational credentials are of considerably greater importance than initially indicated (in table 3.3). For example, the benefit of the B.A.—initially seen as almost $6,000 relative to a high school diploma—rises to more than $12,000 with additional influences controlled. And the A.A. payoff, which originally appeared to provide only a slim edge beyond a high school diploma, now approaches $6,500. The initially smaller increments to each level of educational attainment result mostly from the fact that, after completing their highest degree, holders of lesser credentials had more work experience than holders of more advanced credentials. In effect then, the payoffs to educational credentials are partly masked by the offsetting influence of postdegree work experience.

All in all, our analysis indicates how the chain of cumulative disadvantage extends into the labor market, even under a system such as open admissions. Men who held full-time jobs in college were disadvantaged not only because the demands of employment diminished ultimate educational attainment and thus earning power but also because predegree work experience added little to subsequent earnings. Moreover, among those with comparable degrees, working in college added to the time needed for degree completion, thus reducing postdegree work experience and further limiting earnings. To these disadvantages must be added earlier ones stemming from the continuing consequences of socioeconomic origin and the detrimental effect of public-sector employment. Together all of these influences account for more than half of the earnings inequality between blacks and whites and nearly half of the gap between Hispanic workers and whites. But the part that remains unexplained is substantial: blacks still earned about $3,100 less than whites, and Hispanics trailed by more than $3,800.

The influences upon women's labor-market success (table 3.5) are similar in some ways to those that we observed for men and different in others. Educational attainment is the most important determinant of both occupational status and earnings, and, as with men, is the main source of inequalities between whites and minorities. Social background had a modest effect on both status and earnings, though for women advantages were transmitted by parents' education rather than by their income: women whose mothers had at least some college education held jobs of slightly higher status, and those whose fathers completed at least some college earned more. The educational levels of white women's parents typically exceeded those of minority women, so a part of the ethnic disparities in status and earnings are accounted for in this way. Public-sector employment was associated with lower status and earnings, just as it was for men. Minority women held public-sector jobs more often than whites, thus explaining part of ethnic inequality. Holding a full-time job while in college provided no boost to a woman's postcollege level of socioeconomic success, but experience accumulated after the completion of education made a difference, especially for earnings: each year of work added about $450. This was about a third of the benefit that men received. As with minority men, black and Hispanic women had more postdegree experience than whites, but it did not overcome whites' typically higher level of educational attainment. For example, minority women with A.A.'s (their modal credential) had about a year's more work experience than whites, but the earnings difference in favor of the B.A. (the modal credential for white women) was more than $2,500. To cite another example, black women who had some college but did not earn a degree averaged about 4.5 more years of work experience than whites with B.A.'s, but this experience advantage of about $2,000 is more than offset by the credential advantage to whites of $4,000.

These analyses for women highlight further the importance of educational attainment, for with other factors controlled, the influence of credentials increases. Without controls the average earnings of B.A. holders, for example, were about $4,800 greater than those of high school graduates; with controls the gap widens to more than $6,000; for the A.A., the difference of $1,800 rises to more than $3,600.

Notwithstanding the great importance of education as a determinant of

Table 3.5 Determinants of Occupational Status and Earnings: Females

	Occupational Status Scores				Annual Earnings (Dollars)			
	Model 1		Model 2		Model 1		Model 2	
	Unstandard-ized	Standard-ized	Unstandard-ized	Standard-ized	Unstandard-ized	Standard-ized	Unstandard-ized	Standard-ized
Ethnicity[a]		.266***		.150***		.218***		.126***
Black	-10.01		-5.97		-4,370		-2,631	
Hispanic	-6.54		-2.26		-3,685		-1,849	
Father's ed. (at least some college)			1.47	.043			1,550	.081**
Mother's ed. (at least some college)			2.48	.066*			899	.042
Parents' income[b]				.044				.002
<$10,000			.81				36	
$10,000–14,999			1.73				13	
Educ. attainment[c]				.391***				.328***

	(1)	(2)	(3)	(4)	(5)	(6)
Some college		2.29			2,116	
A.A.		4.02			3,652	
B.A.		9.77			6,223	
M.A.		14.93			7,635	
Advanced		24.06			12,367	
Work exp. before highest degree		.08	.019		76	.032
Work exp. after highest degree		.44	.110*		454	.201***
Public sector job		-3.45	-.097***		-1,902	-.095***
Constant	61.10	47.89		24,140	14,848	
R^2 (adjusted)	.069	.196	.046		.108	
N (unweighted)	1,629	1,555		1,555		

Source: Follow-up survey.

[a] The reference category is whites.

[b] The reference category is $15,000 or above.

[c] The reference category is high school diploma.

*p < 0.05

**p < 0.01

***p < 0.001

job status and earnings for women, the analyses show that credentials have less impact on women's success than they do on men's, both for status and particularly for earnings. Among males the net gain in occupational status of B.A. holders over high school graduates, for example, is fifteen points, while for women it is about ten points; the status payoff of an M.A. is about twenty-one points for men but fifteen points for women. For earnings, women's payoff from the A.A. is about $3,600 compared with $6,500 for men; the B.A. advantage for men was more than $12,000, but it was only about $6,000 among women. So not only did women earn less than men, but they also realized smaller advantages in status and earnings for the educational credentials they earned.

This assessment of women's performance in the labor market indicates that even though the opportunity created by open admissions made an important socioeconomic difference for the lives of many, cumulative disadvantages, to which minority women were especially subject, affected their success in the labor market. Women who worked at full-time jobs in college had even less to show for this experience than did men, and this work extended their college careers and diminished educational attainments, thus lowering their eventual job rewards. New disadvantages arose in the labor market in the form of lesser rewards for working in the public sector. But even when minority women were comparable to whites in social origins, educational credentials, work experience, and employment sector, they still were worse off: blacks earned $2,600 less than whites, and Hispanics trailed by $1,850.

Though our analyses have helped to account for much of the initial ethnic inequalities in occupational status and earnings, unexplained disparities still remain. Among men, only slim residual differences in job status separate whites from minorities, but the earnings gap remains more substantial. Among women there are significant remaining inequalities in status and earnings. In effect, then, even when minority workers are comparable to whites in all of the ways measured in our analyses, they still hold less-rewarded jobs.

In an effort to account for some of this remaining gap, we examined other variables sometimes thought to be associated with labor-market outcomes. One such variable is college grade point average. Perhaps those who earned higher grades might be more skilled or better able to assimilate on the job experiences, or might perform better on preemployment tests that are often used as a criterion in selecting candidates for entry-level jobs. We also considered, following Granovetter (1974), whether the social networks available to whites might help them in job search activities more than the ties available to minorities. Accordingly, we carried out additional regression analyses that included sources of help in job finding (acquaintances, friends, relatives, newspaper ads, employment agencies, etc.), and college grades. Neither of these factors helped to explain ethnic differences in labor-market success.

Another source of ethnic inequalities may be discrimination by employers in making decisions about hiring, raises, promotions, and the like. Of course, assertions about discrimination can almost always be disputed in statistical studies; one can never claim to have measured all of the variables that may influence success in the labor market, and thus it can always be argued that remaining ethnic differences may be due to unmeasured factors other than discrimination. Although we have no information on specific experiences, we did ask respondents whether they had ever been victims of discrimination in these employment-related areas. In each area black and Hispanic men were far more likely than white men to report that they had experienced discrimination. Indeed, differences were often dramatic. For example, 7 percent of whites but 40 percent of blacks and more than a quarter of Hispanics said that they were victims of discrimination in pay and raises; 14 percent of whites, but more than half of blacks and more than a third of Hispanics perceived that they had been discriminated against in promotions. Among women, ethnic differences were also visible: minority women more often perceived discrimination in hiring, pay and raises, and promotions, but consistent with the narrower differences that we have noted in women's pay, ethnic contrasts in the frequency of such reports are less sharp then they are for males. Although we are unable to go beyond individual perceptions, actual instances of differential treatment have, not infrequently, been reported in the media, and discrimination undoubtedly continues to be a source of ethnic inequality in labor-market rewards.[19]

Our analyses cast further light on the continuing debate about community colleges and their role in providing opportunity (for discussions see Brint and Karabel 1989; Dougherty 1987, 1994; Grubb 1992a, 1992b, 1992c). The socioeconomic benefits to A.A. holders placed them between those with high school diplomas and those who received a bachelor's degree. Relative to B.A. recipients who were comparable to them in other respects, community college graduates were substantially behind. Men lagged by about seven points in status and around $5,500 in earnings; among women the deficit was about six

---

[19]For the case of highly educated blacks see the volume by Cose (1993). For issues concerning discrimination in hiring young inner city blacks see Kirschenman and Neckerman (1991).

points in status and nearly $2,600 in income. On the other hand, holders of the A.A. were better off than those with only a high school diploma. But how well A.A. holders were doing relative to those who had some college experience depended on gender: male community college graduates were ahead, but women A.A.'s did not have a significant edge in occupational status or earnings.[20] This amounts to saying that for women, having an A.A. was no more valuable than two or three semesters of college without any degree (on average, women with some college had earned around 35–40 credits).[21] Overall then, though the A.A. degree conferred benefits beyond the rewards gained by high school graduation, the constraining effects of community college entry on B.A. attainment that we saw in Chapter 2 translated into clear labor-market disadvantages, which were greater for women than for men. And in either case, because blacks and Hispanics were more likely than whites to have started college in two-year schools, the disadvantages fell more heavily upon them.

To summarize, because educational attainment is the single most important influence on job success, the opportunity created by open admissions undoubtedly boosted the socioeconomic position of many individuals whose college entry depended upon the program. In doing so, the policy helped to narrow ethnic disparities in status and earnings. Nonetheless, substantial ethnic inequality persisted. Most of this disparity was due to a variety of disadvantages that, taken together, handicapped minorities more than whites in the quest for credentials. Disadvantages of prior education hurt academic chances in college. Other burdens, such as low income, added to the likelihood that students would need to hold a full-time job while going to school, a necessity that diminished educational attainments and counted for very little in terms of subsequent job rewards. Full-time work also extended the time needed to finish school, especially for those who earned a B.A. In turn, one of the costs of delayed degree completion was a loss of postdegree work experience: at equal levels of educational attainment, those who took longer to finish had less time in the labor market. New disadvantages were created within the

---

[20]The findings of Grubb (1992b, 1992c) indicate that the A.A. degree is more valuable than "some college," which he finds to be no more valuable than a high school diploma. For the latter comparison, our results are consistent with his in terms of job status, but in terms of earnings, some college is worth more than a high school diploma for women. The net $2,122 advantage to men just misses statistical significance at the 0.05 level (p=.07).

[21]Monk-Turner (1985, 1990) has noted that community college attendance for women may add to their occupational disadvantages relative to men.

labor market in the form of lesser job rewards in the public sector, where minorities were more likely to work; they probably suffered as well from discriminatory practices. Overall, then, though open admissions contributed importantly to individuals' socioeconomic chances, especially those of minorities, it could not completely overcome prior socioeconomic and educational disadvantages and labor-market processes that worked to reinforce ethnic inequalities.

Although both men and women benefited from open admissions, women's occupational success, particularly in terms of earnings, was more limited than men's. Women earned less, and the dollar leverage provided by educational credentials appears to have been more limited. Because the policy seems to have done more for men, the issue of gender differences deserves a closer look.

Gender, Fields of Study, and Earnings

Comparison of the labor-force position of men and women reveals a paradox: though overall, women held jobs that were comparable in status, they earned, on average, $6,850 less than men. Put another way, women were earning 77 cents on the male dollar. To examine the sources of this gap, we began with a multivariate analysis of earnings that included gender as well as the same variables (family income on entry to CUNY, parents' educational level, ethnicity, respondent's educational attainment, work experience, and employment sector) used in the earlier analyses conducted separately for men and women (tables 3.4 and 3.5). The results showed that very little of the gender gap in earnings—only about $500—was explained by these variables. This finding is not surprising, for educational attainment is by far the most important influence on earnings, and the attainments of men and women are similar.

But whereas levels of degree attainment are comparable, there is considerable evidence that men and women differ in their choices of fields of concentration in college (Jacobs 1989, chapter 6). In other words, evidence suggests the presence of sex typing in college majors. Differences in choice of field are in part a consequence of gender socialization and in part the result of perceptions by men and women of what employment opportunities are realistically available. Although major fields do not predestine individuals to specific jobs, evidence suggests that fields of concentration do influence occupational destinations and that by the time higher education is completed, major fields have narrowed occupational possibilities (see Jacobs 1989, 110–12).

Some studies indicate that the college major fields in which women have been overrepresented are linked to subsequent employment in female-dominated occupations (Bielby 1978; Daymont and Andrisani 1984) so that part of the gender gap in wages may be a consequence of sex-typed college majors (Angle and Wissman 1981; Astin 1977; National Center for Educational Statistics 1982, 187; U.S. Bureau of the Census 1987b). We examined this possibility by conducting an earnings analysis that includes, with the exception of the educational attainment variables, the same factors used in the earlier analyses. In place of educational attainment we constructed a new set of variables consisting of major fields at each degree level.

How men and women are distributed across major fields can be seen in table 3.6 (the major field distributions are not presented according to ethnicity because, somewhat surprisingly, there were only minor ethnic differences). Considerable gender typing is visible across the different areas of concentration. Among A.A. holders, men are much more likely than women to be found in the natural science–math area, including fields such as engineering technology and data processing, while women predominate in health and social service and monopolize secretarial studies. To cite the widest differences at the B.A. level, males are much more likely to have earned a degree in business or in a quantitative field, while women were more concentrated in education and in health–social service fields. Among holders of the M.A., men were far more often found among business majors than were women. Although men were also well represented in education, women were more than twice as likely to be found there. At the advanced-degree level, almost 60 percent of the men were to be found in the practicing professions (law, medicine)—far more than the proportion of women (38 percent).

Although there are some exceptions to the pattern, generally speaking the highest earnings are linked with those major fields in which males are predominant. At the B.A. level, the two majors associated with the highest earnings, business and natural sciences–math, contain 45 percent of the men but only 19 percent of the women. Earnings were lowest for education majors (lagging almost $8,000 behind those of business majors), and women were more likely than men to be found there. At the M.A. level, the earnings of those who had concentrated in business far outdistanced those in other fields, and men's representation in business was much greater than women's. At the other end, the earnings of education majors trailed business by almost $13,000. On average, the earnings of those who held advanced degrees in the higher professions (law, medicine, etc.) far exceeded those of other advanced-

Table 3.6 Influence of Major Fields on Earnings of Full-Time Workers, by Gender

	Dollar Increments[a]	Percent in Major	
		Men	Women
A.A. degree			
Health–social services[b]	$4,877	9	30
Natural science–math[c]	4,260	33	7
Business	4,026	31	22
Secretarial	2,539	0	19
Art–humanities–social science	1,167	15	16
B.A. degree			
Business	11,281	27	11
Natural science–math[c]	9,028	18	8
Health–social services	7,250	6	17
Arts–humanities–social science	5,834	40	41
Education	3,397	5	18
M.A. degree			
Business	19,454	27	7
Natural science–math[c]	9,999	13	3
Health–social services	8,970	15	22
Education	6,539	22	47
Arts–humanities–social science	5,463	18	13
Advanced degree			
Higher professional[d]	21,465	58	38
Other professional[e]	11,759	30	37
Unadjusted gender difference	6,847		
Diff. with all controls except major	6,338		
Difference with major controlled	5,165		

Source: Follow-up survey.

Note: The regression includes all of the variables listed in tables 3.4 and 3.5. For ease of presentation, coefficients for these variables are not presented.

[a]The reference category consists of those with high school diplomas. Major fields were not available in the data for those whose educational attainment was "some college." The coefficient for this group is not shown. The coefficients for degree holders with missing major field data are not presented. Dollar amounts are unstandardized regression coefficients.

[b]Includes education.

[c]Includes computer science and engineering.

[d]Includes law, medicine, etc.

[e]Includes degrees in fields other than law, medicine, etc.

degree holders, and men were overrepresented relative to women in these most remunerative fields. Concentrations at the A.A. level do not align as well with the general trend, but the gap between the highest- and lowest-paying majors is quite narrow relative to the other degree levels. Women are far more likely than men to have majored in health or social services, the best-paying fields for that degree. But offsetting women's strong representation in those areas is their monopoly in secretarial studies, a field leading to low earnings.

In considering these findings, the question arises: are the differences in major field payoffs more a function of gender than of the market value of a particular major? To examine this possibility, we compared the salaries of men and women in the same major-field areas, and we found that even within the same concentrations, the salaries of men typically exceeded those of women. But we also found that the salary rank order of major fields was generally the same for men and women; for example, at the M.A. level a business concentration produced the best payoffs for both men and women (though the men earned considerably more than the women), while education produced the slimmest yield for both (with the men somewhat ahead in earnings). In part, then, women appear to earn less because they are women, but major field clearly makes a difference. Indeed, with field controlled, the earnings gap between men and women is reduced by about $1,700 (or about 25 percent).

No doubt some of the remaining difference of more than $5,000 is due to differences between men and women in attitudes toward work and related factors (see England and McCreary 1987). But some of this economic inequality is probably due also to employer discrimination. Although we have no direct evidence about men's and women's experiences on the job, our data on perceptions suggest this conclusion. There were large gender differences in reports of discriminatory treatment in pay scales and raises and in promotions: 12 percent of men but 39 percent of women reported that they had experienced discrimination in pay and raises; corresponding figures for promotions were 20 percent and 36 percent.

Overall, then, though there has been a general trend, both nationally and at CUNY, toward less sex segregation in college majors (Jacobs 1989; Crook 1989), considerable sex typing is evident for the period reflected by our data. In part women may seem responsible for a portion of the economic consequences, for college major appears to be a matter of individual choice. But as with aspirations in general, choices are partly a result of socialization in family, school, and peer group contexts, so they are more socially determined than they appear.[22] Colleges and universities, through counseling, advising, and other support services could undoubtedly intervene to add momentum to the trend away from sex segregation in college majors.

Gender inequality adds another complication to the already complex socioeconomic outcomes of open admissions. The policy made an important contribution to the labor-market success of many individuals and particularly improved the prospects of minorities. Because more women than men came to CUNY under open admissions, socioeconomic benefits to the former were appreciable. Nonetheless, the magnitude of these benefits was limited by labor-market forces that continue to produce gender inequality. Moreover, some of women's disadvantage can probably be attributed to the college contexts that still tend to perpetuate gender disparities in choices about major fields. In light of these economic disadvantages, it appears that men realized more economic benefit from the open-admissions policy than did women.

The Difference That Open Admissions Made

Our analyses to this point lend support to a fundamental assumption underlying the policy: that providing educational opportunity for economically and educationally disadvantaged minority students, who otherwise would have had no chance for college, would ultimately translate into socioeconomic benefits. Because educational attainment is by far the most important determinant of job status and earnings, many of the students who owed their college entry to the program held better jobs and were earning more as a result. But how much of a difference did the policy actually make? In terms of labor-market success, where would they have stood if open admissions had never come into existence, and just how much better off were they because of the program?

[22]Subjects such as mathematics and science furnish an example. In junior high school girls are more likely than boys to be placed in high-ability group math and science classes, and boys, conversely, are more likely to be placed in low-ability classes and remedial math courses (Catsambis 1994). In spite of these more positive experiences in their middle school years, girls have less-positive attitudes toward these fields. Probably as a consequence, in high school girls are less likely to enroll in advanced math and science courses. Differences favoring males in math and science achievement seem attributable in part to such differences in course work exposure. One may reasonably speculate that these differences are in part responsible for the lower likelihood that girls would major in math or science-related areas in college, thus eliminating their chances of entering remunerative occupations that require high-level quantitative skills.

These questions are more complicated than they may seem. To keep matters as simple as possible in addressing them, we have chosen to focus on earnings as the indicator of benefit. Although the lore about CUNY's contribution to life chances among generations of New Yorkers has certainly recognized occupation as a component of upward mobility, the rhetoric of the CUNY mission has emphasized the importance of the university as a pathway out of poverty. And in debates about open admissions, questions have often focused on whether the policy was worth the cost. Earnings, rather than job status, appear to resonate most naturally with the terms of public discourse.

In examining just how much of an economic difference open admissions made, we shall consider a number of questions. Perhaps the most basic refers to the open-admissions students: how much did the policy add to the earnings of those individuals whose entry to CUNY's senior and community colleges it made possible?

It is best to acknowledge at the outset that any analysis of this question necessarily must be speculative. In order to address it we have made a number of assumptions, some of which may have led us to overstate the benefits of open admissions, others to understate them. To begin with, we must estimate what earnings would have been if the open-admissions policy had never been initiated. There is no self-evident procedure for doing this. As with almost all social interventions, the open-admissions policy was not a true experiment, containing a control group of randomly chosen CUNY applicants who were denied admission to the university (and to any other institution) in order to provide a baseline for judging the impact of the CUNY initiative. In the absence of such a control, we have chosen as a baseline group that subset of open-admissions students who withdrew from CUNY with less than a semester's worth of credits. These early leavers had no educational credential beyond a high school diploma and very little college experience. We have taken their actual earnings to represent what open-admissions students would have earned if the policy had never been initiated.[23]

[23]Using early dropouts in this way may have produced an overestimate of the dollar benefits attributable to open admissions. The dropouts may have differed in some important respects from the open-admissions students who went further in higher education, usually earning some kind of degree. Although the latter had only modestly higher educational aspirations, it is possible that their achievement motivation was greater from the outset. Consequently, even if open admissions had not occurred, these more persistent open-admissions students might have had more success in the labor market. Of course, achievement motivation or other personality factors also may affect educational attainment, and once this is taken into account, their direct influence on earnings

We are also faced with a question in specifying the beneficiaries of the open-admissions policy. Although open-admissions students, by definition, owed their CUNY entry to the program, in its absence some might have gone elsewhere to college. Obviously, there is no precise way of identifying those open-admissions students who would have gone elsewhere, but there is reason to think that whites would have predominated in this group. According to Jaffe and Adams (1971), open admissions siphoned students from several middle-level private colleges in the New York City area. These appear to have been reasonably able students who, although they could not meet CUNY admissions standards in the pre–open admissions era, flocked to the university afterward in order to take advantage of the free tuition.[24] These students were overwhelmingly from middle- and upper-middle-class backgrounds, and undoubtedly no more than a handful were of minority origins, because family incomes of the latter were typically so low that even when their academic records were strong enough for a private institution in the area, very few could have afforded tuition.

These ethnically linked realities of college attendance have led us to make different assumptions about the importance of CUNY's policy for white and minority open-admissions students. Among minorities, we assumed that without the program none would have attended college. To make this assumption for whites, many of whom would have gone to college anyway, would have led to an overestimate of open admissions' benefits for them. Accordingly, we defined white open-admissions students as beneficiaries only if their academic records were especially weak. We designated those with high

---

may be reduced. Jencks and his colleagues (1979) have noted that personality factors do have an independent influence on earnings, but this effect is small relative to the influence of educational attainment.

We do not have a battery of personality measures available to assess this issue in our sample. Notwithstanding this lack, it must be said that because educational attainment is the most important determinant of earnings, it is unlikely that an estimate of the dollar benefits of open admissions could be entirely or even mostly attributable to personality differences between early dropouts and other open-admissions entrants.

In a sense, our choice of comparison group might even be considered conservative relative to the use of high school graduates who never attended college at all, for the latter would, no doubt, have even less of the achievement-related personality traits.

[24]According to Jaffe and Adams (1971, 163), an official of Fordham University's admissions office remarked, "What kid is going to pay two thousand dollars a year for an uncertain education when he can get the same uncertainty at City for almost nothing?"

school averages of less than 75 as the "weak" ones whose college attendance depended on the program.[25]

We have not counted regular students as beneficiaries of open admissions because, as we noted in Chapter 2, their high school records generally would have qualified them for entry before open admissions. Not treating them as beneficiaries may have produced an underestimate of the policy's value, for our data suggest that some regular students, especially minority ones, enrolled only because the policy encouraged them to believe that CUNY was truly open to them. For example, a third or more of black and Hispanic regular senior college students felt that the policy made college possible or encouraged them to attend. Even among regular-admissions whites, nearly 20 percent had such perceptions.[26]

To summarize, we have used the earnings of open-admissions entrants who left CUNY early as the indicator of how open-admissions students would have fared without the policy. We have assumed that all minority open-admissions students were beneficiaries of the program, but that white open-admissions students were beneficiaries only if their high school averages were especially low. We have also assumed that regular students did not benefit from open admissions, though it is likely that some of them did. This assumption probably led to an underestimate of the policy's benefits. Although our estimates of benefit are thus somewhat imprecise, we think that the assumptions on which they are based allow us to convey a reasonable sense of the economic benefits conferred by open admissions.

Table 3.7 presents estimates of the dollar payoffs to open admissions ac-

---

[25]Our assumptions about who would not have gone to college may seen tenuous in the case of senior college minority open-admissions students, for, at least in a mechanical sense, their high school records would generally have qualified them for a CUNY community college even without the policy. But we have chosen not to further complicate our procedure by adding another set of projections about the educational attainments and subsequent income of senior college open-admissions students had they initially entered two-year colleges. Our assumption that senior college open-admissions minority students wouldn't have gone to college (not even a two-year one) without the program may be the more realistic one: in responding to questions about their perceptions of open admissions, the majority of senior college open-admissions blacks and Hispanics said that the policy had made college possible for them or had encouraged them to go. So in treating these students as if open admissions enabled them to attend college, we probably are not very far off the mark.

[26]We could not designate these students as program beneficiaries because data on perceptions of open admissions' personal benefit were collected only for respondents who entered in the 1970 cohort.

Table 3.7 Estimated Dollar Benefits of the Open–Admissions Policy, by Gender and Ethnicity

	Males		Females	
	White	Minority[a]	White	Minority[a]
	Benefits to Open-Admissions Students			
Actual earnings	$28,903	$23,454	$22,266	$19,078
Estimated earnings without open admissions	26,711[b]	20,714[c]	20,897[b]	16,669[c]
Difference	+2,192	+2,740	+1,369	+2,409
	Benefits to All Students			
Actual earnings	31,138	24,336	24,181	20,063
Estimated earnings without open admissions[d]	30,407	22,294	23,893	18,523
Difference	+731	+2,042	+288	+1,540
	Ratio of Minority to White Earnings[e]			
Actual ratio		.78		.83
Estimated ratio without open admissions		.73		.78

Source: Follow-up survey.

[a]Consists of blacks and Hispanics.

[b]Mean earnings for white open-admissions students with high school averages of less than 75 who dropped out of college without completing fifteen credits.

[c]Mean earnings for all minority open-admissions students who dropped out of college without completing fifteen credits.

[d]To make these estimates we constructed distributions in which the mean earnings of open-admissions students who were early dropouts (as shown in the top panel of the table) were assigned to each open-admissions entrant. For each regular student actual earnings were used. Using these distributions, we calculated the mean for each ethnic and gender category.

[e]Ratios calculated from the figures shown in the second panel of the table.

cording to ethnicity and gender. (To simplify the presentation, we have combined black and Hispanic respondents to form the category *minority*.) These estimates of dollar benefit are calculated, of course, for those former students who were full-time workers. The table contains three panels. The first provides an assessment of what the program did for open-admissions students. It compares their actual earnings with the dollars that we estimate they would have earned if CUNY's policy had never been initiated. (We remind the reader that the estimates are represented by the earnings of open-admissions students who dropped out without completing even one semester of college.) The difference between actual and estimated earnings provides the measure of economic benefits that the program conferred upon open-admissions students. Among both whites and minorities, open-admissions entrants typically were better off because of the opportunity that the program gave them, and benefits to minorities exceeded those to whites. Among men, for example, whites received almost $2,200 more per year on average than they would have without open admissions, while minority respondents earned over $2,700 more. Minority open-admissions women received about $2,400 more per year, a boost that exceeded whites' by more than $1,000.

Although these estimates of economic benefit to open-admissions students may seem quite modest, one must keep in mind that our calculations of actual earnings include individuals at all levels of educational attainment—the ones who never earned a degree as well as those with A.A.'s, B.A.'s, or higher. If we had included in our calculations of actual income only those who received credentials, payoffs would be larger. According to our estimates, for example, minority male degree holders earned almost $4,600 more than they would have without the open-admissions policy, and minority females with degrees earned almost $3,900 more. But in evaluating what open admissions did for students whose college enrollment was made possible because of it, we must take into account not only those who earned credentials but also those who did not.

By helping open-admissions students, the policy was designed to improve more generally the economic situations of disadvantaged groups. Although the program brought about very large increases in minority enrollments—proportionately, far larger than those seen among whites—many minority entrants were academically strong enough to have gotten into CUNY even without the program. Overall, then, taking into account both the open-admissions students and the regular ones, how much did the policy actually do to improve the earnings of minorities, who had been identified as especially needing opportunity? The question of how much the payoffs to open-admissions students added to the overall economic standing of the groups to which they belonged is addressed in the second panel of the table. To estimate what earnings would have been for each group in the absence of open admissions, we took the actual earnings of regular students in each group and assigned the earnings figure for early dropouts in that group (first panel) to each open-admissions entrant. Using these values, we calculated the overall mean earnings for each ethnic and gender category. The difference between this dollar value and the average actual earnings for all members of each group is the measure of the open-admissions aggregate dollar payoff. All groups were better off because of open admissions, but the earnings boost to minorities was substantially greater than the one to whites. Among men, minorities received an increment of more than $2,000, almost triple that of whites. Among women, the boost to minorities—over $1,500—was more than five times that experienced by whites. That open admissions made a larger difference for minorities partly reflects the far greater proportion of open-admissions entrants in their ranks. As a consequence, the leverage of the policy in boosting earnings throughout the minority contingent was greater.

Ultimately, the egalitarian thrust of open admissions was to be seen in what it did to affect the relative economic standing of whites and minorities. To what extent did it help to narrow earnings inequalities between groups? Results pertinent to this question are presented in the third panel of table 3.7, which shows the ratios of minority earnings to the earnings of whites. The ratios tell us how much minorities earned for each dollar earned by whites. According to our estimates, without open admissions the earnings of minority men would have been only 73 percent of white men's earnings; with the program, they amounted to 78 percent. A narrowing of the gap among women is also apparent: if there had been no policy, minority women would have earned 78 cents on the white women's dollar. With open admissions they earned 83 cents.

In estimating the economic benefits of open admissions, we remind the reader that we have been working with a sample of 1970–72 entrants who held full-time jobs in 1984. To gain a sense of the broader economic ramifications of the policy, we have projected our estimates to the population of open-admissions students who were employed full-time. As we saw in table 2.12, more than 47,000 individuals entered CUNY as open-admissions students during those years; 31,000 of them were white, and 16,000 were minority students. We have used the proportions of open-admissions students in each ethnic and gender category who were employed full-time in our respondent sample to estimate the numbers in the population who held full-time jobs in 1984.[27] These are shown in table 3.8, along with our previous estimates of dollar benefits for open-admissions students. Projecting these estimates to the numbers in the population provides aggregated estimates of dollar benefits. Payoffs seem very substantial, amounting to almost 67 million dollars for the population of open-admissions students. That is to say, they earned almost 67 million more than they would have if there had been no open-admissions policy. And although only 43 percent of former open-admissions students who were working full-time were from minority groups, half of the payoff went to them.

These estimates of benefit—calculated at a single point in time—convey only a limited sense of the economic consequences of open admissions. First, 1984 was a relatively early year in the work careers of these individuals, who were typically in their early thirties when their earnings were measured. Because earnings rise more steeply with work experience for those with college credentials than for those without degrees (U.S. Department of Education 1990, 48–53; Murphy and Welch 1989), the gap between our respondents' actual earnings and their estimated earnings in the absence of open admissions would be expected to have widened as time has passed.

In other words, the payoffs of the policy undoubtedly grew larger in subsequent years, so that the lifetime earnings of open-admissions entrants will be substantially greater than they would have been if CUNY's policy had never been initiated. Moreover, these estimates do not take account of subsequent cohorts that entered CUNY after 1972. Although changes in the open-admissions policy after 1975 resulted in typically lower educational attainments among those in later entering classes (a point that we shall elaborate in Chapter 9), the edge that open access provided to the earning power of these later cohorts must be added to what we have already taken into account. From this perspective, open admissions has undoubtedly made a substantial economic difference.

The open-admissions policy aimed to reaffirm CUNY's mission to provide an avenue out of poverty for disadvantaged groups. This aim reflected a

---

[27]In estimating the proportions of white open-admissions students in the population who held full-time jobs, we have applied the criterion used in table 3.7: white students with high school averages of less than 75.

Table 3.8 Employment and Earnings, by Gender and Ethnicity

Estimated number of 1970–72 open-admissions entrants working full-time in 1984, with projected aggregate dollar benefits of the open-admissions policy

	Number Working Full-time	Average Dollar Benefit[a]	Aggregate Dollar Benefit
Minority males	6,250	$2,740	$17,125,000
Minority females	6,599	2,409	15,896,991
Total minority benefit			33,021,991
White males	12,205	2,192	26,753,360
White females	5,132	1,369	7,025,708
Total white benefit			33,779,068
Total benefit to all open-admissions students			$66,801,059

Source: Follow-up survey and table 2.14.

[a] Figures taken from the top panel of table 3.7.

widely shared belief in American society about the socioeconomic value of a college education.

Our review of the labor-market experiences of former students reveals a complex picture of successes intertwined with deeply rooted ethnic and gender inequalities. More than a decade after they had entered CUNY, relatively few were out of work, although minority workers were slightly more likely to be unemployed than were whites. Nonetheless, joblessness among the CUNY respondents was, for each category of ethnicity and gender, lower than it was in the comparable category in the New York–area labor market—a result due, at least in part, to the higher level of educational attainment that open admissions had made possible in the CUNY contingent. The majority of former students held full-time jobs; among men the overwhelming proportion were so employed; most women were also working full-time outside the home, though because of child-rearing responsibilities, they were less likely to be doing so than the men.

Relative to the New York work force, these full-time workers were even more heavily concentrated in the white-collar positions that have come to dominate the labor-market profile of the postindustrial city. Within this broad occupational sector, however, considerable ethnic inequality is apparent: whites far more often held jobs at the upper professional and managerial level, while blacks and Hispanics were clustered in the lesser white-collar positions (clerical, sales, and technical work)—the ones with lower job status and earnings.

Educational attainment is by far the most important influence upon occupational status and earnings. Because white workers mostly earned B.A.'s or higher and minority workers typically earned no more than an A.A., a substantial portion of ethnic inequality in labor-market success is explained by these differences in educational credentials.

These results reveal a further unfolding of the process of cumulative disadvantage that we noted in the previous chapter. As we said there, ethnic inequalities in socioeconomic and high school background between white and minority students influenced academic experiences in higher education: minority students were more likely to be placed in two-year colleges and, within them, in vocational curricula; they more often took noncredit remedial courses, thus extending their undergraduate careers; because their family economic resources were typically meager, they more often had to work full-time in college, and that obligation depressed their college grades. Full-time work in college also added to the time needed for degree completion; it especially prolonged the completion of the bachelor's degree. Time to B.A., in turn, was the single most important influence on the attainment of graduate degrees. In concert, these disadvantages, to which minority students were disproportionately subject, diminished their ultimate educational attainments, which in turn translated into lower earnings and occupational status. Furthermore, work experience compiled before degree completion did not compensate for the disadvantages it created. It added little to subsequent job success; postdegree work experience was by far the more important influence on earnings, and the increased time to degree associated with full-time work during college meant less time in the labor market with the degree in hand. Although minorities generally had more postdegree experience than whites because they didn't go as far in education, their experience edge did not come close to offsetting the much larger payoffs to whites' higher levels of degree attainment. Moreover, among individuals with comparable credentials, minorities had less work experience than whites.

Past disadvantages of social background not only were implicated in the educational attainment process but continued to have a direct influence on job success, albeit only a modest one. Coming from a low-income family (for males) or having parents whose educational attainments were low (for females), had a negative effect on labor-market success. Minority students were the ones most likely to come from such families.

New disadvantages for minority individuals arose from the labor market itself. Holding a public sector job produced a penalty in status and income, and minorities were more likely than whites to work there. Even when whites and minorities were comparable in all of the respects that we have been reviewing, disparities remained in status and especially in earnings. Although we cannot document it directly, we think that part of this remaining gap is a consequence of discrimination in the labor market.

In addition to ethnic inequalities in labor-market success, we have seen inequalities based on gender. Although women held jobs equal in status to those of men, they lagged substantially behind in earnings. Higher education is at least partly implicated in women's disadvantage, because males and females tend to be found in different fields of study that are linked to gender-segregated jobs. Women's jobs command lower salaries. But even when men and women occupy positions with the same job titles, the latter receive less compensation. Minority women are especially disadvantaged by gender inequality, which compounds the penalty imposed by ethnic status.

Open admissions could not, then, overcome completely the handicaps of social origins and educational background that depressed the educational attainments of disadvantaged students in higher education, thus leading to diminished work rewards. The effectiveness of the policy was further constrained by conditions outside of education's domain: by disadvantages arising from the labor market itself.

But beyond the limitations that we have reviewed, open admissions substantially advanced the occupational chances of many students who owed their college opportunity to the policy. Those who earned degrees received significant payoffs in status and earnings. The program helped narrow the gap separating whites from minorities. Many millions of dollars in additional earnings of open-admissions students must be counted as a benefit of the policy. This economic payoff undoubtedly has continued to grow in subsequent years, as the earnings of credentialed individuals increased at a faster pace than they would have if they had not gone to college, and as subsequent entering cohorts began to take their places in the labor market.

When the open-admissions policy was being drawn up in the late 1960s, critics feared that many millions of dollars would be wasted on the program, that the city and the state of New York would never realize a return on this large investment. Although a systematic cost-benefit analysis lies beyond the scope of our work, it seems clear that the public has reaped benefits from the program, which enabled many thousands of individuals to become more substantial taxpayers.

CHAPTER FOUR

Getting Ahead

The Development of Work Careers

How did the work careers of former CUNY students take shape? Undoubtedly they had traveled diverse routes in getting to where they were in 1984. Some who were not working at all in the late 1970s held full-time jobs by the mid-eighties, and some who had been working full-time at an earlier point subsequently switched to part-time work, became unemployed, or dropped out of the labor market. Among those who were working full-time in both periods, many started relatively inauspiciously—holding clerical and technical jobs at modest salaries in the lower tiers of the white-collar world. Some of these individuals were successful in moving into better-paid, more responsible managerial and professional work. Others made little progress, appearing to be stuck in their initial low-end jobs.

What accounts for differences in the ways that individuals' work careers developed? What role did educational attainment play in career advancement—in promotions and pay raises? We know from the last chapter that credentials were the most important influence on labor-market outcomes, but it is not clear just how this came about. Differences in educational attainment may have produced visible differences in early job rewards, or perhaps education's effects, not so noticeable at first, may have emerged more clearly over time. In effect, holders of lesser credentials may have found themselves restricted to dead-end jobs—ones that are unconnected with opportunities for promotions and raises—while higher degrees enable their recipients to enter jobs that are a part of career ladders, thus providing opportunities for advancement.[1]

[1]Job shifts can occur in different ways, such as promotions or job changes within an organization, or by moves to a different organization. Moreover, such organizational characteristics as policies to promote from within can affect promotion chances independently of individual characteristics such as educational attainment. Analysis of careers in terms of organizational features or according to interindustry differences in labor market structure are beyond the scope of our analyses. For further discussion of such issues, see Rosenfeld (1992), Hall (1986), and Spilerman (1977).

Table 4.1 Labor-Force Participation in 1978 and in 1984, by Ethnicity and Gender

Percentages, Except as Noted

Labor Force Status	Males			Females		
	White	Black	Hispanic	White	Black	Hispanic
Full-time						
1978	84	78	88	78	76	75
1984	93	88	92	62	78	67
Part-time						
1978	8	13	8	9	10	12
1984	3	4	1	13	8	10
Unemployed						
1978	1	3	3	1	2	3
1984	2	5	6	1	5	6
Not in labor force						
1978	7	5	1	12	12	11
1984	2	4	0	24	9	17
% holding full-time job in both years	79	72	84	52	63	56
N (unweighted)	1,525	247	169	1,795	436	258

Source: Follow-up survey.

Note: Sums may not equal 100 percent due to rounding.

Some have identified community colleges and their A.A. degrees as leading to jobs that hold little promise for advancement, at least by comparison with B.A. institutions. In this view community colleges serve to reinforce inequalities of status and earnings, since poor people and minorities are over-represented in them (Bowles and Gintis 1976; Brint and Karabel 1989; Dougherty 1987, 1994; Monk-Turner 1990, 1985; Pincus 1980, 1986). Although quite a bit of evidence indicates that community college graduates are found in less-rewarded jobs, analyses focus on only one point in time, so we cannot tell whether these graduates are in fact consigned to the dead-end sector of the labor market. These students may have started behind B.A. recipients, and the upward slope of their increases in job status and earnings simply may have been more modest.

Gender inequity is another important issue to be considered in an examination of career development. As we saw earlier, women earned less than men with comparable educational credentials. Perhaps this difference arose because women received narrower dollar increments. This would be consistent with the idea that predominantly female occupations provide fewer promotion opportunities than predominantly male ones (Rosenfeld 1992).

This chapter will assess the role of educational attainment, ethnicity, gender, and other factors in accounting for former students' career development. As we have said, these respondents were in their early to mid-thirties when they were followed up, an age at which, research suggests, evidence of career advancement is generally visible if it is to occur (Rosenfeld 1992; Rosenbaum 1979; Hall 1986). We shall begin with an assessment of labor-force participation over the six-year period from 1978 to 1984, considering stability and change in employment status (full-time work, unemployment, absence from the labor force, etc.) at these two points.

Next, among those who were employed full-time in both years, we shall examine the association between the types of jobs held in 1978 and 1984. For example, among those who worked in the lower white-collar tier of the labor market (in technical and administrative support jobs) in 1978, what proportions had moved into top-tier professional and managerial positions by 1984? Then we shall examine in more detail how educational attainment, ethnicity, and other factors may have influenced changes in occupational status and in earnings over this period.

Changes in Labor-Force Participation

Over the period from 1978 to 1984, clear trends are visible in patterns of labor-force participation (shown in summary form in table 4.1).[2] These patterns are closely associated with gender and to a lesser extent with ethnicity. The outstanding feature of men's labor-force status is that more than 70

---

[2]For simplicity of presentation, the table shows aggregate 1978 to 1984 changes, but not the flow of individuals from one labor-force category to another. Where inspection of the more detailed tables revealed changes across categories that seem important, we shall describe them in the text.

percent held full-time jobs in both 1978 and 1984. Although Hispanics were most likely to exhibit this pattern (84 percent were full-time in both years), and blacks were least likely, ethnic differences are not large. Despite the high proportion working full-time in both years, there were a fair number in 1978 who were not in the labor force or were in part-time jobs (mainly because they were still in school). As they completed their educational careers, they moved into full-time work or were looking for work, so the proportion in the labor market was greater in 1984 than in 1978. More men were out of work in 1984 than in 1978, and those who previously had held full-time jobs contributed the most to the ranks of the unemployed. Few were chronically out of work, that is, unemployed at both periods.

The pattern for women contrasts sharply with that of men. They were not only less likely than men to hold hold full-time jobs in 1978, but over time they moved into part-time work or dropped out of the labor force entirely. Among white females fewer than seven in ten who worked full-time in 1978 were still doing so in 1984 (compared with nine in ten white men). Moreover, women who were part-timers or out of the labor market in 1978 were much less likely than men to move later into full-time jobs. Most likely, marriage and especially children influenced women to take part-time jobs or induced them to leave the labor force. Thus, the processes that helped (in the last chapter) to explain women's 1984 employment status seem also to have been operating in 1978. Although we have no information on the timing of marriage and/or children, many women in 1978 and more by 1984 undoubtedly had family responsibilities. Black women were more likely than white or Hispanic women to work full-time in 1984, but there had been essentially no ethnic differences in 1978. While many whites and Hispanics were disengaging from full-time work, black women's ties to it remained more stable.

As a result of the gender difference in labor-market trend, disparities between men and women in full-time employment widened greatly between 1978 and 1984. The most dramatic example is seen among whites: in 1978 white men were 6 percent more likely to hold a full-time job than white women, but the difference had grown to more than 30 percent by 1984. A similar pattern, on a smaller scale, exists among Hispanics and blacks; black males were 2 percent more likely than black women to work full-time in 1978, but by 1984 they were 10 percent more likely.

Because of women's initially lower levels of full-time employment and because of the gender difference in the trend of labor-market participation, a smaller proportion of women than of men held full-time jobs in both 1978 and 1984. Nonetheless, despite the fact that many women were moving into part-time work or came to devote all of their efforts to family responsibilities, more than half—and in the case of black women more than six in ten—held full-time jobs at both time periods.

These individuals—men and women—who were full-time workers in both 1978 and in 1984 are the ones whose career development we shall consider. Focusing on this pool, thereby excluding others who moved between part-time and full-time work, is not a serious limitation, for one of our primary concerns is to examine the influence of educational attainment on the development of careers. To include part-timers (in 1978, 1984, or both) might obscure the role of educational credentials. In other words, to get a clear sense of the influence of education on career development, we have limited the analysis to those with the strongest attachment to the labor force—full-time employees in both periods.

Our analyses will focus on those who had completed their education by 1978. Although we have made much of the fact that educational careers are, for many students, intertwined with work, we want to estimate the effects of credentials on occupational mobility without mixing different temporal configurations of education and work. Including only respondents who had completed their education by this time eliminates most individuals who earned postgraduate degrees. (A strong majority of postgraduate credentials were awarded after 1978.)[3] Because the remaining number of such degree holders is small, we have excluded them from consideration. In effect, then, we direct our attention to those whose highest degree was a B.A. or less (including those who held an A.A., those who had a semester or more of college experience short of a degree, and those who held only a high school diploma).[4]

The period that we shall examine—1978 to 1984—is an interval when our respondents typically went from their mid- to late twenties into their early to mid-thirties. This is a critical period when career trajectories become established, as the literature has pointed out (e.g., Blau and Duncan 1967, 183–88; Rosenbaum 1979).

[3]About 20 percent of undergraduate degrees also were earned after 1978.

[4]We remind the reader that those for whom the high school diploma is designated as the highest level of educational attainment had in fact entered CUNY as freshmen. They did not, however, complete even one semester's worth of college credits. Those designated as having had "some college" had a semester or more of college experience.

Getting Ahead

We begin our examination of career development by considering the types of jobs full-time workers held in 1978 and in 1984. We shall look first at the broad categories used by the U.S. Census Bureau, just as we did in Chapter 3. It was apparent there that former CUNY students are heavily concentrated in the two white-collar sectors of the New York City labor market—in the top sector, which includes managerial and professional jobs, and in the second tier, which includes the lower-level clerical, technical, and sales positions. To what extent was there, over time, movement of individuals from one occupational category to another, and, particularly, into the more highly rewarded upper-tier positions?

There was considerable stability overall in respondents' occupational classification over this period (table 4.2).[5] Among men in upper white-collar jobs (managerial and professional level) in 1978, for example, far more than half in each ethnic group were still there in 1984. Among women in the lower white-collar tier in 1978, a clear majority—60 percent of whites, 81 percent of blacks, and 84 percent of Hispanics—were still there in 1984.

Nonetheless, considerable movement did occur, mostly in the direction of higher occupational standing. By 1984, for example, the proportion of men in professional and managerial positions had increased over their proportion in 1978. There were comparable changes among women. Most of the increase in the proportion of top-tier job holders is accounted for by moves out of the lower white-collar sector. Among all ethnic groups, an upward flow—out of these jobs and into the top level—predominated over downward moves into blue-collar jobs.

Clear ethnic inequalities are visible in the extent of upward moves: minority individuals were less likely to move up than whites. Thus, among men who held lower white-collar jobs in 1978, 42 percent of whites but only about a fifth of blacks and a quarter of Hispanics had made it into managerial and professional jobs by 1984. Overall, minority workers who held lower-level white-collar or blue-collar jobs in 1978 were less likely than whites to have made it into a higher job category by 1984.

Ethnic disparities are also visible in downward mobility: about 30 percent

[5]The number of cases in table 4.2 is smaller for each ethnic and gender group than the number in table 4.1 because the former includes only those who completed their highest degree before 1978 and who were working full-time in both years. Also, recipients of postgraduate degrees are not part of this analysis.

Table 4.2 Relation of 1978 Occupation and 1984 Occupation, by Ethnicity and Gender

Percentages, Except as Noted

| | 1984 Occupation | | | | | | | | | | | | | | |
| | Managerial–Professional | | | Technical–Sales–Adm. | | | Blue-collar & Other | | | Total in 1978 Category | | | Number of Cases | | |
1978 Occupation	W	B	H	W	B	H	W	B	H	W	B	H	W	B	H
Males															
Managerial–professional	22	13	13	3	3	4	2	3	5	26	19	22	222	25	23
Technical–sales–adm.	22	13	14	28	44	40	3	6	3	53	63	57	405	73	52
Blue-collar & other	4	2	1	4	2	6	12	15	14	20	19	21	131	22	18
Total in 1984 category	48	28	28	35	49	50	17	23	23	100	100	100	758	120	93
Females															
Managerial–professional	24	15	19	3	0	3	0	0	0	27	15	22	153	33	25
Technical–sales–adm.	26	13	10	41	63	58	1	2	2	68	78	69	359	126	78
Blue-collar & other	1	0	1	2	3	4	2	4	4	5	7	9	25	11	6
Total in 1984 category	50	29	30	47	66	65	3	5	6	100	100	100	537	170	109

Source: Follow-up survey.

Note: W = white, B = black, H = Hispanic. Sums of cell percentages may not equal row and column totals due to rounding.

of black men, 41 percent of Hispanics, but only 19 percent of whites who started in the top white-collar tier fell into lower white-collar or blue-collar jobs. In sum the most visible trend is that most individuals remained in the same occupational category; those who moved tended to improve their labor market situations rather than to see them diminished, and whites were more likely to move up than minority workers.

Because the occupational categories we have been using to describe change are very broad, we may be missing some of the job mobility that can occur within each category. For example, individuals in the top tier of white-collar work could be promoted from one managerial job to another at a higher level. Such changes could become visible only with a more detailed measure—one that is provided by the social-status scores (the socioeconomic index or SEI) that we used in the last chapter. Moreover, those whose job title does not change—teachers are an example—might advance in terms of earnings. These traditional socioeconomic indicators, job status and earnings, can help us develop a more detailed portrayal of career development.

To begin with, the ethnic inequalities that we have seen in the upward movement of individuals are consistent with more detailed job-status data (table 4.3 for men, 4.4 for women). Although on average people advanced modestly in job status, whites tended to gain more. Among men there were only small ethnic differences in the occupational status of jobs held in 1978; by 1984 minority men had moved ahead very little, while the job status of whites rose modestly. As a result, ethnic differences—not much in evidence initially—became more apparent. Consistent with this pattern of change in job status, earnings inequalities also widened: in 1978 white men were about $3,000 ahead of minority men, but because whites experienced larger increases, the earnings gap grew, in constant dollars, to more than $6,000 by 1984.

Among women there is a comparable pattern of ethnic difference in the development of occupational status: a relatively small 1978 gap in favor of whites had grown larger by 1984. The ethnic pattern for earnings is also similar to the one we observed for men: white women's earnings rose more than those of blacks and of Hispanics (whose real earnings actually decreased slightly), so that the economic gap had widened by 1984. Although gender differences in job advancement seem minimal (SEI scores increased similarly for men and women), earnings gains among women were considerably more modest than among men. Indeed, white and black women received pay raises that were only about half those of men, and, as we said, Hispanic women actually suffered an overall decline in earnings.

Table 4.3 1978 and 1984 SEI and Earnings for Males, by Educational Attainment and Ethnicity

Educational Attainment	Occupational Status Scores			Earnings[a]		
	1978	1984	Difference	1978	1984	Difference
High school	42.5	46.9	4.4	24,199	26,149	1,950
White	43.4	49.1	5.7	24,976	27,470	2,494
Black	38.5	41.0	2.5	21,496	22,558	1,062
Hispanic	42.2	40.3	−1.9	22,672	21,931	−741
Some college	44.9	51.5	6.6	24,522	27,377	2,855
White	43.8	52.2	8.4	25,172	28,613	3,441
Black	44.7	47.6	2.9	22,607	23,832	1,226
Hispanic	50.9	51.5	0.5	22,523	23,471	948
A.A.	48.8	53.1	4.2	24,831	28,023	3,192
White	48.1	53.5	5.5	25,878	29,156	3,278
Black	52.9	53.3	0.5	22,012	25,489	3,477
Hispanic	47.0	47.7	0.7	21,307	22,679	1,372
B.A.	57.7	63.1	5.5	25,382	33,790	8,409
White	57.6	63.2	5.6	25,501	34,089	8,588
Black	59.8	61.2	1.3	27,324	31,77¹	4,448
Hispanic	57.1	62.7	5.6	21,372	28,031	6,659
Total	49.7	55.2	5.5	24,831	29,644	4,813
White	50.1	56.5	6.4	25,376	30,838	5,461
Black	46.5	48.6	2.1	22,568	24,651	2,083
Hispanic	50.0	51.1	1.1	22,187	23,900	1,713
Total cases[b]	899			840		
White	702			664		
Black	111			101		
Hispanic	86			75		

Source: Follow-up survey.

[a] 1978 earnings have been converted to 1984 dollars.

[b] Ns are unweighted.

Table 4.4 1978 and 1984 SEI and Earnings for Females, by Educational Attainment and Ethnicity

Educational Attainment	Occupational Status Scores			Earnings[a]		
	1978	1984	Difference	1978	1984	Difference
High school	49.1	52.5	3.4	19,600	20,149	550
White	52.3	58.5	6.1	19,887	21,870	1,983
Black	44.9	45.2	0.3	20,266	19,188	−1,077
Hispanic	46.5	47.3	0.8	18,099	16,906	−1,194
Some college	51.9	56.7	4.8	21,385	23,180	1,795
White	52.6	59.5	6.9	22,079	23,990	1,912
Black	47.9	51.4	3.6	18,864	21,299	2,435
Hispanic	53.9	49.5	−4.4	21,486	21,630	144
A.A.	51.2	53.1	1.9	22,099	22,112	13
White	51.4	54.0	2.6	22,154	22,275	120
Black	49.0	49.6	0.9	21,053	21,209	156
Hispanic	53.5	54.5	1.0	23,359	22,837	−523
B.A.	54.7	62.1	7.4	22,108	26,015	3,906
White	55.5	62.9	7.5	22,290	26,628	4,371
Black	48.9	55.6	6.7	18,861	20,937	2,076
Hispanic	51.1	58.1	7.0	26,413	24,106	−2,307
Total	52.4	57.4	4.9	21,574	23,670	2,096
White	53.7	60.0	6.3	21,949	24,766	2,817
Black	47.8	50.4	2.6	19,799	20,774	975
Hispanic	51.7	52.0	0.3	21,887	21,134	−753
Total cases[b]	773				671	
White	517				456	
Black	153				131	
Hispanic	103				84	

Source: Follow-up survey.

[a]1978 earnings have been converted to 1984 dollars.

[b]Ns are unweighted.

Educational attainment appears to have accounted in part for career advancement. Men with bachelor's degrees received the largest pay raises between 1978 and 1984, gaining more than $8,000. Although the B.A. increment is greatest among white men, minority men with B.A.'s also made the largest gains relative to their coethnists with less education. Overall, the relation between credentials and pay raises is positive and linear: the gains to B.A. holders exceed those received by A.A. recipients, the gains to the latter outdistance the ones for individuals with some college but no degree, and, in turn, their earnings advance exceeds that of high school graduates. Ethnic differences generally are narrower when educational attainment is controlled, indicating that disparities in credentials account for some of overall group inequality in economic advancement. Overall, then, these findings add some depth to what we learned in the last chapter: dollar returns to educational attainment, especially the B.A., seem only partly determined by early differences in earnings; they appear rather to reflect larger or more frequent pay raises given to those with the highest educational credentials.

The clear dollar benefit to B.A. recipients is not apparent for men's job status. Indeed, the largest status gain occurs among those who had some college but never earned any degree. Holders of B.A.'s hardly gained more than those with high school diplomas. Only among Hispanic men does there seem to be a clear benefit from a B.A. relative to other credentials. Overall, differences among educational levels in status gains form no clear pattern. Ethnic differences generally persist, even with educational attainment controlled: for each degree level, whites gained more in status than did blacks or Hispanics (except at the B.A. level, where the advances of whites and Hispanics were the same). At first the absence of a positive relationship between education and status gains might seem to conflict with the findings in the last chapter, where we saw that job status and credentials were positively associated. However, the findings are ultimately consistent, because those in Chapter 3 reflected differences in the absolute levels of status, whereas here we are dealing with change in status scores; in both 1978 and 1984 B.A. recipients clearly held the highest-status jobs, but status increments varied little by educational level.

For women the B.A. confers a more consistent advantage than it does for men: it makes a difference in terms not only of earnings but also of job status. The status boost to minority women seems especially marked. For example, among blacks a B.A. is associated with a status advance more than six points greater than the one experienced by those with only a high school diploma.

Holders of A.A.'s experienced only very small increments that seem—in the case of minority women—indistinguishable from those accruing to high school graduates. At every educational level except the B.A., whites typically gained more than minority women, but the B.A. appears to be an equalizer: at this level mobility in job status is essentially unrelated to ethnicity.

With regard to women's pay raises, the B.A. generally provides the biggest dollar boost. Whites with this degree clearly experienced the largest rise relative to other levels of educational attainment. Among black women, B.A.'s did well, but so too did those who had some college experience but no degree. Hispanics are an anomaly: at most levels of educational attainment and particularly for the B.A. holders, pay raises essentially failed to keep up with increases in the cost of living; we don't know why. While there was a clear linear rank order among men in the relation of credentials and the size of earnings increments, there is no such order among women. Controlling for education has no consistent effect on the size of ethnic differences: within educational level, differences among white and minority women are as large or larger as they are when education is not controlled.

These findings need clarification, especially with regard to ethnic differences, for even when educational attainments were comparable, whites seem to have outpaced blacks and Hispanics in promotions and raises. We have taken a closer look at these disparities by examining a broader range of potential influences on career development, including some that we assessed in Chapter 3. Among them are two aspects of social origins—parents' educational attainment and income—which could have affected career gains.

Another factor is work experience. As in the previous chapter, this variable is separated into two components. The first expresses years of experience before completion of the highest degree, while the second reflects experience subsequent to degree completion.[6] Differences in each type of work experience might have obscured some of the influence of education on getting

[6]Years of experience before highest degree was calculated as the difference between the year of first full-time job and the year of highest degree attainment. Experience after highest degree was calculated as the difference between year of highest degree and 1978. We took 1978 as the cut-off point in calculating work experience because all respondents obviously had the same amount of potential work experience between 1978 and 1984. Some who worked full-time at both points may have had a different labor-force status for some periods within this interval, but we do not have the job-history information to enumerate such temporary shifts. 1978 was not necessarily the year of a respondent's first full-time job. Indeed, almost all of them had worked full-time before then; 1974 was the modal year of first full-time employment.

ahead. That is, some of the effects of education may have been muted by the fact that respondents with lower levels of educational attainment (less than a college degree) had more work experience than those who went further in education. Such experience may have offset in part the leverage for career advancement provided by college degrees.

Chapter 3 showed that employment sector had a strong influence on status and earnings in 1984: those in the public sector were less rewarded. This explained some of the ethnic inequalities in status and pay: minority workers were doing less well partly because they were more likely to be found in public-sector jobs. But although public-sector jobs provided lower pay and less job status in 1984, it is less clear whether they were initially less rewarded or whether they might have been about equal to private-sector jobs initially, but subsequently provided less advancement.

To assess the role of such factors in explaining ethnic inequalities in getting ahead and to clarify the influence of educational attainment, we carried out multivariate analyses of their influence on 1978–84 changes in job status and earnings. As is customary in analysis of change scores, we controlled for the influence of 1978 job status in assessing status gains, and for the case of pay raises, we controlled for the influence of 1978 earnings.[7] Because virtually all respondents first held a full-time job before 1978, and because the status of this first job could have affected where they stood in 1978, we also included this factor in both the status and earnings analyses.[8]

Results for men (Appendix B, table B.3) help to clarify the influence of educational attainment on occupational advancement. Although educational level initially did not appear to be associated with gains in status, our expanded

[7]In working with change scores, it is necessary to control for the possible effects of the score at time 1 upon the score at time 2. The intuitive rationale for this is given by Kessler and Greenberg (1981, 8): "The notion that the value of a variable at one time is a source of the value of that variable at a later time is recognized in the popular adages that 'success breeds success' and 'the rich get richer and the poor get poorer.'" In practice, the idea that the value of a variable at one time can affect its value later on is subject to such further complexities as the "regression toward the mean," a phenomenon wherein the score for a variable at time 1 is negatively related to the difference score. Thus groups whose income is initially high, for example, might experience a slower increase than groups whose initial income is low. When score at time 1 is controlled in a regression equation, one can better assess other sources of change over time. More detailed discussions of the analysis of change scores may be found in Allison (1990), Kessler and Greenberg (1981), and Augustyniak et al. (1985).

[8]We collected job title information for the first full-time job and converted it to a status (SEI) score. We did not collect earnings data for that job.

analysis shows that with a larger set of potential influences controlled, B.A. recipients stand out as having gained the most between 1978 and 1984. (For example, compared with those whose highest degree was the high school diploma, B.A. recipients gained 6.6 more status points.) Holders of A.A.'s trail B.A.'s; indeed, two-year graduates are indistinguishable from those with high school diplomas only or those who had some college experience but never completed a degree. Although our analysis does not show it directly, differences in work experience seem to be part of the reason that education initially was not associated with status advancement; those with limited degree attainment—less than a B.A.—had more of a chance to compile postdegree work experience than did those who went further in education, and this served to obscure some of the differences between B.A.'s and others.[9] With experience controlled, however, education is revealed as having a stronger influence. The analysis also identifies other influences on status advancement. One is father's education: those whose fathers had at least some college advanced a bit more in job status than did otherwise comparable men whose fathers had never enrolled in college. Employment sector also makes a difference: those in public-sector jobs did not move ahead as much as workers in private employment.

Initial job status disparities between whites and minorities narrow when all of the variables in the analysis are controlled.[10] Educational attainment accounts for most of the differences; that is, whites more often earned B.A.'s than minorities, and receipt of this degree had an important influence on status gains. Minorities also were more likely than whites to be found in public-sector jobs in 1978, and they less often had fathers with college experience. With these factors taken into account, about a third of the white-black difference is explained, as is a quarter of the Hispanic-white gap.

The importance of educational attainment, and in particular the B.A. as a determinant of men's pay raises, is also confirmed by these analyses. B.A.

[9]Work experience subsequent to completion of highest degree does influence gains in status, but experience is highly correlated with educational attainment. Those with only high school diplomas or some college have much more postdegree experience than those with B.A.'s. When the dummy variables representing education are entered into the equation, the influence of experience disappears.

[10]Because SEI for 1978 job is controlled in model 1 of table B.3, the ethnic difference in model 1 of that table is not identical to the ethnic difference that can be calculated from table 4.3. The analogous point applies to the regression for earnings change, where model 1 controls for 1978 earnings.

recipients received raises almost $6,800 larger than the ones that went to those with only high school diplomas, and more than $5,000 larger than those to A.A. recipients.

Even though educational attainment is the single most important influence on wage increases, other factors—primarily the same ones that affected gains in occupational status—also play a role: having a father who attended college added around $2,000 in salary increases. We saw in Chapter 3 that public-sector workers earned less than those in private employment. This analysis reveals that part of the reason they were worse off is that they did not do as well in getting raises.[11] The status of one's first full-time job also influenced salary increments: a higher-status initial job seems to have assured job holders of larger subsequent gains. A difference of fifteen points in the status of the first job, for example, translated into a difference of a thousand dollars in pay raises.[12]

Overall, more of the differences in raises among ethnic groups is explained than was the case for status gains. Indeed, about 60 percent of blacks' slimmer dollar increment relative to whites is explained by the variables in the model, as is 35 percent of Hispanics'. Black and Hispanic men were less successful than whites in getting ahead financially mostly because of their lesser educational attainments, but also because of their greater likelihood of working in the public sector and of having gotten a first job of lower status, and the smaller chance of having a father who went to college. But these are not the only reasons for the disparities, for even after taking these variables into account, minority respondents still lagged behind whites.

Parallel analyses for women also add to our understanding of the determinants of career development. As with the men, educational attainment is the most important influence on occupational status, and the B.A. provides the most leverage for getting ahead (table B.4). If anything, with other variables controlled, the B.A. stands out as adding even more to occupational advancement than it did initially. Below this educational level there is little to choose between a high school diploma, an A.A., or college exposure without a degree. In other ways, influences on women's status gains are somewhat different than was the case for men. In contrast to males, for example, employment sector had no significant influence on job advancement. Overall, when a larger number of variables is controlled, ethnic gaps are narrowed: about a

[11]About 90 percent of workers were in the same employment sector in 1978 and 1984.

[12]A difference of fifteen points on first job is about the size of the standard deviation for SEI.

third of the difference separating whites from blacks and Hispanics is explained.

The analysis of pay raises confirms that women's economic mobility is limited relative to men's. Consequently, educational attainment has less influence on dollar increases among women than among men. It is true that female B.A. recipients get a larger boost than respondents below this level, and there is little to choose among attainment levels below the B.A. Still, the typical pay raise for a woman with a B.A. was only about $2,400 greater than that received by one with a high school diploma. (For men the comparable gap was almost $6,800.) Women's 1984 salaries more closely resembled their 1978 earnings than did men's. Other factors, such as having a father who attended college or having a high-status first full-time job, added to subsequent salary increases, but employment sector had little influence.[13] As in the case of job status, the variables we have examined help to explain about a third of the disparity in raises separating white from black and Hispanic women.

These analyses extend our understanding of education's influence on occupational status and earnings. The clear association between educational level and 1984 job status that we described in Chapter 3 was already quite well established in 1978. The difference between, say, the average 1984 job status of respondents with a high school diploma and those with a B.A. was already apparent six years before. Although it is true that B.A. holders outdistanced others in terms of promotions, for the most part, inequalities of job status were in place much earlier in our respondents' careers.

Disparities in earnings between educational levels, in contrast, were not very wide in 1978. But the influence of education made itself felt: the upward slope of earnings was considerably steeper for bachelor's recipients than for those further down the education ladder, so that six years later the distance between B.A.'s and others had widened dramatically. Although this B.A. effect is stronger for men, it appears as well for women.

It seems then that our respondents advanced in their careers more through pay raises than through promotions, at least as the latter are measured by the SEI. To a degree, we think that this index underestimates status gains. Al-

[13]Public employment also reduced women's pay raises, but this influence falls just short of statistical significance at the 0.05 level. The actual level is 0.09. Significance at 0.05 would undoubtedly be reached had the number of women approximated the number in the earnings regression in Chapter 3.

though it is a very useful measure, the SEI may insufficiently register the nuances of promotions, dependent as it is upon the occupational titles used by the Bureau of the Census. A college teacher promoted from assistant to full professor, for example, would still have the same status score, because the occupational titles used in the census do not distinguish academic ranks. On the other hand, earnings would surely have increased substantially.

The earnings results add to our confidence about the aggregate estimates of the dollar benefits of open admissions that we made in the last chapter. We suggested there that those benefits were likely to grow in future years because earnings climb more steeply for college graduates than for nongraduates. The analyses of this chapter show that the widening of the dollar gap between B.A. respondents and others was well under way at the cut-off point of our data.

These analyses also help us to understand better the ethnic inequality in status and earnings that we examined in the last chapter. We can now see that some of the disparity arises because blacks and Hispanics were less likely to be promoted and received fewer (or smaller) pay raises. Their more modest career progress is partly explained by their educational attainments: because blacks and Hispanics were less likely to receive a B.A., they were less successful in getting ahead.

The payoffs to the A.A. degree deserve special mention, given the controversy about the contribution of community colleges to individuals' life chances. Although the last chapter showed that in 1984 A.A. recipients were earning more and had jobs of higher status than those who had only a high school diploma, we have seen in the present analyses that this advantage was not caused by greater career advancement but rather by initial placement in better-paying, higher-status jobs. In terms of socioeconomic gains, then, the A.A. provided no more of a boost than a high school diploma or even college exposure with no degree. These results seem consistent with a view of two-year schools as leading to jobs with limited potential, located in the lower reaches of the white-collar world. Because minority students were more likely than whites to start in community colleges, these institutions are implicated in their slower career advancement.

Educational attainments are not the only source of ethnic inequality in the development of work careers. As we have seen, family background, the status of one's first job, and employment sector also affected job advancement and help to explain some of ethnic disparities. But even with all of these factors controlled much of the difference between whites and minorities remains unexplained. Other processes that we were unable to measure adequately may be responsible for some of this remaining inequality. For example, some undoubtedly moved ahead by receiving promotions and raises through moves to new jobs in new organizations. Possibly, whites may have been better able to make interorganizational moves.[14]

Part of ethnic disparities also may have resulted from employer discrimination in promotions and raises, and some of inequality in work rewards is likely a reflection of this.[15] But ultimately, although educational attainment exerted a strong influence on job advancement, we cannot account for the major portion of ethnic inequalities in getting ahead.

An understanding of women's socioeconomic standing is clarified by these analyses. Over time they displayed a different relation to the labor market than did men. Between 1978 and 1984 a declining proportion held full-time jobs. Their disengagement from paid employment was largely due to family and child care responsibilities. Men moved in the opposite direction, toward an increasing likelihood of holding a full-time job. Notwithstanding the general trend for women, more than half held full-time jobs at both points. Not only did these women have jobs in 1984 that were comparable in status to those of men, but they had moved ahead to about the same extent as men. As we saw in the previous chapter, however, women earned less than men. We now see that the inequalities visible in 1984 were produced in part because women received fewer or more modest raises. As a result, gender differences widened over time. Put another way, in 1978 women's salaries were more similar to those of men than they were in 1984.

Overall, many students who came to CUNY in the era of open admissions experienced considerable upward mobility in their work. Their gains were more visible, however, in terms of pay raises than in terms of advances in job status. The main significance of educational attainment for the latter was in enabling individuals to enter higher-status jobs.

Notwithstanding the presence of ethnic and gender inequalities in the extent of career advancement, the open-admissions policy must be counted as having made an important contribution to the chances of getting ahead, especially for minority students. The policy raised minority educational level,

[14]In this connection we had thought that whites who started work in public-sector jobs might have moved to the better-rewarded private sector more frequently than minorities; our data, however, show little ethnic difference in sector migration.

[15]But discrimination did not affect career mobility in any obvious way, for among minority respondents there were no consistent differences in actual socioeconomic gains separating those who did and those who did not perceive that they had been victims of discrimination.

so that even though there was a substantial ethnic gap in B.A. attainment, a considerable number of blacks and Hispanics attained this degree who would not have in the absence of the program. Given the importance of the B.A. for career advancement, the open-admissions program undoubtedly helped minority students to make more progress in work than they otherwise would have.

CHAPTER FIVE

The Quality of Work Experience

The focus on status and earnings in Chapters 3 and 4 reflects the traditional interest of social scientists who study labor-market standing. Indeed, what is known about socioeconomic attainment derives largely from the extensive research on occupational status and earnings. (The most prominent studies include Blau and Duncan 1967; Sewell and Hauser 1975; Featherman and Hauser 1978; and Jencks et al. 1979.) Notwithstanding the importance of these characteristics of jobs, there are other important aspects of work that deserve attention. These aspects concern what people actually do on the job: how much thought and judgment they must exercise, whether and to what extent they oversee the work of others, and how much responsibility they have in making decisions. Research shows that individuals prefer intrinsically engaging, challenging work to that which is easily mastered, offering little room to develop and utilize new skills (see Jencks et al. 1988; Kusterer 1978; Ronco and Peattie 1988). Furthermore, jobs that require solving problems, making decisions, doing complex tasks, and the like are associated with better working conditions, more organizational influence, opportunities for upward mobility, and higher salaries (see Hout 1984a; Kohn and Schooler 1983; Parcel and Mueller 1983; Spenner 1983). Jobs with these and similar demands enrich work skills that, in turn, improve prospects for advancement into positions with even greater nonmonetary and monetary rewards.

Examining the influence of educational attainment on access to intrinsically engaging jobs is an especially relevant concern in evaluating the results of higher educational opportunity. Although students may initially enroll in college mainly to better their odds for higher earnings and a prestigious job, the college experience broadens students' orientation towards work and its range of potential rewards. Studies of the impact of college on students indicate that seniors place less emphasis than freshmen on extrinsic work rewards (income, job security, status), and more emphasis on such intrinsic qualities as opportunities for self-expression, use of special talents, and independence

An earlier version of this chapter was published in *Sociological Forum* (Hyllegard and Lavin 1992).

(Bowen 1977, 109; Feldman and Newcomb 1973, 17–19; Pascarella and Terenzini 1991, 560–61; Strumpel 1971).

Once in the labor force individuals with higher education continue to expect work to be a source of intrinsic satisfaction (Hall 1986; Kanter 1978; Zuboff 1988). Like other college-educated workers, those who entered CUNY in the early 1970s desired interesting work. Responses to questions about the importance of work and success in our follow-up survey revealed that more than 80 percent of degree holders (A.A. or higher) disagreed with the statement that the salary a job pays is much more important than whether the work is interesting, and nearly 65 percent rejected the idea that job security is the most important aspect of work. Furthermore, more than 40 percent strongly preferred a job that demands their initiative.

This chapter examines the effect of educational attainment on access to nonmonetary job rewards among white and minority men and women. We shall focus on two dimensions of work: job authority and work complexity. Job authority implies managerial responsibility in such hierarchically structured workplaces as the many large private firms and public agencies in New York City. The primary responsibility of those with authority is to plan, manage, and monitor the work of others. As members of the managerial staff they must be knowledgeable about organizational rules and procedures and capable of using judgment and discretion in solving problems, making decisions, and the like. Because they are responsible for the performance of their organizational unit, they are compensated with higher salaries. Moreover, those who perform well are apt to move up the ranks into positions with greater pay, status, and power (see Caplow 1983; Hall 1975; Zuboff 1988).

Whereas job authority involves overseeing the work of others, work complexity pertains to the level and scope of cognitive difficulty inherent in task situations and is most prominently exemplified by the professions and high-level technical occupations. The work of architects, engineers, lawyers, and physicians, for example, typically involves the use of independent judgment, analytical skills, and the application of a substantial body of theoretical knowledge to solve problems, make decisions, and the like. The extensive research of Melvin Kohn and his associates (for example, Kohn and Schooler 1983) has demonstrated that work complexity—the degree to which tasks require thought and independent judgment—is a pivotal property of work that distinguishes challenging jobs from more routine, less demanding ones. It is an especially pertinent index of socioeconomic advantage in the modern, postindustrial economy, given its heavy reliance on the ability to carry out complex tasks that involve data and people in an increasingly word-oriented, information-intensive work environment.

Such important work qualities as complexity and authority are especially relevant to issues of equity. How do minorities and women compare with whites and males in the attainment of intrinsically challenging, high-quality jobs? What is the role of educational attainment and other variables in influencing access to jobs with these characteristics? These are the questions addressed in this chapter.

A Perspective on the Attainment of High-Quality Jobs

Chapters 3 and 4 identified a number of variables that influence occupational status and earnings. We believe that these factors also affect the attainment of jobs that have authority and involve complex work, but we want to discuss just why this is so. We view access to such jobs as primarily determined by educational credentials. Because graduate or professional degrees (M.A., Ph.D., LL.B., and so on) are prerequisite for employment in most professional occupations and for an increasing share of high-level managerial and administrative positions (Useem and Karabel 1986), they undoubtedly facilitate access to jobs with challenging task demands and/or decision-making responsibility. A bachelor's degree is frequently required for employment in many technical and middle-level managerial occupations, as well as a number of professional ones (nursing and teaching, for example). In light of our findings in the previous two chapters, an associate's degree seems much less likely to lead to intrinsically challenging work. Because blacks and Hispanics on the whole have lower educational attainments than do whites, their odds of obtaining high-level work are diminished. Differences in credentials therefore should explain a substantial portion of ethnic disparities in job complexity and authority.

As Chapter 3 showed, employment experience after completion of schooling has some bearing on occupational status and earnings. It may also be connected to complexity and authority. This expectation would be consistent with human capital theory, which argues that work experience represents an investment in work skills that enable one to perform more demanding, complex tasks (Mincer 1974, 1989). Studies of how managerial careers unfold reveal that whereas education is often very instrumental in being hired, promotion into positions with greater power and responsibility is determined far more by organizational tenure (Bills 1988; Caplow 1983; Kanter 1977). This finding leads us to believe that work experience after completing college has a greater effect on these job qualities than time spent at work before finishing one's degree.

Employment sector, a variable of the labor market that was shown in the previous two chapters to affect status and earnings, is likewise related, we believe, to work complexity and authority. As we said in Chapter 3, the emergence of a service-based economy and the attendant increased demand for a better-educated, more highly skilled work force appears to be especially pronounced in the private sector of the nation's major urban centers. In part this emphasis prevails because private organizations are subject to greater competitive pressure to lower costs and thus typically introduce advanced production technologies more rapidly. On balance, these technologies—various computer-aided labor processes, for example—appear to increase the cognitive demands of work (Adler 1986; Hirschhorn 1984; Zuboff 1988) and may add to the number of managerial jobs (Attewell 1990). It seems likely, then, that work complexity and job authority may, on average, be higher in the private sector of the economy than in the public.

Although we expect work complexity and job authority typically to be higher in the private sector, minorities and women may have greater success in gaining access to jobs involving such work in the public sector, partly because public employers have more aggressively sought to reduce employment-related discrimination (Farley 1984; Kaufman and Daymont 1981; Kaufman 1986). Consequently, the public sector has become very important to the chances of minorities and women for professional, technical, and administrative employment (Carnoy and Levin 1985; Collins 1983; DiPrete 1987; Farley 1984; Hout 1984b; Sokoloff 1980; Wilson 1980). Occupational opportunities apparently are distributed more equitably in the public sector, but job rewards tend not to be as good as those in the private sector—certainly the two previous chapters have shown status, earnings, and promotions to be lower in the public sector. We shall explore the process of obtaining access to challenging and responsible work in each employment sector. In doing so we gain a fuller understanding of how sector of employment influences group differences in socioeconomic success.

In sum, this chapter explores the effect of educational attainment on access to challenging work and job authority among the ethnic and gender groups who attended CUNY after it began its open-admissions program. Along with educational credentials, we examine other factors that may contribute to group differences in such jobs: work experience before and after degree completion and sector of employment.[1] All analyses are for jobs held in 1984 and include only full-time workers.

Work Complexity

Before considering our results a few words are in order about the meaning and measurement of work complexity. As used here, work complexity refers to the degree of thought and independent judgment required by work with data and/or people.[2] This concept typically is measured by scores assigned to occupational titles. The scores are based upon ratings produced by trained occupational analysts, who conducted extensive on-site observations of the task requirements of occupations, including their complexity of involvement with data and with people.[3]

We assigned scores of work complexity in relation to data and people to the occupational titles reported by respondents to our follow-up survey. To simplify matters we produced a single, overall measure of complexity by combining the information on data and people to create a single index of work complexity.[4]

In order to see how the work complexity variable distributes occupations, we divided its range of scores into thirds. Occupations high in work complexity (in the top one-third of the distribution) include architecture, dentistry, engineering, high-level administration and management, law, medicine, and teaching. The prominence of professional and high-level managerial occupa-

[1]We had thought that parental education and income might help explain how jobs with complex work and authority are distributed. When we included these variables in our preliminary analyses, however, they did not exert significant influence.

[2]Work with things—machinery, materials, and the like—can also be complex. As Kohn and Schooler point out, artists work with materials typically requires a great deal of thought and independent judgment. Yet relative to work with data and people, complex work with things is much more the exception than the rule (Kohn and Schooler 1983, 22). This principle seems particularly true in the modern postindustrial economy, in which communicative, interpersonal, and numerical skills are the primary competencies required in the performance of work.

[3]These scores were obtained from the *Dictionary of Occupational Titles* (U.S. Department of Labor 1977). The *DOT* is described in detail by Cain and Treiman (1981) and Miller et al. (1980).

[4]The *DOT* rates the complexity of occupational tasks in relation to data and people on seven- and nine-point scales, respectively. We created a single measure of work complexity by factor analyzing the data and people information, using the factor scores to produce an overall work complexity index. The resulting variable has a mean of 0, a standard deviation of 1, and scores range from a high work complexity value of 2.47 and a low value of minus 2.89.

tions in the upper range of work complexity is consistent with other research. Spaeth (1979, 1984), for instance, characterizes professional and upper-echelon managerial work as highly complex because it entails self-direction and abstract conceptualizing. By contrast, workers in the middle third of the variable distribution were typically in technical and midlevel managerial occupations (for example, they were air traffic controllers, assistant managers, police officers, and sales managers) that generally have a narrower range of task responsibilities and/or more specific cognitive demands. The more routinized jobs (for example, they were bank tellers, bus and truck drivers, cashiers, and security guards) appear in the bottom third of the complexity distribution.

There are substantial differences in the proportions of white and minority workers who hold jobs in the top one-third of the work complexity distribution (as shown by the means in the bottom row of table 5.1).[5] Whites are nearly twice as likely to hold the most challenging jobs.

The relation between educational attainment and work complexity exhibits a threshold effect: relative to the high school diploma, neither some college nor an associate's degree augments complexity. The B.A. appears as the minimum credential necessary for entry to jobs that provide more challenging work and seems especially important for minority chances of holding a challenging job. Relative to an A.A., for example, the B.A. is associated with roughly a sixfold increase in the proportion of Hispanic men and women doing complex work and almost a fivefold increase for black women. Among holders of graduate degrees there are further substantial increments in the proportion with the most complex jobs. Holders of an M.A. for example, are generally about twice as likely to be doing complex work as those with a B.A.

Differences in work complexity among ethnic groups are associated with educational attainment. Among those with high school diplomas whites are more likely than minorities to be doing complex work. These inequalities evaporate, however, among holders of bachelor's and master's degrees (and are even reversed in the case of Hispanic women at the B.A. level). With educational attainment controlled, gender differences favoring males are significant among whites at the A.A., B.A., and advanced- or professional-degree levels. There are no gender differences among blacks and Hispanics. Work complex-

---

[5]All differences referred to in the discussion of this table are statistically significant, as determined by difference-in-proportions tests for all key pairs of interest (see Blalock 1979). The same is true of table 5.2, which presents group differences in job authority.

Table 5.1 High Work Complexity, by Educational Attainment, Gender, and Ethnicity

Educational Attainment	Percentages						
	Males			Females			
	White	Black	Hispanic	White	Black	Hispanic	Total
H.S. diploma[a]	14.0	1.9	10.2	23.5	2.2	5.1	11.3
	(78)	(30)	(16)	(38)	(33)	(17)	(212)
Some college[b]	20.8	14.0	12.5	18.7	1.8	2.5	15.5
	(181)	(56)	(42)	(118)	(53)	(35)	(485)
A.A.	26.1	16.1	5.6	10.3	5.6	5.7	14.4
	(170)	(51)	(28)	(160)	(110)	(63)	(582)
B.A.	34.5	34.4	32.6	25.8	26.4	44.8	32.0
	(577)	(61)	(58)	(434)	(117)	(39)	(1,286)
M.A.	64.1	66.6	63.3	67.6	75.2	72.4	66.5
	(247)	(25)	(14)	(329)	(55)	(32)	(702)
Advanced[c]	87.2	—	—	75.3	—	—	84.1
	(178)			(62)			(248)
Mean	38.5	20.5	21.4	35.7	19.3	20.9	36.3
	(1,431)	(224)	(160)	(1,141)	(376)	(193)	(3,525)

Source: Follow-up survey.

Note: Table counts those in the top one-third of the work-complexity distribution. Percentages are weighted; frequencies (shown in parentheses) are unweighted.

[a]Respondents dropped out before completing one semester of college (fewer than fifteen credits).

[b]Respondents never earned any college degree but completed one or more semesters.

[c]Because of small Ns, minorities with advanced or professional degrees are not reported.

ity appears to be more strongly related to education and ethnicity than to gender.

As we said earlier, variables in addition to educational attainment—work experience, for example—may also influence access to complex work. Further, it is possible that substantively complex jobs are more typical of the private than of the public sector. To get a fuller picture of what determines work complexity, we conducted a further analysis, looking at the effects of ethnicity, gender, educational attainment, years employed before highest degree, years employed after highest degree, and public-sector employment. The analysis both confirms and clarifies our understanding of the influence of educational attainment on work complexity (table B.5).[6] It indicates that educational attainment is the single most important determinant of work complexity, with holders of advanced, professional, and master's degrees enjoying large increases in complexity. To a lesser extent, bachelor's degree recipients also tend to be highly placed in this dimension of work. Standing well below B.A. recipients are A.A. holders, who, when the additional variables are taken into account, do obtain more-complex work than those whose highest credential is a high school diploma. The increment associated with an A.A., nevertheless, is quite modest.

As we anticipated, employment sector exerts substantial influence on access to challenging work. Workers in the public sector have less-complex work than their otherwise comparable private-sector counterparts. Post-degree work experience has a smaller influence: as it increases, so too does work complexity. Our analysis also reveals that women are as likely as men to obtain complex positions. This finding is consistent with our earlier analyses of occupational status, implying that women are not disadvantaged on these dimensions of occupational stratification. Lastly we see that whites' advantage over blacks and Hispanics is mostly explained by these variables, particularly by differences in educational attainment. But also contributing to blacks' and Hispanics' typically lower job complexity is their disproportionate employment in the public sector, where work tends to be less challenging.

Not only is work in the private sector generally more complex, there is reason to believe that minority workers and women have more difficulty obtaining high-level positions there than in the public sector. As we have seen, evidence indicates that public employers have more actively worked to reduce employment-related discrimination (Farley 1984; Kaufman and Daymont 1981; Kaufman 1986). By extension, the process of attaining complex jobs may be more equitable in the public sector. We examined this issue by carrying out separate analyses for public- and private-sector employees.[7] They

[6]The analysis reported in table B.5 is for the full range of the work complexity variable, not just the top one-third. Two regression models are presented: the first shows the unadjusted differences in work complexity among ethnic groups; the second reports ethnic differences controlling for the effects of the other explanatory variables.

[7]Because of missing data on employment sector, the combined number of cases of these regressions is less than the aggregate regression reported in table B.5. The same is true in the parallel analyses of job authority (tables B.7 and B.8).

show clear contrasts in the process by which individuals gain access to complex work (table B.6). In the public sector, there are no significant ethnic differences when educational attainment is controlled. In the private sector, however, even after educational attainment is controlled ethnicity continues to matter: whites do more-complex work relative to minority workers with comparable education.

That ethnic inequalities persist in the private sector when differences in educational attainment and other characteristics are controlled suggests that this sector is less meritocratic than the public. If so, these inequities may be due in part to discriminatory processes (cf. Kaufman and Daymont 1981; Waldinger 1986–87). Employers may have preferred to hire and/or promote whites into higher-level jobs. As we have done in previous chapters, we looked at our self-report data on perceptions of discrimination in promotions and hirings. Here our main concern was to see whether ethnic perceptions of discrimination vary by sector. In both sectors blacks and Hispanics were more likely than whites to report discrimination, but the disparity was far greater in the private sector. Among respondents in the public sector, for example, blacks were 19 percent more likely than whites to report discrimination in promotions, whereas in the private sector they were 37 percent more likely. The comparable figures for Hispanics were 8 percent versus 19 percent. These results lend support to the idea that access to jobs with challenging work is more equitable in the public than the private sector.

Our analyses of each sector also reveal an interesting gender contrast in work complexity: relative to comparable males, females have more-complex work in the public sector; in the private sector they have less. Following from our discussion in Chapter 3, we believe the source of this difference is to be found in gender differences in college major and subsequent occupations. In part because of sex differences in socialization and experiences in schools (curricular placement and counseling practices that steer females away from math and science courses, for example), females often aspire to and are over-represented in the so-called helping professions—teaching, social work, nursing, and so forth—which are disproportionately located in the public sector. Our data fit this pattern, showing that females most often majored in education or in health and social-service fields (see table 3.6), and that many were employed in related occupations. Indeed, 30 percent of publicly employed women are schoolteachers, whose work is particularly complex in relation to people. Another 13 percent hold other public-sector professional positions (as librarians, social workers, and the like) that typically involve complex work. In this sector, males are found in less-complex semiprofessional and technical occupations (as police officers, correction officers, and firemen, for instance). On the other hand, males were much more likely to major in business and engineering—fields associated with private-sector occupations. Hence they are more strongly represented in positions with complex work in the private sector. Males are more than two and a half times as likely as females, for example, to occupy the most-complex, higher-level managerial positions (21 percent to 8 percent). They also hold an edge in professional employment, while most clerical jobs are held by women.

These findings further our understanding of gender and occupational stratification. Not only do gender-typed college majors contribute to occupational sex segregation, but the way these occupations are distributed over the labor market's public and private sectors also makes a difference. In effect, females obtain challenging work in the public sector because the professional positions traditionally occupied by women are in education and other services provided by the state. Women are not somehow unfairly advantaged in public employment; rather, that is the sector where upper-level positions consistent with their sex-typed occupational preferences are concentrated. Even though they have made gains in occupations traditionally dominated by men (see England and McCreary 1987; Jacobs 1989), the pattern of employment seen in the CUNY data is common. Indeed, national and New York State census data indicate that females are disproportionately employed in public-sector professional occupations, whereas males are overrepresented in managerial employment in the private sector (U.S. Bureau of the Census 1984b, table 279; 1983b, table 220).

In sum, our analyses show that access to complex jobs is strongly influenced by educational attainment, especially a bachelor's or graduate degree. Because blacks and Hispanics lag behind whites in the attainment of these credentials, they are less likely to do challenging work. But lower educational attainment is not the only source of minority group disadvantage. Even when differences in education and other characteristics are taken into account, whites still fare better in the private sector of the economy, where most jobs are found and where work tends to be more complex. Although meritocratic standards appear largely to determine how complex jobs are allocated in the public sector, the advantage accorded whites in private employment seems at least partially to result from discrimination. Although there is no overall gender difference in work complexity, women tend to fare better in the public sector, where they hold a disproportionate share of professional positions;

males are advantaged in the private sector, where they are more likely to be in higher management. This pattern stems, we think, from the relation between gender-linked college majors and employment in sex-typed occupations and from the way these occupations are distributed over the public and private employment sectors.

Job Authority

The uppermost level of work authority is where decisions are made that affect the overall scope and direction of an organization. High-level managers, for instance, make the important decisions concerning firms' investment strategies. In assessing the job authority of former CUNY students who were only in their early to mid-thirties when we administered the follow-up survey, it seems unrealistic to focus on access to the highest reaches of management. On the other hand, some can be expected to have gained access to the ranks of middle management, where responsibilities for the day-to-day functioning of organizations lie, particularly supervising employees. Supervisory authority may entail a range of responsibilities, including organizing and monitoring others' work, conducting job-performance evaluations, making decisions about pay and promotions, and hiring and firing employees.

In order to assess the distribution of authority among the former CUNY students, we had asked respondents whether they supervise the work of others, have authority to hire and fire employees, and work without close supervision.[8] A job authority scale ranging from a low of 0 to a high of 3 was created by adding the number of positive responses to these questions.[9]

In examining the proportion of those with high work authority (as represented by a job authority scale value of 2 or 3), the most visible finding concerns ethnicity; on average whites are more likely to hold jobs high in authority (table 5.2). About half of white men and women occupy such

[8]Supervising others' work and having authority to hire and fire are obvious indicators of job authority; not being closely supervised is more ambiguous. Its importance is suggested by the way work is structured in complex organizations. Spaeth's (1979) research on the dimensions of work in upper-echelon occupations shows an increase in autonomy as one ascends the authority hierarchy. In other words, those with more authority tend not to be closely supervised.

[9]Only respondents who answered all three questions are included in the authority scale. Assessments of the construct validity of the job authority variable suggest that it is a valid indicator of the concept. Those with high authority, for example, tend to have high salaries and hold managerial or administrative job titles.

Table 5.2 High Job Authority, by Educational Attainment, Gender, and Ethnicity

Percentages

Educational Attainment	Males			Females			Total
	White	Black	Hispanic	White	Black	Hispanic	
H.S. diploma[a]	38.9	20.9	24.9	38.7	4.8	38.7	31.7
	(69)	(27)	(15)	(33)	(31)	(16)	(191)
Some college[b]	42.5	25.3	29.8	56.2	37.7	19.4	41.6
	(164)	(49)	(40)	(108)	(46)	(31)	(438)
A.A.	44.8	39.4	26.2	41.9	30.3	24.0	38.8
	(153)	(46)	(25)	(144)	(95)	(55)	(518)
B.A.	50.2	34.1	45.7	50.9	34.6	36.1	48.3
	(545)	(58)	(50)	(398)	(109)	(34)	(1,194)
M.A.	52.3	31.5	33.3	41.0	24.8	22.5	43.6
	(230)	(22)	(13)	(304)	(51)	(27)	(647)
Advanced[c]	64.7	—	—	60.6	—	—	62.6
	(167)			(59)			(245)
Mean	48.9	29.4	33.6	47.8	28.5	28.7	44.3
	(1,328)	(204)	(145)	(1,046)	(340)	(170)	(3,233)

Source: Follow-up survey.

Note: Table counts those with a job-authority score of 2 or 3. Percentages are weighted; frequencies (shown in parentheses) are unweighted.

[a]Respondents dropped out before completing one semester of college (fewer than fifteen credits).
[b]Respondents never earned any college degree but completed one or more semesters.
[c]Because of small Ns, minorities with advanced or professional degrees are not reported.

positions, whereas among minorities the proportion never exceeds one-third. Even when education is controlled, differences in job authority remain. In some cases they are reduced in magnitude, but disparities typically persist.

Other variables are tied to authority in a less consistent way. Although there are no overall gender differences, for example, in some comparisons males have more authority, in others females do. Similarly, there is no linear relation between education and this dimension of work. Credentials appear on balance to improve opportunity for job authority, but in certain instances those with less education are more apt to wield authority than those with higher credentials.

In order to clarify education's role and to gain a better idea of the sources of ethnic disparities, other variables that influence job authority need to be controlled. As discussed earlier, we expect access to such jobs to be affected by work experience before and after degree completion and by employment sector. An additional variable that is particularly relevant to whether or not one has supervisory responsibility in the workplace is labor union membership. As numerous commentators have observed, unions have conceded to management the right to run the enterprise in exchange for higher wages, fringe benefits, and job protections for their members (see Aronowitz 1973; Freeman and Medoff 1984; Jacoby 1985; Piore 1974). And although unions do negotiate work rules to protect workers from abuses, higher-level supervisory functions—hiring and firing, access to confidential information, and the like—remain the prerogative of management and represent the main criterion for excluding an employee from a collective-bargaining unit. Hence it is highly probable that union membership diminishes work authority (empirical support for this is reported in Kluegel 1978).[10]

Our analysis using a larger set of variables gives us a clearer picture of influences on job authority (table B.7). Education emerges as having a consistent effect. An A.A. provides a small edge over a high school diploma and B.A. recipients have a substantially larger edge, equal to the advantage held by M.A. recipients. Holders of advanced or professional degrees obtain positions with the most authority.

Each year of work experience before and after completion of schooling increases job authority, with postdegree experience the more valuable of the two. As expected, employment sector makes an important difference: private-sector employees have more authority than otherwise similar public-sector employees. Similarly, union members are far less apt than nonmembers to exercise supervisory responsibility.

Males have somewhat more authority than comparable females. Because

---

[10]We have not controlled for union membership in our multivariate analyses of work complexity because there is no obvious reason for expecting the heavily white-collar, unionized workers in our sample to hold jobs of lesser complexity than their nonunion counterparts. In fact, virtually the same proportion of unionized (38.6 percent) and nonunion (37.8 percent) employees hold professional, technical, and related jobs, as defined by the Census Bureau's occupational classification system.

men and women hardly differ on the variables for which we have controlled, we suspect that this advantage, like that for complex work, is rooted in gender differences in degree majors and occupational placements—namely, that men more often earn business degrees and gain employment in management, whereas women are overrepresented in education and social-service curricula, which tend to place them in nonsupervisory jobs.

Much inequality in job authority among ethnic groups is explained by this analysis. Inequality is attributable in part to the lower educational achievements of blacks and Hispanics. Also diminishing the work authority of minority members is their greater likelihood of union membership (51 percent of blacks, 40 percent of Hispanics, but only 29 percent of whites are unionized workers).[11] The overrepresentation of minorities in the public sector comprises another key source of ethnic disparity in acquiring authority.

Because blacks and Hispanics have more work experience before and after completion of schooling than whites, these variables partly offset the negative effects of the other factors. Work experience hardly counts as much of an asset, however, for while minority members were in the work force, whites more often remained in school pursuing higher degrees that provided much greater leverage in obtaining high-quality jobs. In effect, having more work experience because one completes fewer years of education is a telling indicator of social disadvantage.

All in all, our analysis adds considerably to the explanation of ethnic differences in job authority. Nevertheless inequities favoring whites persist.

Based on the previous analysis of public- and private-sector differences in the attainment of complex work, the process of acquiring authority may also differ by sector. The evidence that job authority on average is lower in the public sector and that minorities are more likely than whites to work there suggests that the public/private dimension needs further examination. We explore this issue through separate analyses of job authority for public- and private-sector workers (table B.8).

---

[11]Labor union representation is proportionately larger among our respondents than nationally. In 1983, for example, 22 percent of white and 32 percent of black wage and salary workers nationally were represented by unions (percentages are not available for Hispanics; U.S. Bureau of the Census, 1991a, table 697). We believe the higher rates among our respondents are largely due to the high concentration of public-sector workers in urban centers, who in turn are far more apt than other workers to be unionized. National data for 1983 indicate that 46 percent of public wage and salary workers are represented by unions, compared with 19 percent of those in private employment (U.S. Bureau of the Census 1991a, table 697).

In the public sector, initial ethnic differences vanish with controls. What determines whether an employee has authority—regardless of ethnicity, gender, education, and work experience—is union membership, which dramatically limits access to such work. This finding implies that minorities and women are not unfairly excluded from this sector's authority ranks. It is not surprising that unionization diminishes access to positions of authority. What is curious is the absence of an effect for educational attainment, particularly because a college degree is often a prerequisite for administrative employment (see Collins 1979; Useem and Karabel 1986; Zuboff 1988). We think that the reason for this absence is that the educational attainments of managerial or administrative employees are being offset by the similar educational attainments of professional and semiprofessional employees with little or no supervisory responsibility. In other words, the expected effect of education is being masked by the offsetting influence of the large number of highly educated employees who generally do not oversee other workers (social workers, teachers, health care professionals, and so forth).

Unlike in the public sector, ethnic differences favoring whites are evident in the private sector despite the strong role played by educational attainment and the other variables. This disparity suggests that private-sector employers give preference to whites over similarly qualified blacks and Hispanics when staffing administrative or supervisory ranks. This finding is consistent with studies of specific firms that document ethnic inequalities in management (Baron 1984; Kanter 1977; also see Waldinger 1986–87) as well as with other analyses of job authority (Kluegel 1978; Mueller and Parcel 1986).

As we saw for work complexity, men tend to fare better than women in the private sector. Gender differences in authority are not apparent in the public sector, however. So although women generally do more complex work than men in this sector, they do not exercise greater authority. As we have said, this condition likely prevails because many of these women are employed in such professional fields as counseling, nursing, and teaching, where administrative authority is often low (Grimm and Stern 1974; Strober 1984).

In sum, these analyses indicate that college credentials—especially a B.A. or higher degree—enhance opportunity for job authority. Indeed, students who earned only an associate's degree fared poorly in competition for such positions. And although minorities are well ahead of where they otherwise would have been without degrees, ethnic differences in educational attainment are responsible in part for minority workers' obtaining jobs with lower average authority than whites. Also contributing to blacks' and Hispanics' poorer authority chances is their overrepresentation in unionized jobs, their higher rate of public-sector employment, and the more favorable treatment accorded similarly qualified whites in the private sector.

Our investigation of the quality of work experience sharpens the picture that has been emerging in earlier chapters. It is consistent in its findings about the importance of educational attainment, but the analyses add new detail to our understanding of access to desirable jobs. In particular they point to the significance of employment sector. They suggest that the public sector is fairer but has less to offer in terms of job rewards. In the better-rewarded private sector, on the other hand, whites tend to hold higher positions than blacks and Hispanics with comparable education and work experience. Whatever the precise labor-market dynamics may be, this inequity seems to be at least partially due to discrimination. Certainly our data on respondents' perceptions of unfair treatment support this view.

So although educational attainment has helped to reduce ethnic disparities in occupational status, earnings, and obtaining work that involves complex duties and exercise of authority, it is not in itself enough of a force to eliminate such disparities completely. Even though a large number of blacks and Hispanics have capitalized on the opportunity provided by open admissions by earning bachelor's and advanced degrees, often overcoming poor high school academic preparation and impoverished economic circumstances to do so, many have had to face additional obstacles in the private-sector labor market. And though such disparities are not evident in the public sector, private-sector inequalities have a greater impact because most jobs are located there.

Our analyses also help to clarify gender differences in job rewards. They suggest that the persistence of gender-linked occupational preferences results in the disproportionate placement of women in the helping professions, where work is often challenging and associated with high occupational status, but at the same time typically entails little if any administrative power and—because these positions are concentrated in the public sector—relatively modest earnings. Males, by contrast, have greater access to private-sector managerial and professional positions.

CHAPTER SIX

Marriage and the Formation of
a College-Educated Class

Consolidating the Gains of an Open-Admissions Policy

Because open admissions helped to boost educational attainments and subsequently added to occupational standing and earnings, it was an intervention that succeeded, at least partly, in interrupting the inheritance of disadvantage that is endemic in minority communities. But the ramifications of the policy extend beyond the results for its immediate beneficiaries, the students who entered after the program was initiated in 1970.

Indeed, the benefits of open admissions for that generation of students could be thought of as just a starting point. The large majority of the students that the program attracted were the first generation in their families to attend college. By extending a collegiate opportunity to them, the program was designed, at least implicitly, to establish an educational momentum that would carry over to their children. In effect, open admissions was intended to produce gains that would flow across generations, so that a self-sustaining critical mass of college-educated men and women would develop in heretofore educationally disadvantaged communities.

Such a result would be consistent with a quarter-century of studies on status attainment. This research teaches us that although there is considerable social mobility in American society, the intergenerational transmission of status remains substantial (Blau and Duncan 1967; Featherman and Hauser 1979). The inheritance of status occurs mostly through educational attainment: the children of higher-status families typically attain more education than those of lower status. Subsequently, their higher educational credentials translate into greater rewards in the labor market. An intervention such as the open-admissions policy may be seen as an effort to capitalize on social reproduction to increase the likelihood that the newly won advantages of its beneficiaries would translate into a more favorable set of life chances among their children.

In this chapter we consider the contributions that open admissions may have made to the development and growth of a college-educated class of men and women, especially among those of minority origin. In examining this issue, we focus upon our respondents' children, assessing the marital, educational, and economic contexts in which these children were living and the implications of these contexts for their life chances. We begin by looking at ethnic and gender differences in marital status, determining the proportions of respondents who were married, divorced, separated, or never married. Then, for each ethnic and gender group, we consider how children were distributed across these marital contexts: what proportions were living with both parents, with parents whose marriages had terminated, or with a single parent who had never been married? We examine also how parents' marital status and educational attainments are associated with family income. In assessing how children are distributed among various configurations of marriage, parental educational level, and household economic resources, we hope to provide a sketch of the likely consequences for the life chances of the next generation.

In some ways our respondents comprise an appropriate group for the assessments we shall be making. They were mostly in their early thirties when we followed them up, an age by which the propensity to marry is fairly well established, though not completely so.[1] They had largely completed their formal schooling, and quite a bit is known about their employment situations and those of their spouses, if they were married. Moreover, though they had not completed their child-bearing careers, they were far enough into their reproductive years and had in fact produced enough children to provide a sense of the family contexts in which these offspring found themselves.

Nonetheless, it is best to acknowledge at the outset the speculative nature of the analyses that follow. We do not have all of the data needed to explore fully the questions that we have raised. Although we know who was married, who was divorced or separated, and who had never been married, we do not know when either the marriages or the separations occurred. We know the employment status and earnings of our married respondents' spouses, but we don't have information on those spouses' educational attainments, so we are

---

[1]The median age at first marriage in the U.S. in 1984 was just over 25 for men and 23 for women (U.S. Bureau of the Census 1991b). Probably the age of marriage among our respondents is somewhat higher than this because they were above average in educational attainment, and higher levels of attainment appear to be associated with delayed marriage.

unable to characterize family educational contexts as precisely as we would like. Although we know whether our respondents have children and how many they have, we don't know when they were born, or their gender, and we have no data on any aspect of their early educational experiences. Even if we had this schooling information, the children generally were quite young in 1984. Hardly any could have been old enough to allow an assessment of their entry to or accomplishments within higher education.[2] Consequently, we can only speculate about the influence of parental marital status, educational level, and family income on children's success in school. Such speculation is, however, rooted in a considerable research literature: quite a bit is known about the impact of such variables on children's achievement, and so, in our effort to paint a broad picture of the social consequences of the open-admissions policy, it makes sense to consider their likely effects for our respondents' offspring.

A substantial body of research indicates that children from single-parent families, typically female-headed households, are disadvantaged relative to children from two-parent households (Jaynes and Williams 1989, 523–26; McLanahan 1985; McLanahan and Sandefur 1994). Offspring from single-parent families compile lower grades in high school, and they are at greater risk of dropping out; if they do graduate, they are less likely to enroll in college; they are also less likely to graduate from college. A number of factors have been identified that help to explain why children from single-parent families do less well. Three of the most important have to do with the loss of economic, parental, and community resources (for review, see McLanahan and Sandefur 1994).

The absence of a parent, generally the father, typically leads to a substantial decline in economic resources. Indeed, in 1992 about 45 percent of families with children headed by single mothers were below the poverty line; for two-parent families, the figure was about 8 percent (McLanahan and Sandefur 1994, 23). Even children from economically advantaged households experience sharp declines in income with the loss of a parent. There are numerous reasons why the typically superior economic resources of two-parent families might add to children's educational chances and eventual earnings. Parents

---

[2]A few of our respondents probably had children when they were in high school, say in 1966–68. These children would have been close to college age when we surveyed their parents in 1984. For notable work on teenage parents and on the long-term outcomes for their children, see Furstenberg (1976) and Furstenberg et. al. (1987).

with more income may be able to live in neighborhoods with public schools of stronger quality, or they may be able to send children to private schools. They may be better able to afford tutoring if children are having school difficulties or to help prepare them for college admissions tests (coaching for the Scholastic Aptitude Test, for example). As family income increases, so, too, does access to such cultural resources as books, magazines, computers, and interesting vacations or trips. Money can help assure that students are able to remain out of the labor market, thus helping them to complete secondary school and college in a timely fashion. Overall, then, higher family income is associated with higher levels of children's educational attainment and, subsequently, with greater occupational rewards.

More fragile economic resources are not the only reason that single-parent families are disadvantaged. Another is that they have less social capital available for child rearing. For example, the absence of a parent tends to weaken control over children's behavior: the supervisory activities of the single parent may be diluted by such competing responsibilities as full-time employment (Astone and McLanahan 1991). Reduction of time allocated to parental supervision may lead to school difficulties, such as disruptive behavior and suspensions, cutting classes, and the like. Such problem behavior no doubt contributes to lower test scores, lower grades, and increased high school dropout rates among children from one-parent families (see McLanahan 1985; Mulkey et al. 1992). Moreover, in the two-parent family, there is often a process of "peer review" wherein one parent may help to control the parenting behavior of the other, sometimes protecting the child from neglect or even abuse.

Father absence can also affect children by weakening or disrupting their ties to community resources. In part, this disruption may be an effect of reduced income. Lowered income may force the single-parent family to move to a new community, for example, with diminished quality of housing, public safety, and quality of schools. But apart from this income effect, even if families do not move, divorce and separation often disrupt ties to friends and relatives that provide emotional support and access to information about the community. Children may often suffer stress from these changes in social networks.

For such reasons, children in single-parent families are subject to disadvantages. As we said earlier, we do not have data on children's eventual educational and economic outcomes. Nonetheless, our information on marriage, family income, and parental education does allow us to consider some important aspects of the family configurations in which children were living.

The Distribution of Children Across Marital Contexts

Our assessment of socialization contexts begins with an examination of marital status.[3] About half of our male respondents were married (table 6.1). Differences among whites, blacks, and Hispanics were narrow. The marriages of some had ended in divorce or separation. This was most likely to have occurred among Hispanics (17 percent were separated or divorced), and it was least likely among whites (7 percent). Blacks were in the middle. Between 35 and 40 percent of men had never married.

Among women there are very large ethnic variations in marital status. Consistent with what is generally known about differences among women (Farley 1984; Wilson 1987; Schoen and Kluegel 1988; Mare and Winship 1991), whites were by far the most likely to be married. Indeed, the proportion of married whites was almost double that of blacks (60 percent compared with 32 percent) and was substantially greater than that of Hispanics (44 percent). Because a higher percentage of black women had never married and also because their marriages more often ended in divorce or separation (a few were widowed), two-thirds of black women were unmarried, compared with only 40 percent of whites. Fifty-five percent of Hispanic women were unmarried.

These ethnic differences in women's marital status have received much attention from researchers, especially in connection with discussions of falling marriage rates. One reason advanced for the decline of marriage has been the growing economic independence of women, reflecting greater labor-force participation and increases in wages relative to men, particularly for black women (Mare and Winship 1991). As a result, it is argued, women have less economic incentive to marry. A second view focuses upon schooling. Longer periods of school enrollment delay marriage, so the increase in educational attainment could account in part for lower marriage rates. Another interpretation of falling rates, especially for black women, has been provided by Wilson (1987). According to this theory, low marriage rates are due largely to a low ratio of employed black men to black women in the same age group. This ratio, called the "male marriageable pool index," is an indicator of the supply of economically attractive men—men in sufficiently stable economic situations to support or help support a family. In the 25–34 age group in 1980

[3]In subsequent discussion about cross-tabulations, we do not allude to differences unless they are statistically significant, as determined by difference-in-proportions tests for all key comparisons of interest (Blalock 1979).

Table 6.1 Marital Status, by Gender and Ethnicity

Percentages, Except as Noted

Marital Status	Males			Females		
	White	Black	Hispanic	White	Black	Hispanic
Married	56	50	48	60	32	44
Widowed	0	0	0	0	2	1
Divorced	5	6	10	9	12	17
Separated	2	4	7	2	11	4
Never married	38	40	35	29	42	33
% not married	45	50	52	40	67	55
N (unweighted)	1,591	260	181	1,873	477	291

Source: Follow-up survey.

Note: Columns may not total 100 percent due to rounding.

there were 58 eligible black males for every 100 black females; among whites the ratio was 88 to 100 (Wilson 1987, 97, table 8.4). This huge disparity, a consequence of higher rates of joblessness, incarceration, and mortality among black males, is undoubtedly responsible in part for the diminished marriage possibilities of black women relative to white women. (Undoubtedly it also helps to explain the lower marriage rates of Hispanic women.)[4]

Because of falling marriage rates, the historical increase in divorce rates, and growth in the number of never-married individuals who become parents, the proportion of single-parent families, especially those headed by women, has been rising. The trend is apparent among both whites and minorities, but it has been especially pronounced among the latter, particularly for blacks (Jaynes and Williams 1989).

Ethnic differences consistent with this trend are apparent among our respondents (table 6.2). Although married persons were generally the most

[4]Although other influences on low marriage rates, such as women's increasing economic independence, cannot be discounted, Lichter et. al. (1991) state that their results clearly reinforce the view that the supply of economically attractive men plays a large role in defining young women's marriage prospects.

Table 6.2 Parenthood, by Marital Status, Gender, and Ethnicity

Percent Having One or More Children

Marital Status	Males			Females			Total		
	W	B	H	W	B	H	W	B	H
Married	58	83	78	65	76	77	62	80	77
Separate[a]	12	43	21	26	80	74	20	72	56
Never married	1	9	7	2	41	23	1	30	16

Source: Follow-up survey.

Note: W = white, B = black, H = Hispanic.

[a]Includes those who were separated, divorced, or widowed.

likely to be parents, substantial percentages of those who were divorced or separated also had children. Minority individuals whose marriages had terminated were much more likely than whites to have children; minority women were especially likely: three-quarters or more were mothers, compared with a quarter of white women. Among those who had never married, minority men and women were more likely than whites to be parents. The proportion of never-married black women with children was strikingly high: 41 percent were mothers; more than a fifth of Hispanic women were, compared with only a tiny fraction of never-married white women. Overall, among those who were single—that is, who had never married or whose marriages had terminated—minorities, particularly women, were especially likely to be parents.

The extent to which children were living in single-parent families can be more precisely gauged if we shift our emphasis from the marital status of parents to how their children were distributed among marital categories (table 6.3). Few of the children born to whites (5 percent) were living with only one parent. On the other hand, 40 percent of black children were doing so, as were more than a quarter of Hispanic children. The major part of this ethnic disparity is accounted for by single minority women, since they were much more often parents than were single minority men. Of all the black children in single-parent households, 90 percent were living with their mothers; among Hispanic children, the figure was 85 percent.

Table 6.3 How Children Are Distributed According to Marital Status, by Gender, and Ethnicity

Percentages, Except as Noted

Marital Status	Males			Females			Total		
	W	B	H	W	B	H	W	B	H
Married	97	90	90	93	43	63	95	60	73
Separate[a]	2	6	6	6	37	27	4	25	19
Never married	1	4	4	1	21	10	1	15	8
N of children	812	241	146	1,282	452	248	2,094	693	394

Source: Follow-up survey.
Note: W = white, B = black, H = Hispanic. Columns may not total 100 percent due to rounding.
[a]Includes those who were separated, divorced, or widowed.

The Economic Consequences of Marital Contexts

As we said earlier, the literature suggests that economic deprivation associated with single-parent status, particularly among single mothers, is an important factor in the intergenerational transmission of disadvantage. Whether as a consequence of out-of-wedlock births or marital dissolution, single-parent families are likely to be far worse off in terms of economic well-being (Farley 1984; Jaynes and Williams 1989; Mare and Winship 1991; Weiss 1984; Wilson 1987). Indeed, increases over the past 30 years in female-headed families appear to be a major reason for the rise in the proportion of children living in poverty (Wilson 1987).

Two-parent families typically have higher income largely because of the potential of married couples to have two wage earners. Part of this edge is due also to the fact that husbands typically earn more than their wives. Nationally, for more than half of the children living with two parents, both were employed (U.S. Bureau of the Census 1991b). Our data are consistent with that finding (table 6.4). In 70 percent of black couples with children and half of Hispanic ones, both parents were working; in a large proportion of these families, both spouses held full-time jobs. Even among white couples, least likely to be dual wage earners, both spouses were working in 40 percent of the families.

Table 6.4 Two-Spouse Employment, by Gender and Ethnicity

Percent of Couples
in Which Both Spouses Are Employed

	Males			Females			Total		
	W	B	H	W	B	H	W	B	H
Employed	35	70	37	44	72	59	40	71	50
Employed full-time	17	56	28	20	57	43	18	56	36
N (unweighted)	484	104	68	710	111	102	1,194	206	170

Source: Follow-up survey.

Differences in parents' marital status are associated with large disparities in household income. Nationally, the mean income in 1984 for two-parent families was about $30,000, but for single mothers it was about $9,900. For the few single fathers it was about $20,000 (U.S. Bureau of the Census 1985).[5] This pattern is visible for white, black, and Hispanic groups. Our data are broadly consistent with the national picture, as can be seen in table 6.5, which compares the family income of parents who are married with those who are single.[6] In all cases, but especially among women, there is a stunning advan-

[5]These disparities are not due entirely to the influence of marital status. Differences in educational attainment between married and single parents could also have an influence, but it is unlikely that all or even most of the gap could be explained by factors other than the number of wage earners.

[6]Incomes of our respondents are higher than the national means largely because of their above-average educational levels and the higher wage rates in metropolitan areas. In both the national data that we have cited and our own records, family income includes earnings of husband and/or wife, but not of other adults living in the household who might be contributing income. Moreover, family income does not include such other sources as public assistance or child support payments from ex-spouses. Although these omissions lead to some understatement of income, it seems unlikely that they affect our conclusions about economic differences between single- and two-parent families. Bianchi (1981), for example, included all sources of household income (both earned and from other sources) and found income ratios of married couples to single heads of household that were similar to the ones we have reported. Single mothers have been increasingly likely to provide for their children without the aid of additional household adult wage earners. In 1960, for example, almost 40 percent of black female householders with children had earnings

tage to those who are married. Among black female-headed families, for example, average income was only a little more than $18,000, whereas for families of black women who were married it was almost $43,000.[7] Looked at in a slightly different way, the family income of black and also Hispanic single mothers was only 43 percent that of married couples. Families of white single mothers were even worse off relative to those of married couples, earning only 37 percent as much. Because of men's higher earnings, inequalities separating married and single men were less but still substantial: family incomes of white single fathers were only 56 percent of family incomes of married ones; the ratios for blacks and for Hispanics were 58 and 46 percent, respectively.

The income differences that we have been reviewing could be exaggerated if fewer people share income in single-parent families. The absence of a spouse, for example, while reducing resources also reduces the demand on resources that are available, and single-parent families also tend to have fewer children. We took account of differences in family size by using a measure of per-capita income. Even after this adjustment, however, single-parent households were still worse off. Among black and Hispanic women, for example, there was a difference of nearly $4,000 in per-capita income separating families of married couples from female-headed households. Among white women the disparity in per-capita income was more than $6,700.

Another aspect of the earnings of married couples sheds further light on the question of economic well-being in families. Research and theory in the sociology of the family teach us that a principle of homogamy is an important basis of mate selection. According to this principle, people are more likely to marry others who are similar to them in such characteristics as ethnicity, social-class background, religion, and educational attainment. Much evidence points to educational homogamy as a primary factor in mate selection and suggests that its role has been increasing (Kalmijn 1991; Mare 1991). There may be a number of reasons why people who marry tend to be similar in their educational attainments. In part, highly credentialed individuals may be at-

---

from others in the household. By 1976 this proportion had fallen to just under 20 percent (Bianchi 1981, 64–65). According to Ruggles (1994), the percentage of extended households among blacks declined steeply after 1960. The decline was especially steep for black single mothers, 21.5 percent of whom lived in extended households in 1980. According to Hofferth (1984), black female-headed families are less likely to receive money from extended kin networks than are white female-headed families.

[7]We have chosen to report mean rather than median income to maintain consistency with earlier presentations. Calculation of the mean and the median produces very similar results.

Table 6.5 Family Income for Respondents with Children, by Marital Status, Gender, and Ethnicity

Marital Status	Males			Females			Total		
	W	B	H	W	B	H	W	B	H
Married	$47,918	$43,218	$40,769	$49,256	$42,799	$39,236	$48,576	$42,904	$39,813
	(351)	(78)	(36)	(520)	(85)	(70)	(871)	(163)	(106)
Not married[a]	26,809	25,183	18,826	18,093	18,353	16,725	20,570	19,307	16,877
	(15)	(19)	(7)	(46)	(136)	(45)	(61)	(155)	(52)
Income ratio not married/married	.56	.58	.46	.37	.43	.43	.42	.45	.43
Per capita income									
Married	14,758	12,237	11,845	14,626	12,161	11,926	14,678	12,149	11,898
Not married[a]	11,604	10,719	7,186	7,869	8,247	8,195	8,595	8,550	8,043

Source: Follow-up survey.

Note: W = white, B = black, H = Hispanic. Ns (in parentheses) are not weighted.

[a]Includes those who were separated, divorced, widowed, or never married.

tracted by each other's labor-market prospects. But educational level may also signify the acquisition of tastes, styles, ways of thinking, and values. Similarities in such cultural capital are likely to provide fertile soil for the growth of intimacy (DiMaggio and Mohr 1985).[8] Because educational homogamy is an important basis of mate selection, an additional economic influence of open admissions may have occurred among those who married: educational attainment is associated with earnings, so if respondents' marriage partners had educational attainments similar to their own, then the higher the level of one's credentials, the greater will be the earnings of one's spouse if he or she is employed. In effect, then, a higher educational level "buys" a higher-income spouse.

Although we have no data on the educational attainments of respondents' spouses, we used information on their earnings to examine the hypothesis that their educational attainment would be associated with their spouses' salaries. We focused the analysis on two–wage earner couples in which both were employed full-time. In general, we found that the higher a person's educational attainment, the higher was the salary of his or her spouse. Among Hispanics, for example, women without college degrees had spouses who earned an average salary of about $21,750. The figure rose to more than $25,000 among husbands of women who had completed an A.A., and for women who earned a B.A. degree or higher, spouses' average earnings were nearly $29,000. Black women who did not earn a college degree had husbands who earned an average of about $21,650, compared with more than $25,300 earned by husbands of those who completed a B.A. or more. This relationship appeared also among men, but probably because earnings increments for educational attainment are more modest for women, increases in men's educational attainments were not associated with increases as large in their wives' earnings as for women's attainments and their husbands' earnings.[9]

These results suggest that open admissions helped to produce an unanticipated benefit among two–wage earner couples: those who used the opportunity that the policy provided to increase their level of educational achievement also found more economically valuable mates, further augmenting family

---

[8]A good introduction to the concept of cultural capital may be seen in an article by David Swartz (in Dougherty and Hammack 1990, 70–80).

[9]Among black male respondents we found no association between their educational attainments and the earnings of their wives.

income. For married parents who were working full-time, family income among white respondents without a college degree was about $47,000, compared with $51,000 for A.A. holders and $56,500 for those with a B.A. or higher. Among Hispanic respondents the family income for those without a degree was about $42,000, for A.A. recipients almost $45,000, and for those with the B.A. or better nearly $47,000. These economic benefits to parents obviously provided additional resources for their children.

Of course, we have no concrete information about the effects of economic differences between single- and two-parent families on actual living standards—on the amount of space in peoples' apartments or houses, for example, or on the kinds of neighborhoods in which they could afford to live. We were able to make a further assessment, however, albeit a somewhat indirect one. For persons with children, we examined the association between marital status and satisfaction with facets of respondents' lives that seemed dependent to an important extent on economic resources. We asked, for example, how satisfied people were with their income, their home or apartment, the neighborhood in which they lived, and the schools in their community. Among men and women of every ethnic group, single parents were more likely to be dissatisfied with each of these than were married couples.[10]

In summary, the economic well-being of families was strongly associated with marital status and with ethnicity. Children in single-parent families were considerably worse off than those living with both parents. Because minority parents were far more likely than whites to be single, either because their marriages had ended or because they had never married, the economic burdens of the single-parent household fell most heavily on minority children. In addition, other costs that have been identified in the research literature as consequences of father absence and the stress of marital disruption also would have affected them disproportionately. As a result of educational homogamy in mate selection, moreover, greater educational achievement added leverage to the earning power of two-parent families. Because some minority respondents were boosted by open admissions, they probably had higher-earning spouses than they otherwise would have, and their children undoubtedly

[10]For example, 45 percent of single mothers were dissatisfied with their income, compared with 25 percent among married mothers. Analogous figures for fathers were 28 percent and 18 percent. Twenty-six percent of single mothers were not satisfied with the neighborhood in which they lived, compared with only 8 percent of married mothers. For fathers the percentages were 34 and 11.

reaped the economic benefits. But because the educational attainments of whites typically were greater and because minority individuals generally earned less than whites even when they held comparable educational credentials, white children were more advantaged by homogamy.

Education and Cultural Resources

Whether children live with both mother and father or with a single parent is not the only aspect of the domestic context that may affect their life chances. The educational attainments of their parents, by influencing family cultural resources, including expectations for educational attainment, can also make a difference (see Pascarella and Terenzini 1991, 545–47). College-educated parents can provide resources that contribute to school success. They are more likely to read to their children, who probably benefit when they begin reading in school (Hill and Stafford 1980). Typically, more-educated parents are better able to help with school assignments. They may instill better work habits, a characteristic of students that teachers reward with higher grades (Farkas et al. 1990). Partly because of their higher educational status, college-educated parents are likely to feel more comfortable with teachers than are those with less education, and as a result they interact with them more frequently and effectively on behalf of their children (Lareau 1989). Linguistic styles in families with more-educated parents may be more compatible with the structure of discourse most rewarded within schools, thus resulting in better academic evaluations (for a review of home-school language issues see Mehan 1992). In general, college-educated parents are likely to possess more information and cultural knowledge that will allow children to feel comfortable with the curricular demands of school and in interaction with teachers. In effect, their offspring are better able to exchange cultural capital for good grades (Bourdieu 1973; DiMaggio 1982).

Children of more-educated parents also develop a clearer picture of the structure and demands of higher education. Not only can their parents share their knowledge about the process of college attendance, but the children themselves are more likely to know people who have been to college and to have access to college counselors and other educators who can help them translate aspirations into appropriate activities, showing them, for example, how to choose colleges and how to apply (see Swidler 1986, on the notion of "cultural tool kits"). Undoubtedly, they more often come to see expectations for higher education as a "natural" part of the life course.

Still, it is not entirely clear just what levels of parental attainment are likeliest to affect children's college-going. At least it is arguable that the most strategic distinction is between parents who have and have not had college experience—that any taste of college, even a brief sojourn at a four-year institution or even a two-year school, without the completion of any degree— is the critical event that makes the college entry of one's children likely. Because all of our respondents had at least a brush with higher education, wide differences in matriculation among offspring might not be expected.

But more important than mere college entry is how far children will go in higher education. It is now widely understood, both from our analyses and from those of others, that level of entry—to a four-year college or to a two-year school—influences ultimate educational attainment, job status, and earnings (Brint and Karabel 1989; Dougherty 1987, 1994; Monk-Turner 1990; Pincus 1980, 1986). And college quality—from highly selective, prestigious institutions to more accessible ones of lesser status—may make a difference for careers (Karabel and McClelland 1987; Karen 1991; Useem and Karabel 1986). We think that having a parent or parents whose educational attainment is at the B.A. level or higher provides a critical threshold for family cultural resources. The liberal arts curricula of B.A. programs generally provide their graduates with more cultural capital than is provided by community college vocational programs or the truncated liberal arts curricula in these institutions. Consequently, children of parents holding at least a B.A. may have an edge in their primary and secondary schooling. This, in turn, adds to their chances of starting in a four-year school, perhaps even in a more selective one, increasing the likelihood of substantial achievement in higher education.[11]

To gain a sense of the family educational contexts in which children found themselves, we have examined how they were distributed according to their parents' attainments (table 6.6). To begin with, there are sharp disparities

[11]Our earlier analyses of educational attainment and occupational status show that the B.A. degree typically provides a more substantial boost to occupational status relative to what the A.A. degree adds over the high school diploma. That is, occupations typical of B.A. holders are more clearly demarcated from those held by A.A. recipients than are the latter from the jobs of those with only high school diplomas. Moreover, friendship circles may tend to be bounded in the sense that people draw their friends from a pool of those with comparable educational attainments and occupational levels (for a discussion of structural influences on friendship see Wright and Cho 1992). Among those in the occupational categories associated with B.A. or higher credentials, high educational expectations are more likely to be normative—not only held within the family but also reinforced through friends and neighborhoods.

Table 6.6 Distribution of Children, by Parent's Educational Attainment, Gender, and Ethnicity

Percentages

Educational Attainment	Males			Females			Total		
	W	B	H	W	B	H	W	B	H
H.S. diploma	15	21	29	11	24	18	13	23	23
Some college	19	26	24	22	24	20	20	24	23
A.A. degree	15	23	16	15	26	35	15	24	27
B.A. or higher	51	31	31	52	26	27	51	28	28

Source: Follow-up survey.
Note: W = white, B = black, H = Hispanic. Columns may not total 100 percent due to rounding.

separating white from minority children. Most striking overall is that half of white children but less than 30 percent of minority offspring had parents with B.A. degrees or higher. If a white child had a parent with a college degree it was far more likely to be a B.A. or advanced degree than an A.A. The credentialed parent of a minority child, on the other hand, was about as likely to have an A.A. as a B.A. At the other end, only a third of white children but nearly half of minority ones had parents who never received any college degree. These results are not unexpected, because they reflect in large part the greater educational attainment of whites that we reviewed in Chapter 2. But because individuals at the lower end of the educational scale (without a degree or with an A.A.) had more children on average than those at the upper end (B.A. or higher), ethnic inequalities in our respondents' educational attainments are accentuated in the distribution of their children across educational contexts. Of course, these are not final results: part of the reason for the smaller average number of offspring among those with higher credentials is that they were in school longer, and extended study likely delayed childbearing. Subsequently, the respondents who went further in education may have narrowed the fertility gap.[12]

[12]Whites with a high school diploma had an average of 0.83 children, those with an A.A. an average of 0.78, and those with a B.A. or higher an average of 0.55. Analogous figures for blacks are 1.13, 1.08, and 0.86. For Hispanics they are 1.00, 1.05, and 0.78.

Notwithstanding the ethnic inequalities in the likelihood of a child's having college-educated parents, there is little doubt that open admissions made an important difference for our minority respondents' offspring. Because the policy tripled the number of B.A.'s that blacks earned and doubled those awarded to Hispanics (see table 2.14), their children experienced a more favorable set of family educational environments overall than they otherwise would have.

The potential influence of family educational environments cannot be fully appreciated in isolation from the marital contexts that we discussed earlier. How marriage and parental educational attainments might jointly affect children's life chances can be considered by examining where children are located among different marital and educational configurations. This distribution may be seen in table 6.7, which distinguishes three levels of parental educational attainment: no college degree, A.A. degree, and B.A. or higher. It also distinguishes two categories of marital status, married and single (in which the never married are combined with those who are separated, divorced, or widowed). Our earlier discussion implies that the optimal context for children's life chances is the one in which the parents live together and each holds at least a B.A. degree.[13] White and minority children have vastly different probabilities of being in this context. Half of white children were found there, whereas, partly as a consequence of minority parents' lesser educational attainments and partly because they were more likely than whites to be single parents, only about a fifth of minority children were living in this situation.

If a two-parent family with educational attainment at the B.A. level or higher is the configuration with the most promising potential for children's life chances, then the household of the single parent without any college credential is the least favorable one.[14] Children in such households would

[13]Although we have no information on the educational attainments of our respondents' spouses, the principle of educational homogamy in mate selection and our previous analysis of spouse earnings in relation to respondents' educational attainment lead us to think that there is, in general, similarity in the credentials held by spouses. To simplify the discussion, we constructed table 6.7 as if both spouses had the same level of educational attainment.

[14]Although the B.A.-level married couple is a configuration that seems to have clearly different implications for children's outcomes than the single parent with no college credential, not all configurations are so easily contrasted. For example, if we compare the children of married couples having no degree with the offspring of single parents who have a B.A. or higher, the implications are not easily apparent. The relative weight of parent absence versus parents' educational attainment in influencing such outcomes as school grades, test scores, school dropout, college entry, ultimate educational attainment, and earnings is not well understood.

Table 6.7 Distribution of Children, by Parent's Marital Status, Educational Attainment, Gender, and Ethnicity

| | Percentage of Children in Each Context | | | | | | | | |
| | Males | | | Females | | | Total | | |
Marital Status	W	B	H	W	B	H	W	B	H
Married									
No degree	33	45	48	29	17	24	31	27	33
A.A.	15	20	12	13	12	23	14	14	20
B.A. or more	49	24	29	51	14	16	50	18	21
Not married									
No degree	1	4	6	4	33	14	3	21	11
A.A.	0	2	3	2	12	12	1	9	8
B.A. or more	2	5	2	1	13	11	1	10	7
N of children	812	241	146	1,282	452	248	2,094	693	394

Source: Follow-up survey.

Note: W = white, B = black, H = Hispanic. Columns may not total 100 percent due to rounding.

seem triply disadvantaged: their well-being is diminished by the meager cultural resources that are a likely consequence of their parent's truncated exposure to college and by lower family income, which results not only from single-parent status but also from the absence of college credentials. Only a very small fraction of white children (3 percent) were living in this context. A more substantial proportion of black children—21 percent—were found there, as well as more than 10 percent of Hispanic ones. Among black female parents, this configuration was the modal one, containing a third of their children. Overall, more than half of all black children in single-parent families were living with a parent who had not received any college degree. The comparable figure for Hispanic offspring was about 40 percent. Indeed, the children of single mothers suffer an additional disadvantage imposed by the lower earnings of women relative to men. And the economic well-being of the children belonging to single black or Hispanic mothers is even further diminished by the dollar penalty that is associated with minority status.

In this analysis of family and educational contexts in which the offspring of former CUNY students found themselves, the picture is incomplete. Marriage still lay ahead for some never-married individuals, the marriages of others were undoubtedly headed for dissolution, some divorced or separated persons would remarry or reconcile with a former spouse, and the members of the respondent cohort had not yet passed through their child-bearing years. As a consequence of these conditions, some children who had been living in single-parent households would find themselves in reconstituted families, and others who were living in two-parent households would end up in ones headed by single parents. But even though the processes of marital formation and dissolution, as well as child bearing, were still occurring, inferences about the influence of family contexts on children may reasonably be made.

This examination of marital and child-bearing patterns adds depth to our understanding of the social consequences of the open-admissions policy. In Chapter 2 we saw that the educational opportunity created by the program translated into greater educational attainment, adding substantially to the proportions of minority students who received collegiate and postgraduate degrees. And as we saw in Chapter 3, these educational credentials increased earning power. As a result, many of our respondents' children had access to cultural and economic resources that otherwise would not have been available to them. In effect then, they faced a better future because of the advantages that open admissions made possible for their parents.

The benefits of open admissions were significantly influenced by the ways in which educational attainment was configured with marital contexts. Among those with the more valuable credentials (B.A.'s or more), marriage can intensify cultural and economic effects. That is, the cultural capital that individuals acquired as a part of the college experience is probably a more influential resource for children when it is shared by couples with similar educational backgrounds. And the combined economic benefits of their parents' greater educational attainments will likely add further to children's well-being, increasing their educational attainments and eventual labor-market success. Single parents—even those with the more valuable educational credentials—probably will not have been able to do as much for their children. Being single will likely diminish the influence of parental educational attainment on children's school success, and the economic penalty typical of the one-parent family is not offset by the additional earning power conferred by their credentials. This disadvantage holds true especially among minority single mothers, who care for the great majority of all single-parent children.

Thus, our examination of marriage, educational attainment, and parenthood suggests another way in which the benefits of social policies are often constrained by a larger context of disadvantage. On the one hand, educational opportunity led to greater educational attainment, which in turn added to the prospects of many children. But at the same time, even among parents with the most valuable educational credentials, minorities, particularly women, were disadvantaged by a marriage market and other factors that increased their chances of being single parents, probably diminishing the benefits of their attainments for their offspring. In short, the lower probabilities of marriage and the greater chances of marital dissolution among minorities no doubt reduced the number of minority children living in college-educated two-parent families. But it is unlikely that these patterns of family formation and marital stability will have neutralized the intergenerational effect of open admissions. Although the policy did not make as deep a dent as it might have, it still added to the number of college-educated minority men and women who married and had children. Further study is needed to assess this contribution, but it probably augmented the life chances of the respondents' offspring. To the extent that it did, it helped to consolidate educational and economic gains across generations.

CHAPTER SEVEN

Nonmaterial Outcomes of Higher Education

Attitudes, Values, and Life Satisfaction

Our heavy emphasis to this point on educational and socioeconomic outcomes of open admissions is partly an expression of City University's historic identity as a pathway out of poverty for the sons and daughters of lower-class, working-class, and immigrant families. It reflects as well the political context from which the policy arose: it was intended as a reaffirmation of CUNY's traditional role during a period when higher education was growing in importance in a changing labor market. It is consistent also with the perceptions of the students themselves about what they wanted from college: vocational aims—the ability to get a better job—were most often cited by entering freshmen as very important reasons for going to college.

This emphasis on the connection between education and work should not blind us to the nonmaterial benefits that college may provide for students. For decades many educators have expressed concern about overemphasis on the vocational functions of college and the devaluation of liberal education. They have asserted that a narrow focus on the acquisition of marketable skills and credentials undermines a broader perspective that credits higher education with providing fertile soil for intellectual and psychosocial growth and development. In this view colleges are—or should be—intellectually empowering: they should nurture the ability to think critically, help to broaden cultural interests, tastes, and perspectives, and stimulate greater concern with civic issues and participation in the political process. Higher education also has been seen as an important catalyst in personal development, which aids in the transition from adolescence to adulthood. Although there is disagreement about how this transition should be characterized, it is generally thought to involve the acquisition of moral sensibility and the development of personal identity, self-esteem, a sense of control over one's life, and feelings of personal well-being.

Whether college produces such benefits for students and, if so, what elements of the experience might have that effect are questions that have stimulated a huge volume of research over the past four or five decades.[1] This body of work has been reviewed, critiqued, and synthesized in three encyclopedic works—by Feldman and Newcomb in 1969, by Bowen in 1977, by Pascarella and Terenzini in 1991—so we can describe with reasonable clarity some of the outcomes of the college experience.

Before we present our own analyses, some comments are in order about the contributions and limitations of this body of work. First, it has far more to say about white middle-class or upper-middle-class students who entered college at the age of seventeen or eighteen, lived on campus, and graduated four or five years after entry than it does about students—especially minority ones—from economically impoverished backgrounds who enter commuter colleges as adults, many of whom have children, hold full-time jobs, and need more than six years—sometimes more than nine—to graduate.

Another issue that must be addressed is that the literature is very uneven in the amount of attention it devotes to the different tiers of higher education. Research is focused overwhelmingly on what happens in four-year schools that give the B.A. degree. With the notable exceptions of the analyses that we alluded to in previous chapters that compare the effects of four-year and two-year colleges on educational attainments and on socioeconomic outcomes, the literature has almost nothing to say about other ways in which these two kinds of institutions influence their students—for example, in cognitive skills, political attitudes, and psychosocial development. The same shortcoming exists in research on postgraduate institutions. Although studies have assessed the influence of undergraduate colleges on students' entry to postgraduate study, relatively little attention has been given to the subsequent effects of graduate school on individual development.[2] One focus of this chapter will be to compare outcomes among respondents with different levels of attainment in higher education.

The research literature on undergraduates is often hindered by the way that studies are designed. Frequently, college effects on students are inferred

[1]Among the best-known and most influential studies has been the pioneering work of Theodore M. Newcomb and his associates on Bennington College students. They have studied the development of political attitudes over the college career (Newcomb 1943) and subsequently assessed the durability of college effects on attitudes—twenty-five years after graduation (Newcomb et al. 1967) and fifty years after (Alwin et al. 1992).

[2]There have been a number of landmark studies of graduate and professional schooling. For examples, see Becker et al. (1961), Mechanic (1962), Merton et al. (1957), Sibley (1963).

from comparisons of seniors with freshmen. Such cross-sectional studies risk possible confounding factors. Between the freshman and senior years, for example, many students may drop out. If seniors appear much different from freshmen on some characteristic, say political liberalism, it is hard to know whether this represents genuine change over the college career or a winnowing process wherein conservative students were more likely to drop out. Another problem, even with longitudinal studies, which follow the same students over time, is that change may not always be a result of the college experience. Rather, it could be a result of such broader societal influences as war or the economic cycle, or it might be due to human maturation, or simply to growing older. Although control groups of non–college attenders may help to clarify interpretation, they are infrequently used.

Another important issue in assessing college effects concerns their durability. How enduring are changes that may be apparent among college seniors? Is change fragile, visible when students are connected to the immediate collegiate environment, but vanishing as college recedes into the past? Or does it last over the long term—perhaps over a lifetime, as is suggested by a famous case study of political attitudes among Bennington College graduates who were followed for fifty years after they started college in 1935 (Newcomb 1943; Newcomb et al. 1967; Alwin et al. 1992). Analysis of the long-term impact of college is complex because many of its influences may be indirect. Such psychological factors as self-esteem or a sense of personal well-being, for example, may be strongly influenced by one's job situation, marriage, family life, and health, some of which have been affected, at least in part, by educational attainment. This issue is clearly pertinent to our work, because the outcomes that we shall address in this chapter were measured more than a decade after our respondents had started college.

Notwithstanding its limitations, research identifies a number of broad areas in which colleges seem to have at least a modest influence on students. In the realm of cognitive development, evidence suggests that college enhances one's intellectual repertoire (for reviews see Bowen 1977, chapter 3; Pascarella and Terenzini 1991, chapter 4). Not only is there growth in knowledge related to content in the academic major, there is also a broadening of general knowledge about music and the arts, government, science, and the like. The college experience also augments verbal, quantitative, and communication skills. Moreover, it appears to help students develop critical-thinking capacities, including the intellectual flexibility that enables them to assess different sides of complex issues, the ability to question assumptions in arguments, and skill in using reasoning and evidence to analyze problems that may not have verifiably correct answers (Pascarella and Terenzini 1991). Such intellectual qualities presumably enhance the ability of individuals to do complex work and to adapt to changing demands in the workplace and elsewhere. There is reason to think that such cognitive benefits of college endure over the long term (Hyman et al. 1975).

The evidence suggests also that college has a broad liberalizing effect on political, social, and other attitudes and values. Not only do students display growth in aesthetic interests and activities—reading novels, poetry, and plays, visiting museums, and the like—but they also come to be more accepting of individual diversity and able to think in nonstereotypic ways about others who are culturally and ethnically different from them. They develop greater interest and participation in civic and political activities and exhibit increased commitment to the protection of civil rights and liberties (Bowen 1977; Feldman and Newcomb 1969; Pascarella and Terenzini 1991). They tend as well to move from traditional conceptions of gender roles to more egalitarian views about women's roles and opportunities. Some of these findings, however, have been contested. Dougherty and Hammack (1990, 456), for example, point out that some studies (Jackman and Muha 1984, for example) have found very little association between education and prejudice toward race, sex, and social-class groups. They note, moreover, that rather than becoming more tolerant, more-educated people simply may have acquired greater subtlety in the way they express prejudices.

College appears also to influence important aspects of personality development. According to Pascarella and Terenzini (1991), during their college years students tend to attain greater self-understanding, develop a more positive sense of self-esteem, and gain in their sense of control over events in their lives. It appears that these changes are maintained over the long term, but it is not so clear how much of this persistence of attitudes is a continuing influence of the college years and how much may be a result of postcollege experiences having to do with occupational status, income, family life, and the like.

A good deal of research has focused on the association between educational attainment and the quality of life after college (Pascarella and Terenzini 1991, chapter 12). A number of indicators of quality of life have been looked at, including physical health and subjective well-being, happiness, or satisfaction with life. With regard to health, the general conclusion of studies is that a college education is positively linked with subsequent health status and that this association holds even when income, age, and prior health are controlled.

A possible explanation is that because the college educated are better informed about proper health practices—diet and smoking, for example—and about health care services (Hyman et al. 1975), their actual quality of health is superior. With regard to subjective well-being, one might expect that college graduates would report being more satisfied with their lives than those who did not attend college. The literature is not clear about this connection, however. According to Pascarella and Terenzini, evidence suggests only a small positive association between educational attainment and life satisfaction. Moreover, when factors such as income, job status, and marital status are controlled, college graduates seem little different in life satisfaction from those with no credentials beyond high school.

Traditionally, the kinds of outcomes that we have been describing have been viewed as beneficial for students and as socially desirable. Increasing cultural diversity in academe, however, forces a rethinking of this conclusion, at least in some respects. It is by no means clear, for example, that interest and participation in "high culture"—literature, classical music, and fine art—of the Western tradition is an indisputable good, standing alone above other cultural heritages. Although there had been a long-standing consensus that the Western heritage should form the basis of curricula in the humanities, competing claims represented by multiculturalism and critical work in social science have shaken this consensus. Such sociologists as Bourdieu (1977, 1984) have demonstrated the social class–linked nature of cultural knowledge. It could thus be argued that high culture is not intrinsically superior, but, rather, is perceived in this way because it forms part of the status culture of elite groups in society. One of the major functions of the university is to define what constitutes legitimate knowledge. A decisive indicator of legitimacy is inclusion in the college curriculum, and elite culture traditionally has formed its bedrock. Increasingly, however, the content of this curriculum is being contested. Largely because of the growing social diversity of college campuses and because of the increasing power of women, strong arguments have been made for a multicultural perspective—that the literature, art, and music of different groups should be defined as legitimate and thus represented in collegiate curricula. Of course, at the same time others defend the dominance of the Western "canon."[3] Perhaps this national debate between multiculturalists and traditionalists is too recent to have insinuated itself into research on college

[3]Examples of the traditionalist perspective may be seen in Bloom (1987) and Hirsch (1987). For a critique see Aronowitz and Giroux (1988).

effects. Nonetheless, it clearly throws into question any simple assumptions about the desirability of higher education's functions of cultural socialization.

Keeping in mind this caveat, many of the outcomes that we have noted still seem desirable. If they are, then attaining them constitutes an equity issue in much the same sense that job status and income are. If college graduates are in better health, are more likely to have a positive sense of self-esteem, and feel more satisfied with their lives, for example, then ethnic disparities in educational achievement may be associated with group inequalities on these indicators of well-being.

In effect, here is the point of this chapter: we want to explore whether the open-admissions policy influenced access to certain attitudes and orientations, to a positive sense of self, and to feelings of satisfaction with life. We shall consider whether educational attainment is associated with the kinds of nonacademic outcomes that we have described in the previous pages. Among our respondents, what is the level of interest in civic issues and political affairs, of cultural involvement, of affinity for intellectual activity? What is their quality of health, and how do they feel about themselves? How satisfied are they with various facets of their lives? Are variations in these characteristics associated with educational attainment? Are there ethnic disparities, and if so, what explains them?

In addressing these questions, we shall compare individuals who never completed any college degree with those who went on to reach various levels in higher education (A.A., B.A., graduate degrees). Although comparisons across the degree spectrum are not typically made in the research literature, there is some reason to expect differences among educational attainment categories, especially between A.A. and B.A. recipients (we are less sure about holders of graduate degrees, which include a wide range of specialties). Some work—analyses of the community college movement by Brint and Karabel (1989), for example, and a detailed field study by Howard London (1978)—implies that because A.A. holders generally receive less exposure to a liberal arts education than those with B.A.'s, the latter should display more of the characteristics that are thought to be nurtured by a four-year college experience (interest in cultural activities, intellectual orientation, and civic orientation, for example). Our measures of these characteristics were for the most part taken at only one time (1984), so it is possible that differences among individuals at each educational level might be a result either of ways in which they differed to begin with or of disparities in their life situations subsequent to college. We are able, however, to control for at least some of the pre- and postcollege characteristics that might confound any assessment of the influence of educational level.

Attitudes and Orientations

Our exploration of non-material outcomes of higher education includes a variety of behaviors, attitudes, and psychosocial characteristics. We shall begin with an examination of two kinds of behavior: civic or political interest and participation in cultural activities. Then we assess individuals' self-esteem, their sense of control over their lives, and evaluations of their health status.[4]

As we said earlier, a heightened sense of concern with civic issues has typically been found to be one of the changes that occurs during college. We gauged civic interest by responses to four questionnaire items: "I don't spend much time keeping up with political events"; "I read the newspaper almost every day"; "I am registered to vote"; and "I often watch documentaries and public affairs programs on television." Respondents indicated whether each statement was or was not true of them. We developed an index from 0 to 4 based on the responses to the items, with 4 representing the score obtained by an individual with a "civically involved" response on each item. Respondents who gave such a response on at least three of the four items were characterized as having high civic interest.

By this standard more than 60 percent were civically involved (table 7.1). In line with the literature on the effects of college on political and civic interest (Pascarella and Terenzini 1991, 277–79, 287), level of interest is to some degree associated with educational attainment: among whites and Hispanics, B.A. holders displayed a stronger civic orientation than did those with A.A.'s or high school diplomas (there is little difference between the two latter categories).[5] Among blacks, higher levels of credentials are also associated with higher civic interest scores, but differences are very narrow. Graduate-

---

[4]We developed a number of questionnaire items designed to measure individuals' civic orientation, cultural participation, self-esteem, locus of control, preference for thinking about complex problems, and health status. As a check upon our ad hoc assignment of items to these dimensions, we carried out a factor analysis, which largely confirmed our categorizations. We revised our assignment of items in the few instances where factor loadings did not support our initial assignment.

[5]Differences referred to in this and all other discussions of tables in the chapter are statistically significant, as determined by difference-in-proportions tests for all key pairs of interest (see Blalock 1979).

Table 7.1 Strong Civic Interest, by Ethnicity and Educational Attainment

Percentages, Except as Noted

Educational Attainment	Ethnicity			Total
	White	Black	Hispanic	
High school diploma	58	68	63	61
	(567)	(217)	(137)	(921)
A.A.	56	71	66	60
	(432)	(184)	(119)	(735)
B.A.	64	72	76	65
	(1,306)	(203)	(119)	(1,628)
Graduate degree	69	75	69	69
	(992)	(104)	(56)	(1,152)
All degrees	62	71	67	64
	(3,297)	(708)	(431)	(4,436)

Source: Follow-up survey.

Note: Interest was measured by an index combining responses to four questionnaire items. The index runs from 0, signifying little civic orientation, to 4, signifying strong interest. Data in the table reflect those with a score of at least 3. The numbers in each cell correspond to, but are not identical with, those in tables 7.2, 7.3. Ns (in parentheses) are unweighted.

degree holders, perhaps because they are quite a diverse group (containing M.A.'s in various fields, advanced professional degree holders, and Ph.D's), do not stand out from the lower degree levels in any consistent way. Ethnic differences are also apparent: blacks displayed the most civic interest and whites the least, with Hispanics in the middle. Although these ethnic disparities are not very wide, they are consistent: even with educational attainment controlled, minorities appear, almost without exception, to have more civic interest than whites.

In an effort to account for ethnic differences and to take a closer look at other possible influences on civic interest, we carried out a multivariate analysis. In addition to ethnicity, we looked at other demographic and background factors, including gender and two measures of socioeconomic status, parents' education and family income at the time of the student's entry to

CUNY. These would help us understand whether educational attainment is still associated with civic involvement after a fuller set of background factors is taken into account. We included also a set of attitude factors that described students' initial reasons for going to college. Two factors are included: the extent to which students attended for vocational reasons (to get a better job and make more money), and the extent to which they attended for reasons of personal growth (to get a good general education and to become a more cultured person). Those who valued personal growth might have possessed more civic and political interest to begin with. Finally, we added a set of variables that described important aspects of respondents' current life situations: their employment, job, and marital status, their household income, and whether they had children.

Overall, civic interest was not very predictable.[6] Nonetheless, the analysis does help to clarify some of the influences on it (to avoid overburdening the text, the table is not presented). Family income at the time when the student entered CUNY was positively related to involvement. So was gender: women were less involved than men. Students who entered college to get a general education had more civic interest. Aspects of respondents' current life situations, their job status and household income, also had a modest influence: those who held higher-status jobs and who earned more money were more civically oriented. With these variables taken into account, educational attainment still played a role, albeit a modest one.

The analysis sheds additional light on ethnic differences. With all of these variables controlled, minorities appear to have even more civic interest relative to whites than they had to begin with. This seems to be mostly a result of gender differences. That is, women have less civic interest than men, and the representation of women among minorities is larger than it is among whites, so with gender controlled, ethnic differences widen. Although whites generally held jobs of higher status and typically had higher incomes as well, this advantage did not narrow differences between whites and minorities in civic interest. Our inability to account for more of these ethnic disparities suggests that there are important sources of civic involvement beyond those that we have been able to measure. It may be that the political mobilization around issues of opportunity in American society that occurred among minorities

[6]In this regression, we used the entire range of scores on civic interest, 0 to 4, rather than classifying respondents according to whether they scored "high" as we did in table 7.1. The adjusted $R^2=.04$.

(especially among blacks) during the 1960s and 1970s is reflected in our data. This possibility is suggested by other research showing that with socioeconomic status controlled, blacks in the 1980s exhibited more political consciousness and higher voter participation rates than did whites (for review see Jaynes and Williams 1989, chapter 5).

We also assessed interest and participation in cultural activities. Such interest was measured through these questionnaire items: "In the last year I visited an art museum or gallery" and "In the last year I have read novels, short stories, plays, or poetry." Those who responded affirmatively to both items were classified as "participating in cultural activities." We use this measure of cultural involvement with no illusions about its thoroughness. There are obviously many cultural products, like films, theater, dance, classical, jazz, and other ethnically based music (widely available in New York), which would have been covered in a more comprehensive inventory of cultural consumption. But practical considerations (in particular constraints on questionnaire length) precluded such an undertaking. Nonetheless, even our modest effort can shed some light on the relation of education and ethnicity to cultural activity.

As we measured it, about half of former CUNY students were cultural participants (table 7.2). Unlike the case of civic interest, ethnic differences were generally narrow and inconsistent as to direction. We don't know, of course, about the *content* of museums attended or of literature read. A metropolitan area like New York offers an array of ethnically specialized museums and galleries—the Museum of the American Indian, El Museo Del Barrio, the Schomburg Center for Black Culture, and the Jewish Museum, to name a few—not to mention many other famous institutions that present culturally diverse sets of programs, exhibits, and the like. And a vast cultural menu is readily available in fiction, plays, and poetry. So although we don't know the extent to which the tastes of whites, blacks, and Hispanics may have run in different directions, as far as we can tell groups were quite similar in the degree of their cultural participation.

There are visible disparities in cultural participation among those at various educational levels. The critical threshold is the bachelor's degree. Below this level less than half of any group reported being culturally involved (and none of the differences between A.A. and high school diploma holders is significant). At the B.A. level or higher well over half of respondents in almost every group were involved (but only in the case of whites did the participation of graduate-degree holders exceed that of B.A.'s).

Table 7.2 Participation in Cultural Activities, by Ethnicity and Educational Attainment

Percentages, Except as Noted

Educational Attainment	Ethnicity			
	White	Black	Hispanic	Total
High school diploma	43	40	43	43
A.A.	42	46	49	44
B.A.	55	55	65	56
Graduate degree	61	49	59	60
All degrees	52	46	51	51
	(3,455)	(745)	(466)	(4,666)

Source: Follow-up survey.

Note: Participation was measured by an index combining responses to two questionnaire items. The index runs from 0, signifying no cultural participation, to 2, signifying active participation. Data in the table reflect those with a score of 2. Ns (in parentheses) are unweighted.

Are these differences in cultural participation influenced mainly by educational attainment? Might they be affected to an important extent by other differences among individuals, like gender and socioeconomic background, or by such current aspects of their life situations as job status, marriage, income, and parental status? We examined these questions with the same set of variables that we used in the case of civic interests (results are not shown in table form). The analysis shows that cultural participation is a bit more predictable than is civic interest, and that a number of factors influence it.[7] Among them, the most important is gender: women were more involved in cultural activities than were men. Parental educational background also made a difference: those respondents whose fathers had attended college were more likely to be cultural participants. Attitudes that students brought with them to college also had an influence: those who said that they were going to college for reasons of personal growth were more likely to be active cultural partici-

[7]The adjusted R^2=.10.

pants than those who emphasized vocational reasons for attending college. Respondents' current life situations also had an influence, but not entirely in ways one might expect. Household income, for example, which might be thought to provide the means for greater pursuit of cultural activities, played no role. Marriage and in particular having children seemed to deter cultural participation. Being married may have led to other competing forms of leisure activity, and respondents' children were generally at an age that made heavy demands on parental time; probably they were still too young to make museum going a suitable activity.

When all of these influences on cultural activity are taken into account, the initial impressions provided by table 7.2 are confirmed. White and minority respondents were equally likely to be participants in cultural pursuits, and educational attainment remains an important predictor of such interests. The B.A. degree continues as the minimum level of attainment at which cultural participation increases. The educational opportunity provided by open admissions thus seems to have augmented involvement in cultural activities.

As we said, a large research literature attests to the influence of college on the development of cognitive skills—increased general knowledge and the abilities to think critically and to engage in formal reasoning. Although we have no data that assesses such aspects of cognitive development among our respondents, we do have information on a more general aspect of their intellectual orientation: whether they were predisposed to solving complex intellectual problems. We assessed this orientation through two items: "I enjoy thinking out complicated problems" and "I like to try my wits in solving puzzles." Respondents who said that both items were true of them were classified as "liking to think."

Although overall about 60 percent or more said that they liked to think through complex problems and to solve puzzles, we found no clear pattern of association with educational attainment. Minority B.A. holders more often held this intellectual orientation than did those with A.A.'s, but those with high school diplomas appeared as intellectually oriented as the B.A.'s. Also, there is little difference between the responses of B.A.'s and those of holders of graduate or advanced degrees. No consistent pattern of ethnic differences appears, either. A multivariate analysis did little to clarify these results. We are inclined to think that perhaps our items were not sensitive enough to reveal any relationship between educational attainment and liking to think. Those who like to try their wits in solving puzzles, for example, could be referring to anything from the puzzles in the *New York Daily News* to the *New York Times* crossword puzzle to trying to understand data in the media relating to economic conditions, racial tensions, or the validity of the hypothesized "greenhouse effect." The latter problems, which lack clear solutions, are more complex than those posed in intellectual games, but such distinctions cannot be identified in our data.

Psychological Characteristics and Health Status

Among the various psychosocial qualities that have been thought to develop as a consequence of the college experience, self-esteem has been one of the most frequently studied. Individuals with a strong sense of self-esteem are, among other things, characterized as self-confident, as feeling that they can do things well, and as having a positive attitude towards themselves. We measured self-esteem by means of four questionnaire items: "Generally, I'm confident that when I make plans, I'll be able to carry them out"; "Generally, I take a positive attitude toward myself"; "I often feel downcast and dejected"; and "I often feel powerless to get what I want out of life." Those who gave responses indicative of self-esteem to all four items were characterized as having a high degree of that quality.

Between two-thirds and three-quarters of respondents exhibited high self-esteem (table 7.3). Educational attainment is associated with self-esteem only among minority individuals: those with B.A.'s and graduate degrees more often displayed a positive sense of self than those with high school diplomas alone or A.A.'s. For example, around 60 percent of Hispanics with the lesser educational credentials but more than 80 percent of those at the highest educational level had a strong sense of self-esteem. Disparities between educational levels are quite narrow among whites, but they showed a higher level of self-esteem than Hispanics, and they were slightly ahead of blacks. The overall stronger self-rating of whites reflects their more positive sense of self at the lower levels of educational attainment (among A.A. recipients and those with high school diplomas alone).

Differences in self-esteem that appear related to education disappear when other situational factors, especially ones pertaining to work, are taken into account. A regression analysis shows that having a higher-status job and higher household income add to self-esteem. The influence of educational attainment thus appears to be transmitted mainly through its positive effects on

Table 7.3 High Self-Esteem, by Ethnicity and Educational Attainment

Percentages, Except as Noted

Educational Attainment	Ethnicity			Total
	White	Black	Hispanic	
High school diploma	72	64	64	69
A.A.	77	66	59	72
B.A.	74	77	71	74
Graduate degree	78	84	81	78
All degrees	75	70	66	73
	(3,038)	(631)	(385)	(4,054)

Source: Follow-up survey.

Note: Self-esteem was measured by an index combining responses to four questionnaire items. The index runs from 0, signifying low self-esteem, to 4, signifying the highest level. Data in the table reflect those with a score of 4. Ns (in parentheses) are unweighted.

labor-market experiences. Overall ethnic differences seem to be explained as well by the role that education plays in the labor market: minorities did less well than whites in educational attainment, and this served, in part, to create ethnic inequalities in work.

The college experience is also thought to help bring about a related kind of change, referred to as the development of an internalized locus of control. In essence, the idea is that college enables individuals to become more independent minded, to develop some autonomy from parents, peers, and others in making choices about values and behaviors (Pascarella and Terenzini 1991, 215). Students with an internalized locus of control are less susceptible to external influence; they come to feel that they are able to control what happens to them. Externally directed persons, on the other hand, more typically think that what happens to them is determined by chance, luck, or fate. We assessed locus of control using these questionnaire items: "What you get out of life is mostly a matter of luck"; "I am the sort of person who takes life as it comes"; and "Getting a good job depends mainly on being in the right place at the right time." Individuals who rejected at least two of these statements were counted as having a strong internal locus of control.

By this standard, about two-thirds of our respondents exhibited a strong sense that they were in control of what happened to them. Minority-group members were as likely as whites to have an internal locus of control. There was little relationship between educational attainment and locus of control: whites and Hispanics who had earned graduate degrees were more internally focused than those at other levels of educational attainment; otherwise, there were no differences associated with academic credentials. When a larger number of variables is taken into account in a regression analysis, the relation between graduate-degree attainment and locus of control appears to be mediated by occupational factors. Those with high-status jobs and higher income were more likely to exhibit internal control.

Because college-educated individuals generally have a broader knowledge base, they tend to be better informed than others about good health practices and medical services. This greater awareness is one explanation for the finding typical of many studies that educational attainment is positively associated with indicators of physical health (Bowen 1977; Hyman et al. 1975; Pascarella and Terenzini 1991). Of course, economic resources help provide better access to medical care, and this, rather than any direct effect of education, could explain any apparent influence of education on health. We gathered only minimal information about health status among our respondents. They were asked whether they had suffered from a major illness during the past two years. Overall, about 10 percent reported that they had. They also were asked how satisfied they were with their health. More than 60 percent reported being "very satisfied." Those who said both that they had not suffered a major illness and were very satisfied with their health were designated as having "positive health status."

Sixty percent of respondents were so classified. Health status and educational attainment were positively linked, though only modestly so. Generally speaking, recipients of graduate degrees and B.A.'s were more likely to display positive health status than those with only a high school diploma, and B.A. holders tended to be better off than those at the A.A. level. Overall, whites and Hispanics were a bit more likely than blacks to report being satisfied with their health. A regression analysis, using our standard set of control variables, confirms that educational attainment makes a difference, suggesting that education does have an independent long-term direct effect. Earnings also matter: as earnings increase, so does health-status rating.

Life Satisfaction

More than a decade after students had started college, how did they feel about their lives? How satisfied were they with their economic situations, with social life, with the communities in which they were living, and with life in general? Did their educational attainments influence their feelings of satisfaction? Did college graduates feel better about their lives than those who had not gone as far in education? Such questions have been assessed in a number of studies (for review, see Pascarella and Terenzini 1991, 538–41). Somewhat surprisingly, perhaps, research shows that educational attainment (measured as having at least a B.A. degree) has at best only very small effects on life satisfaction. Moreover, when other aspects of individuals' lives—income and marital status, for example—are taken into account, even these small influences disappear. So education plays a modest and indirect role, affecting satisfaction mainly through its influence on other aspects of life, such as socioeconomic ones.

We assessed relationships between educational level, ethnic membership, and life satisfaction of respondents in three domains: their socioeconomic situations, quality of social life, and quality of their living situations. To assess satisfaction in each domain, we asked respondents to indicate whether they were "very satisfied," "satisfied," or "not satisfied" with items corresponding to that area. In the socioeconomic category, they were asked how satisfied they were with their work situation, their income, and their future prospects.[8] To gauge the quality of social life, respondents rated their satisfaction with family life, social life, the amount of time available for leisure activities, the quality of these activities, and their satisfaction with "life in general." Quality of living situation was assessed by asking them how satisfied they were with their home or apartment, their neighborhood, their city or town, and the schools in the community. We produced a scale score for each area by summing the responses to the constituent items ("very satisfied" was given a score of 2, "satisfied" 1, and "not satisfied" 0). Summing the three items that constituted the socioeconomic satisfaction assessment produced a scale ranging from 0 to 6; the scale measuring satisfaction with social life ranged from 0 to 10; and the one pertaining to quality of living situation ranged from 0 to 8.

[8]For this, as well as succeeding dimensions of satisfaction, the items constituting each scale were validated through a factor analysis.

We also combined responses to all of the items in the preceding scales to produce a measure of overall life satisfaction.[9]

Table 7.4 shows the percentages classified as very satisfied in each area, as gauged by a specified minimum score (see table footnotes).[10] The results are consistent with the research literature on the relationship between educational attainment and satisfaction: variations in educational level are not associated with large differences in satisfaction. Moreover, what differences exist are not distributed according to any systematic, consistent pattern. Whites with graduate degrees express more satisfaction with their socioeconomic situations than those with degrees below this level, for example, but in such realms as satisfaction with social life and with one's living situation, A.A. recipients were just as likely to be very satisfied as those at the graduate level, and they were more satisfied than B.A. holders. Among minority respondents, B.A. recipients were generally more satisfied than those with A.A.'s, but there is no positive linear association between educational credentials and satisfaction.

When we look at group differences, a clear ethnic ordering is visible: whites expressed the most satisfaction, followed by Hispanics, and blacks were least satisfied. The gap between whites and blacks was very consistent and quite wide, exceeding 30 percentage points in some comparisons; in not one instance were blacks more satisfied than whites. Although whites were also consistently more satisfied than Hispanics, differences were not as wide as those separating them from blacks.

These ethnic disparities in life satisfaction do not seem to be explained by differences in educational attainment: differences between responses of minority members and whites are often as large or larger when education is controlled as when it is uncontrolled. Of course, other factors could influence feelings of satisfaction, and might, therefore, help to explain some of the

[9]Our analyses of each domain of satisfaction included only those subjects who responded to all items related to that area. On one item, however—satisfaction with schools—nonresponse was much higher than for other items. Individuals who did not have children were overwhelmingly the ones who did not respond. Rather than exclude from the neighborhood and overall satisfaction scales several hundred subjects who responded to every item but this, we assigned to them the sample mean for the item.

[10]Because the number of items differs for each scale and the cut points defining "very satisfied" are not identical as a proportion of the range of each scale, the reader is cautioned against comparing satisfaction percentages *across* the different scales. For example, one should not say that blacks were more satisfied with family and social life (41 percent classified as quite satisfied) than they were with their socioeconomic situations (33 percent quite satisfied).

Table 7.4 Life Satisfaction, by Ethnicity and Educational Attainment

Very Satisfied, Percentages Except as Noted

Educational Attainment	Socioeconomic Situation[a]				Family and Social Life[b]				Quality of Neighborhood[c]				Overall Satisfaction[d]			
	W	B	H	Total	W	B	H	Total	W	B	H	Total	W	B	H	Total
High school diploma	48	32	43	44	53	39	52	50	50	18	32	41	40	16	31	34
A.A.	53	29	34	45	59	39	46	53	56	29	33	47	49	20	29	40
B.A.	49	38	48	48	53	45	50	52	50	28	35	46	41	26	32	39
Graduate degree	58	35	37	56	57	46	52	56	53	26	41	50	47	30	36	45
All degrees	52	33	41	48	55	41	50	53	51	23	34	46	43	21	31	39
Mean scale score	3.59	2.84	3.05	3.44	6.62	5.87	6.32	6.49	5.52	4.09	4.65	5.25	17.30	14.27	15.59	16.74
N (unweighted)	3,352	701	437	4,490	3,436	727	459	4,622	3,461	746	468	4,675	3,352	701	437	4,490

Source: Follow-up survey.

Note: W = white, B = black, H = Hispanic.

[a]This scale consists of three items. Scores can range from 0, signifying the least satisfaction, to 6, signifying the most. Data in the table reflect those with a score of 4 or higher.

[b]This scale consists of five items. Scores can range from 0, signifying the least satisfaction, to 10, signifying the most. Data in the table reflect those with a score of 7 or higher.

[c]This scale consists of four items. Scores can range from 0, signifying the least satisfaction, to 8, signifying the most. Data in the table reflect those with a score of 6 or higher.

[d]This scale consists of thirteen items. Scores can range from 0, signifying the least satisfaction, to 26, signifying the most. Data in the table reflect those with a score of 19 or higher.

ethnic gap. One is household income, which could affect where one can live, how one feels about work, and the kinds of leisure-time activities that one can pursue. Marriage and parenthood might also affect life satisfaction. To take a closer look at these and other possible influences, we carried out regression analyses for each satisfaction area.[11] These analyses confirm the initial finding that ethnicity is strongly associated with how people feel about their lives, and that educational attainment is not associated with satisfaction in any systematic way.[12] They indicate also that other factors play a role, in particular household income, which is positively associated with each area of satisfaction. As we have seen, whites typically earned more than blacks and Hispanics. Partly as a result, ethnic differences in satisfaction are somewhat reduced when inequalities of income are taken into account. Being married generally adds to satisfaction, especially with social life. This factor also helps to account for the lower levels of satisfaction for minority respondents, who were less likely to be married. Single parenthood plays a less consistent role, having a negative influence on satisfaction with one's living situation but not on other satisfaction areas. Even after these factors are controlled, however, most of initial ethnic differences in each realm of satisfaction—especially between whites and blacks—remain unexplained.[13]

That educational attainment does not go very far in helping us to understand life satisfaction is consistent with the literature that we noted earlier. That we are able to account for so little of the ethnic differences, however, is

[11]We regressed each of the four satisfaction scores on the following variables: ethnicity, parents' educational attainment, income at time of matriculation at CUNY, gender, educational attainment, employment status in 1984, occupational status in 1984 (the Duncan socioeconomic index), household income, marital status, parental status, and single-parent status.

[12]We carried out these regressions for the total sample and also separately for each ethnic group. Other than the differences that we noted earlier in the pattern by which educational credentials are associated with satisfaction, these within-group regressions suggest that the pattern of influences on satisfactions is fairly similar across groups.

[13]Above and beyond 1984 income, we thought that salary increases between 1978 and 1984 might have affected satisfaction. In effect, in addition to actual earnings, concrete evidence of progress in work, as evidenced by pay raises, might have affected how satisfied people felt, not only in terms of their jobs, but also in other realms of satisfaction. As we saw in Chapter 4, some showed considerable progress in pay raises, whereas others showed relatively little. Overall, blacks and Hispanics made less progress than whites. To examine the possibility that pay raises would explain some of ethnic differences in satisfaction, we included an earnings-change score in a set of regressions that covered each of the satisfaction areas. These analyses did not add to the explanation of disparities in satisfaction between whites and minority members.

perplexing. Minority respondents, especially blacks, may have perceived themselves as disadvantaged relative to the socioeconomic conditions and quality of living environments of comparably educated whites with whom they work. That is, part of minority dissatisfaction may result from their perception that they are rewarded less than whites, even when they appear similar in terms of educational credentials.

Educational opportunity is typically thought of as an equity issue because it affects socioeconomic life chances. But equity has a broader meaning. If education enhances participation in civic and cultural life, if it promotes psychic well-being and feelings of satisfaction with various facets of living, then, in effect, inequalities of educational attainment affect access to these nonmaterial aspects of well-being.

Overall, a majority of respondents—often a substantial one—was civically and culturally involved, liked to think, had a positive sense of self-esteem and an internalized locus of control, and reported positive health status. Educational attainment had a visible influence on civic involvement and cultural participation, but it had little effect on psychosocial characteristics and life satisfaction. Although ethnic differences are seen for some outcomes, typically they are not very large, except in areas of life satisfaction, where disparities are quite wide. But wide or not, they are largely unconnected to differences in educational level.

In part these results are consistent with the research literature, which indicates that the influence of college on many of these outcomes is weak and often indirect—a function of the effects of education on such subsequent life conditions as earnings. But the absence of many clear educational effects in our data may, at least in part, be a result of the weakness of some of our measures, especially those related to cognitive development and to health status. In addition, the negligible effect of education on many outcomes might be a consequence of the life circumstances under which many students pursued their college careers. Those who attend nonresidential, commuter universities like CUNY have only a truncated exposure to many of the social contexts that are taken for granted in residential colleges—opportunities for development of peer group relationships, for example, and easier access to faculty—which can influence cognitive and social development. Further diminishing exposure to traditional college life were the family responsibilities of many CUNY students, who had to work full-time and consequently attended college only part-time, often in evening classes. The meaning of college is far different in the context of the lives of such students than for full-time residential students. Many are already at points in the life cycle that the traditional collegian, still emerging from late adolescence, has yet to reach. The effects of college would be difficult to disentangle from the complexities of many CUNY students' lives.

Open admissions, then, undoubtedly helped students to develop further in some ways, such as in civic and cultural interests. But both the status of the university as a commuter institution and socioeconomic forces that further limited students' participation in campus life no doubt served to constrain the influence of college.

CHAPTER EIGHT

Open Admissions

An Assessment

The open-admissions policy has been, arguably, the most ambitious effort to promote educational opportunity ever attempted in American higher education. It represents one of the last great examples of the 1960s commitment to the idea that social policy could and should be used to advance equity in U.S. society. Almost overnight the university was transformed from one of the nation's most selective institutions to its most accessible. After the doors of CUNY opened wide, over 200,000 freshmen crowded in between 1970 and 1975—including many of minority origins and from impoverished backgrounds who otherwise would have had no chance for college. These students entered an arena where few from their families and neighborhoods had been before.

More than a quarter of a century has passed since CUNY launched its historic program, offering a seat in college to all students with a high school diploma. Quite a bit can now be said about that policy—about its successes and its disappointments—after following the initial entering classes for a period of fourteen years.[1] In reviewing what happened to these former students, we shall see that there are no easy answers to the question: Was the open-admissions policy a success?

The Benefits of Open Admissions

Open admissions was spectacularly successful in bringing into college thousands of minority students who had been starkly underrepresented. In its first year, 1970, the size of the freshman class grew by 75 percent over that of the previous fall. The representation of black and Hispanic students increased

---

[1]For other issues, like faculty responses to open admissions, only anecdotal information exists. An early study of grading practices offers the only systematic data about faculty responses to the policy. For example, there is no information about changes, if any, in course syllabi, reading assignments, term paper requirements, and the like.

dramatically in the policy's initial years, quadrupling in CUNY's four-year colleges and almost doubling in its community college tier. Open admissions brought about one form of equity: the program attracted so many minority students that in the early 1970s they came for the first time to be represented in CUNY freshman classes in the same proportions that they were in the graduating classes in New York City's high schools. Most of these students would not have gone to college had it not been for open admissions.

What the program did for whites is less well recognized. Under open admissions large numbers of them were attracted to the university. Indeed, even though there was a public perception of open admissions as a minority program, more whites actually got into CUNY because of the policy than did minority students. The benefits of the policy flowed to a broad cross-section of New York City's ethnic communities, both minority and white.

CUNY's policy was designed to do more than simply get students into college. Equally important was where they were placed. The open-admissions blueprint stipulated in different ways—mainly in its admissions criteria and in easing the process of transfer from two-year to four-year colleges—that the creation of access to B.A. programs was a significant priority. This emphasis set CUNY apart from other higher education systems, like California's, where most minority students were tracked into its community college tiers. Open admissions so dramatically increased minority representation in four-year institutions that by 1975 minority freshmen were distributed across the two collegiate tiers in proportions similar to the distribution of whites.

Over the long haul the educational opportunity that CUNY provided translated into substantial academic achievement for many thousands of students. Because of open admissions, the number of blacks who earned B.A.'s more than tripled and the number of Hispanics doubled. Many were able to use the opportunity that the program provided as a springboard to earn postgraduate degrees; open admissions tripled the number of blacks who got M.A.'s and more than doubled the number who earned advanced degrees; among Hispanics, the program came close to doubling the number of M.A.'s and more than doubled the attainment of advanced degrees. Open admissions also added substantially to the achievements of whites.

CUNY's program had been put in place after the occupational trend in New York City toward a postindustrial economy was well under way. Manufacturing jobs had been on a downward slope for some time, while white-collar positions in both the clerical and the professional-managerial tiers represented an expanding sector of the labor market. To an increasing degree, it was necessary to attend college to be eligible for entry to good jobs in this sector—ones that carried the possibility of attaining high status, interesting and challenging work, and decent pay.

In opening CUNY's doors to all high school graduates who wanted to come, many in New York—not only university administrators but also the alumni, politicians, and private citizens who made up the broader CUNY community—hoped that education would ultimately translate into improved life chances in the changing economy. The educational credentials earned under the open-admissions program clearly made a difference in terms of success in the labor market. Indeed, educational attainment was the single most important influence on how well former students did at work. Overwhelmingly they were employed in the white-collar sector of the city's economy. Students who earned A.A. degrees had jobs of higher status and earned more than those without a college degree. Those who completed B.A.'s or postgraduate degrees were significantly better off than those with lesser credentials. Typically, they held the higher-status managerial and professional jobs in the top tier of the postindustrial labor market. These jobs had attributes that people value very much: they provided interesting, challenging, and responsible work, with substantially better pay than the jobs held by those with less educational attainment. Even students who never completed a degree but who earned more than a semester's worth of college credits received an economic bonus, albeit a modest one.

The economic benefit to those who owed their college opportunity to the open-admissions policy was substantial. For one year of the 1980s we estimate that former open-admissions students earned almost 67 million dollars more than they would have earned if CUNY's program had never been instituted. These respondents typically were in their early to mid-thirties when their earnings were measured, so they generally had another thirty years left in their work careers. Even if we make the conservative assumption that in subsequent years there would be no widening of the 67 million–dollar spread between their actual earnings and what they would have been earning had there been no open-admissions policy, the long-term aggregate benefit over the course of their careers amounts to more than two billion dollars. If we assume that 5 percent of this benefit would be paid in taxes, one hundred million dollars in government revenue would be generated by the program. In fact, the earnings slope climbs more steeply for college graduates than it does for those with less educational attainment, so the true dollar benefit is undoubtedly far larger than reflected by these estimates. Furthermore, these calculations, which apply only to open-admissions students in the first three classes to enter under the policy, do not include the benefits that went to the members of succeeding cohorts. In the early 1970s there was speculation about whether open admissions would help to turn "tax-eaters" into taxpayers. Although we have not undertaken any systematic cost-benefit analyses, the policy clearly produced substantial aggregate taxable returns.

By augmenting the pool of minority men and women who received educational credentials, open admissions contributed to the growth of a college-educated class in New York City's minority communities. The policy was a social intervention designed to interrupt the inheritance of socioeconomic disadvantage. In achieving this aim to an important degree, open admissions undoubtedly helped to produce a more promising set of life chances among the children of the students who came to CUNY after the open-admissions program was initiated. Although we cannot specify with precision the extent to which this occurred, the opportunity that the program afforded led to educational and occupational attainments that helped to ensure more advantaged prospects for the children of many former students.[2] Open admissions helped to raise the odds that the advantages to its immediate beneficiaries would be transmitted across generations.

In every respect that it added to the life chances of former students, open admissions must be counted as a success. But along with these positive consequences, we must acknowledge that the program did not entirely erase inequalities that separate minorities from whites in educational attainment and in labor-market rewards. To understand the persistence of inequity, we must consider differences in the ways that educational careers of white and minority students typically developed, how these differences affected college experiences and attainments, and the influence and limitations of these attainments on subsequent experiences in the labor market.

Open Admissions and Cumulative Disadvantage

Typically, minority students are subject to a series of cumulative disadvantages that begin early in life. Although our data do not begin until the students were in high school, disadvantages have much earlier roots—in the economic resources of their families and in their minority status. Such students frequently

[2]Another follow-up survey is now being planned. This survey will provide important data on the educational attainments of the children of our CUNY respondents.

start elementary school already behind whites in the development of academic skills. They are more often placed in lower ability groups or diagnosed as learning disabled, a status that tends to remove them from the mainstream of early academic work.[3] Because minority parents often have lower educational attainment than white parents, the former may be less able to intercede effectively with teachers on behalf of their children regarding such matters as ability-group placement. Partly because teachers tend to have lower expectations for students in lower-track classes, students in these tracks actually learn less. This slower academic progress reinforces teachers' confidence in the validity of their initial track placements. As minority students move through elementary school—not infrequently needing to repeat grades and thus falling behind the modal grade for their age group—tests appear to ratify the judgments of teachers that these students are slow learners. By the time they leave elementary school, they are, on average, academically further behind whites than they were when they started in first grade.

Once minority students reach high school, the typical academic dossiers that they have compiled lead them, more often than whites, to be placed in vocational high schools and in nonacademic curriculum tracks in general high schools. High school tracking limits their opportunity to take academic, college preparatory courses and probably reinforces their negative self-images as poor students. Many become discouraged and do not graduate from high school. Earlier analyses (Lavin et al. 1981) suggest that in our respondents' high school classes, less than half of black high school juniors and only 40 percent of Hispanics graduated by the spring of the following year, compared with almost three-quarters of whites.[4] The pool of minority students eligible for college was thus proportionately reduced far more than was the case among whites. Moreover, even with open admissions, minority graduates were somewhat less likely than their white counterparts to enroll in college. Among those who did, about 90 percent of the minority enrollees went to CUNY. That it was their almost exclusive college destination testifies to the

[3]Minority youngsters are overrepresented among those labeled as learning disabled and are generally more likely to be assigned to special education classes, a placement that prevents them from having access to regular academic classes. For a report on this system in New York City schools see Richardson (1994).

[4]Some who failed to graduate by the spring of the following year did so later. Others entered the job market, met with disappointment, and eventually graduated with a general equivalency diploma (GED). These students were typically already in their twenties when they started college, and faced with other obligations, like the need to hold a full-time job.

profound importance of the university's open-admissions policy, both in meeting and encouraging the aspirations of minority youth.

Disadvantages rooted in earlier educational experiences continued to influence the college careers of minority students. Because of their weaker high school records, they were less often eligible to enter a four-year program. So even though students were more equally distributed across CUNY's senior and community college tiers than in other higher educational systems, minority students still were more likely than whites to start at a community college. Beginning in a two-year school substantially lowers rates of B.A. attainment, so this disadvantage fell more heavily on minority students. Even if they succeeded eventually in earning a bachelor's degree, community college entry added almost a year to the time it took.

Decades of research have shown that high school grades are the single most important influence on how students do in college. Our findings are consistent with this work: low grades in high school—to which black and Hispanic students were subject more than were whites—typically led to lower college grades, which slowed progress to graduation and diminished graduation chances. Placement in nonacademic high school tracks, which also was more typical of minority than of white students, contributed as well to lower college GPA's and thus to extended college careers.

Whatever their level of entry to CUNY, minority students had fewer economic resources than did whites, and so they more often worked full-time, which contributed also to diminished grades, making minority students less likely to graduate. But even among B.A. recipients, full-time employment extended by well over two years the time required to finish.

Because of weaker academic preparation, minority students were more often placed in noncredit remedial courses. These courses also added to the time it took to graduate. Overall, then, the past disadvantages of minority students contributed to the creation of new disadvantages in college, and these led to substantial differences between white and minority students in graduation rates and in the amount of time needed to complete a degree. Sixty percent of white students earned a B.A. or a postgraduate degree, compared with only a third of minority students. Among those who completed a B.A., only 14 percent of whites needed seven or more years to finish, but almost half of blacks and 40 percent of Hispanics required that much time. These often very lengthy periods of time that a disproportionate number of minority graduates needed for degree completion constituted yet an additional disadvantage, for time to B.A. was the single most important influence on the chances of earning a postgraduate degree.

Differences in the receipt of educational credentials, in turn, influenced labor market experiences. Postgraduate degree holders and B.A. recipients were more likely than those with lesser attainments to hold high-status jobs that were intellectually challenging, involved supervisory responsibility, and paid well. Because it was whites who typically went further in education, they outdistanced minorities in these ways. Blacks and Hispanics were more likely than whites to have terminated their schooling at the A.A. level, and the relatively meager returns to these degrees were one reason for the more modest success of minorities in the labor market. And even those minority students who attained the higher degrees typically took longer to earn them, adding to their disadvantage: because whites typically finished sooner than minorities with comparable credentials, they had more time in the labor market with the degree in hand. This head start was an advantage because postdegree work experience was more valuable than predegree experience.

Although educational attainment was the single most important influence on success in the labor market and was responsible for much of the differences between the achievements of whites and minorities, other factors also had their effects. Family background continued to make a difference: having parents with relatively high income and having a father who had at least some college added to earnings. Minority students were less likely to come from such families. The continuing significance of social origins underscores the crucial importance of educational opportunity in helping minorities overcome earlier disadvantages.

Conditions intrinsic to the labor market itself also had an effect. One of the most important factors is the sector of employment. Minority respondents were more likely than whites to be employed in the public sector. This entailed a penalty: holders of public-sector jobs earned less than otherwise comparable workers in the private sector. But even after taking employment sector into account, minority workers continued to do less well than whites. Some of this inequality is most likely rooted in employer discrimination in hiring, in promotions and raises, and in firings. Discrimination appears to have occurred mainly in the private sector, where most of our respondents—including minority workers—were employed.

Although open admissions did not have a specific gender focus, in considering the influence of the program on job market experiences, we must take account of the fact that women did substantially worse than men, even when they held similar educational credentials. This inequality was especially evident with regard to earnings, which are arguably the single most important facet of work, particularly considering the often impoverished backgrounds of our respondents. Minority women were doubly disadvantaged: they were paid less because of the burdens to which minority individuals were especially subject, and they were also less rewarded because they were women. In this sense, they got less benefit from open admissions than did men. The skimpier job rewards to women hurt minorities the most: because women constituted a larger proportion of minority workers than of white ones, their lower pay scale accounts in part for the fact that blacks and Hispanics did less well in the labor market.

In sum, not only did past disadvantages continue to hinder the job success of minorities, but the labor market itself added new handicaps. These hindrances—public-sector employment, lower pay for women, and employer discrimination, all of which lie beyond the institutional scope of higher education—dulled the edge that open admissions provided in improving minority life chances.

The cumulation of disadvantage can be seen also in the extent to which the benefits of open admissions could be consolidated across the generations. The policy's critical role in raising minority educational attainments allowed more minority children to be born to college-educated parents. However, the extent to which this produced advantages for the offspring may be equally dependent upon the social context of the family. The intergenerational transmission of educational advantage could be truncated in a single-parent family, in part because income differences between single- and two-parent families are dramatic—especially if the single parent is female. Because more minority parents than white parents had been divorced, separated, or widowed or had never married, minority children were far more likely to be found in a single-parent family. Among children whose parents earned B.A.'s, virtually all of the whites were living in a two-parent family; although a majority of the black and Hispanic children of B.A. parents also came from two-parent homes, the percentage was smaller. As we have said, research suggests that single-parent families have an attenuating effect on the educational attainment of children. Processes that create such a family pattern represent yet a further illustration of how the web of disadvantage, to which minorities are especially subject, can diminish the effectiveness of a social intervention such as open admissions.

Obviously, then, there is no simple answer to the apparently simple question of whether open admissions worked. The policy made a large difference in improving the life prospects of many thousands of students. It was especially critical in advancing the chances of disadvantaged minority students, for whom CUNY represented the only college opportunity. But as an intervention made at a relatively late stage in students' lives, open admissions could not overcome completely the inequalities that had been established much earlier.[5] These led, in turn, to disadvantages in the labor market, and that market itself imposed additional handicaps, which diminished the influence of open admissions in advancing minorities' socioeconomic attainments.

This catalogue of the policy's limitations should not cause us to lose sight of its substantial achievements. One may imagine the likely consequences had the program never been started. Few of the minority students would have gone to college at all. Many whites, on the other hand, had the resources to attend elsewhere. Without open admissions, ethnic inequalities in educational attainment and in the labor market would have been far greater than they are. In spite of the disparities that remain, open admissions must be counted as having contributed significantly to the promotion of educational and socioeconomic equity.

Our findings have mixed implications for the theoretical issues that we sketched in Chapter 1, which concern the role of education in advancing individuals' chances for social mobility or, conversely, in reproducing social inequality. On the one hand, open admissions did much to advance students' life prospects, and in this way it is consistent with the functional view of education as an institution that may loosen the links between social origins and social destinations. On the other hand, in important respects, our findings are also consistent with the critical view of education: although open admissions gave large numbers of minority students their only chance for college,

---

[5]Of course, each college in CUNY had mounted programs of remediation and other support services to compensate students whose high school academic preparation was weak. Overall, there were few benefits from the remedial effort, in the sense that the academic outcomes of students who needed remediation but did not take any remedial courses were hardly distinguishable from the outcomes of those who did take remediation. When students who took and passed remedial courses were evaluated separately (excluding those who failed all of their remedial courses), they were slightly better off than comparable students who received no help, but differences in college persistence and in graduation were generally very modest. At least for the initial cohorts covered in these studies, it did not appear, then, that the remedial effort did much to advance the academic life chances of underprepared students. For a full discussion and analysis of data pertinent to this question, see Lavin et al. (1981, chapter 9).

they still were more likely to be found in two-year institutions, and this placement diminished ultimate educational attainment and rewards in the job market. Whites, on the other hand, more often started in four-year institutions, which augmented their educational attainment and occupational success. This finding is consistent with the view that advantaged social origins provide a competitive edge in educational attainment so that the more privileged groups reproduce their advantages.

Open Admissions and the Issue of Academic Standards

No assessment of open admissions can be complete without a consideration of the furor over academic standards that accompanied the birth of the policy and which continued to smolder thereafter. Some feared that grading standards would become so lax that CUNY would turn into a diploma mill. CUNY graduates would then march into the labor market only to find their devalued credentials rebuffed by disdainful employers, and the hopes and dreams of those who aspired to postgraduate study would be dashed as CUNY diplomas were laughed at behind closed doors in the admissions offices of America's graduate schools. A story in the *New York Times* (1994) provides a sense of what some feared as a looming reality:

> With final examinations imminent, students . . . are not as nervous as one might expect.
>
> The grade F does not exist here. The C is fast becoming extinct. If a B looms, a student can parachute out of a course on the day of the final exam with no consequences. The median grade for undergraduates last year was an A minus.
>
> Some faculty members are campaigning against grade inflation. They want to revive the C, limit the number of times a student can repeat courses and stop allowing students to fill their transcripts with A's by dropping classes when their grades fall.

This scenario, actually a report about grading at Stanford University, bears no resemblance to the realities at CUNY under open admissions. After the program began, the university could hardly be said to have lapsed into "social promotion," giving students respectable passing grades just for showing up. Substantial differences in grade point averages separated open-admissions students from regular students. By the end of their freshman year, for example, the former had compiled a mean grade average of 2.00, just meeting the level required for graduation, and well over 40 percent of this contingent finished the first year below this threshold. Regular students—the ones who didn't need open admissions to get into CUNY—finished their initial year with a mean grade average of 2.75 (a superiority over the open-admissions group equivalent to three-quarters of a letter grade—roughly the difference between a C+ and a C- average); only about 10 percent of these students were below the minimum standard (see Lavin et al. 1981, chapter 6). That students with weaker high school backgrounds did substantially worse than better-prepared ones is consistent with what one would expect in any university where academic standards were in place.

Similarly, CUNY scarcely turned into a diploma factory. Among the students who were admitted only through open admissions, half of the minority entrants and 40 percent of the whites never got any kind of degree.

The great majority of students who went on to earn postgraduate degrees completed them at institutions outside of CUNY. Although we do not know whether their competitive position relative to graduate school applicants from other colleges declined in the era of open admissions, clearly their CUNY credentials carried weight: they gained admission to many graduate programs, and subsequently many were successful in meeting the academic standards set by these outside institutions.

What we know about former students' experiences in the job market provides no evidence that they foundered while prospective employers looked with disdain on their devalued academic credentials. Rates of unemployment were very low overall, and with each step up the credential ladder, they became lower still. Educational attainment was positively associated with such job rewards as status and earnings, leading to the conclusion that after open admissions, CUNY diplomas continued to be valuable. In one year of the mid-1980s, men who graduated with A.A. degrees from community colleges earned about $6,500 more than high school graduates, and those with B.A.'s exceeded high school graduates by more than $12,000. The boost that CUNY degrees gave to women's earnings was—because of gender inequality in pay—more modest, but still it was substantial.[6]

[6]It is possible, of course, that CUNY degrees might be less competitive in the job market than those from some other institutions. If this were the case, it would be in line with what some research suggests: that those who attend less selective colleges—which, presumably, tend to be less prestigious—receive lesser job rewards than comparable students who attend selective, and presumably more prestigious, ones (Jencks et al. 1979; Karabel and McClelland 1987; Useem and Karabel 1986). We have no data that would indicate how CUNY's diplomas stack up against

Before leaving the matter of academic standards, it should be recognized that there are other criteria that could be brought to bear, but we lack the data to do so. For example, were there substantial changes in the nature of course requirements after open admissions? Did faculty change the amount of reading that was required and the amount of written work that was demanded of students? Were there changes in the intellectual content of course material, and did any such changes reflect a softening of standards? If there were changes in requirements, could the influence of open admissions be disentangled from other determinants—for example, the influence of multicultural and women's studies perspectives on course content in the humanities and social sciences? If one could isolate these various influences, could any consensus be reached about how the changes reflected on academic rigor? We do not have the data that would be required for such evaluations, and if we did, we doubt that there would be much agreement on what they signified. Multicultural influence on the curriculum is one of the most controversial issues in higher education today.

In the data available to us, there is little to support the criticisms that under open admissions CUNY's academic processes unraveled and its diplomas became degraded. But if criticism does not square with evidence, what sense can be made of it? We think that the debate about standards is better understood as a reflection of the conflict that ensues when claims are staked by new and disenfranchised groups for greater access to education (Lavin et al. 1981). It is not surprising that higher education is one of the foremost arenas of conflict, considering how important it has become as a gatekeeper for places in the occupational system.

In many cases new groups, trying to get a foot in the door of higher education, have been disparaged for doing so. When eastern European Jews became the dominant presence at CCNY in the early part of the twentieth century, that institution was reviled as the "Jewish University of America," and when they began to attend the University of Pennsylvania, that school was derided as having the "democracy of the street car" (Vesey 1965, 288). Sometimes college communities, fearing that the prestige of their institutions will be diminished, are embarrassed by the entry of newer groups and take

---

those from other schools or whether there have been changes in their competitive strength. Leaving aside such comparisons, which involve issues beyond open admissions, the conclusion seems warranted that CUNY credentials made a substantial difference for those who earned them.

steps to control their numbers. Early in the twentieth century, for example, Columbia University modified its admissions criteria in an effort to stem the "Jewish invasion" (Wechsler 1977).[7] Efforts to control the entry of Jews into higher education were not, to be sure, accompanied by rhetoric that they were a threat to academic standards. Rather, these college communities were apprehensive that the newcomers would undermine their cultural integrity.

Efforts on the part of more privileged groups to disparage new groups seeking entry to valued institutional arenas are not limited to the Jewish experience. The political mobilization of minorities and women that emerged in the 1960s and 1970s was a crucial factor in their increased representation in higher education. But their efforts encountered resistance, not only with regard to access to college but also with regard to what would be taught. When they insisted, for example, that the cultural legacies of blacks and the accomplishments of women should be accorded legitimacy through greater representation in the curriculum, their demands were frequently disparaged as a threat to academic standards.

We think that the controversy about academic standards is best understood in terms of this history of conflict over academic access. CUNY experienced a large influx of groups that previously were only thinly represented. In skin color, manner of dress, speech, and other aspects of cultural style, the new students were frequently very different from those who preceded them. Although these differences were mostly unrelated to academic competence, it was easier to mark them as open-admissions students. There was nothing to identify whites in this way, unless their deficiencies were blatant. Unlike earlier generations of newcomers who revered their mentors, the new students were not always so deferential. Indeed, faculty were sometimes condemned as "cultural imperialists." Many of the new students demanded ethnic studies departments. The new context was undoubtedly painful for quite a few CUNY faculty members; for some it evoked a sense that their academic lives were crumbling and that their disciplines were being eroded (for discussion see Lavin et al. 1981, 37–40, 275–84, 303).

At CUNY as elsewhere in higher education, the conflict between established groups and newcomers has, to a considerable extent, been packaged in the rhetoric of "academic standards" rather than in some of the cruder disparagements acceptable earlier in this century. In practice, of course, even though the claims of new groups are judged as academically unworthy and as a

---

[7]For a discussion of similar issues at Harvard see Steinberg (1974, chapter 1).

threat to standards, the American higher education system has always had places for those with the economic resources to afford tuition, regardless of their academic qualifications.

Groups that mobilize politically in order to advance their interests often make substantial headway (Karen 1990), but their gains are not irreversible. More established groups, in reaction, often mobilize to protect their interests, and frequently they succeed in countering some of the advances that the newcomers have made. Much of the debate between proponents of equity and advocates of "excellence" can, we think, be understood in these terms.

Even though the open-admissions policy made a positive difference for students, CUNY has received few accolades for its efforts. Institutions that are easy to get into do not stand high in public esteem, partly perhaps because many of their students represent low-status groups striving for a more secure position. Because public support for policies such as CUNY's is always uncertain, open admissions was vulnerable to the attacks that accompanied it from the outset, which rose to an intense pitch when New York was engulfed by fiscal woes in the mid-1970s. The fate of the open-admissions policy and the mission of the university in the 1990s are issues that we turn to in the last chapter.

CHAPTER NINE

Open Admissions in an Era of Scarcity
Changing Educational Opportunities

The open-admissions policy that we have been analyzing throughout this book no longer exists in its original form. The program was undercut by a major fiscal crisis that befell New York City in the mid-1970s. As the city confronted bankruptcy and default, all municipal services were cut back substantially, but the most severe reductions by far were suffered by City University. CUNY was asked to offset part of its dollar shortfall by ending the century-old tradition of free tuition.

The New York crisis was a precursor of more widespread fiscal scarcity that soon engulfed many of America's cities and states. One reflection of austerity was the reduction of local and state funding for colleges and universities. Further contributing to shrinking support for higher education were reductions in direct federal aid, including financial aid for students (see Orfield 1990).

As CUNY entered an era of scarcity, debates that had accompanied the birth of open admissions were resurrected with renewed intensity. The controversy was a harbinger of a broad counterattack that was developing nationwide against the liberal educational initiatives of the 1960s—initiatives that had been part of a broad effort to promote equity in American society. Conservative voices, asserting the need for greater emphasis on educational excellence, all but drowned out those concerned with equity issues (for a sampling of the major statements, see Dougherty and Hammack 1990a, chapter 10). At CUNY debate revolved around a perceived tension between broadened opportunity for college on the one hand and the preservation of academic standards on the other. This tension between "equity and excellence" never disappeared after open admissions began—it simply faded a bit into the background. But under the pressures of fiscal austerity, controversy intensified. Although debate was not informed by systematic evidence about what was actually happening under the open-admissions program (it was still too early to know very much), the fiscal crisis furnished the context in which important policy modifications took place—not only in fiscal policies, but also in academic ones.[1] Among the changes that occurred in the wake of the crisis were these:

Admissions policy. Although the policy of guaranteed admission to the university for all high school graduates continued, entry to CUNY's senior colleges became more difficult. Before the fiscal crisis eligibility for a four-year institution required a high school average of at least 80 or graduation in the top 50 percent of one's high school class. Afterward, an average of 80 or graduation in the top 35 percent was required.

Tuition policy. As part of a state takeover of funding responsibility for the university's four-year colleges, and to relieve New York City's financial burden in supporting the community colleges, CUNY was forced to impose tuition at all of its campuses, beginning in fall 1976.[2] Partly offsetting the new charges was New York State's financial aid policy, the Tuition Assistance Program (TAP). Under the program, tuition was fully covered for full-time matriculated students from low-income families (at that time, families with incomes of about $10,000 or less). For students above this income level, TAP aid covered much smaller proportions of tuition. Part-time matriculated students were especially affected by the policy. Before, they had qualified for free tuition, but under the new policy they were typically ineligible for TAP support. Furthermore, TAP eligibility was limited to a period of eight semesters. As we have seen, substantial percentages of CUNY students needed more than four years to complete their degrees. Students who started college in the late 1970s and in the 1980s faced the loss of aid eligibility as they approached the end of their studies. Of course, TAP was not the only source of financial aid. CUNY students could avail themselves of the array of federal grant and loan programs that were available nationally to all college students. But TAP was (and is) by far the most frequently used source of aid for CUNY students.

Retention policy. In an effort to encourage students who entered CUNY with weak high school preparation, the university had been applying relatively flexible standards of academic progress. Students were not to be dismissed for academic reasons during the grace period of the freshman year, and each

---

[1] A full description of CUNY's fiscal crisis and of the repercussions in the 1970s may be seen in Lavin et al. (1981, chapter 11).

[2] Tuition was charged at the levels in effect at the colleges of the State University of New York (SUNY). By 1980 tuition was $950 per year, considerably above the average of $720 at other public institutions. The disparity was especially wide between the CUNY figure and the average tuition in public two-year institutions, $383 (Grant and Eiden 1982, table 129).

CUNY college implemented retention criteria as it saw fit. In the wake of the fiscal crisis, a more stringent university-wide retention policy was adopted. Students were required to achieve a 2.0 or C average—the minimum required for graduation—by the time they had completed twenty-five credits.[3] Previously, CUNY colleges generally had not required a 2.0 average until students had completed more than sixty credits, and at some schools the 2.0 threshold was set at ninety credits or more.[4]

Another policy change made it more difficult for students to withdraw without penalty from courses in which they were doing marginal or unsatisfactory work. Students who did not meet the new academic progress standards faced a loss of satisfactory academic standing, which would in turn jeopardize their New York State financial aid.

Skills assessment program. Primarily to gauge the need for remedial programs, the university had administered basic skills tests in reading and math to most entering freshmen in 1970 and 1971. In addition, most CUNY colleges used other assessment procedures, including further skills testing and reviews of students' high school preparation. Based upon guidelines that were developed at each college, such information was used to identify students who needed remedial work. Placement in remedial courses was often mandatory, but in some cases students were simply encouraged to register for such work. After 1976 a more far-reaching, centralized policy of skills assessment was adopted. All incoming freshmen were required to take skills-assessment tests in reading, writing, and mathematics. University-wide minimum competency standards were set, and students who did not meet them were required to take remedial courses in their area(s) of weakness. Furthermore, these tests functioned as a gateway to the junior year of college: even if their academic

---

[3]Credit completion is not the same as credits earned. A student might attempt twenty-five credits, but if he or she flunked one or more courses, not all of them would be earned. The new CUNY policy, in effect, stipulated that a 2.0 average would be required after twenty-five credits were attempted. In addition, minimum grade point averages were designated for initial credits attempted. For example, after twelve credits were completed, a grade point average of 1.5 is required for satisfactory standing, and a 1.75 average is required for completion of between thirteen and twenty-four credits.

[4]The new standard was far more stringent than that in effect at many colleges around the country. Most of the colleges in the SUNY system are much more permissive, allowing students to complete at least 60 credits before invoking the 2.0 standard; schools in the California State University system simply require that students attain the 2.0 by the time 120 credits have been completed.

averages were strong enough, students were not to be allowed entry to their junior year unless they had passed all three tests. Graduates of community colleges could not transfer to senior colleges unless they had passed all of the tests.

Assessing the Outcomes of Policy Changes

What has been the impact of these changes in fiscal and academic policies upon educational attainment at the university, especially among the many minority and low-income students toward whom open admissions was targeted? In a variety of ways that we shall describe, like diminished proportions of freshmen placed in four-year colleges and decline in such bottom-line outcomes as graduation rates, the policy changes provide grounds for thinking that opportunity at CUNY has narrowed. We shall examine this fundamental issue in this chapter.

To assess the impact of policy changes at the university on students' academic careers, we shall compare two classes whose entry to CUNY was separated by a decade. The first consists of students who entered in 1970, the initial freshman class to enroll after open admissions was inaugurated. A substantial portion of these students' academic careers—their first six years—occurred entirely within the framework of the original policy. We shall compare this class with one that entered in 1980, which experienced the full force of the policy modifications that we have described. Such a comparison can provide a sense of how policy changes affected college careers, and, ultimately, how these reflect on the fate of CUNY's open-admissions policy.

The data set for these comparisons is not the same as the one we have used in the analyses of the preceding chapters. The most obvious difference is in our use of data for the 1980 cohort. This contingent consists of 31,890 students. For a sample of 11,625, or 36 percent of this population, detailed information was collected on socioeconomic and demographic characteristics, educational background, attitudes about education, the likelihood of having to work while in college, college placement (senior or community college), academic performance, and graduation. The college performance and graduation data cover the ten-year period from fall 1980 through spring 1990. They are drawn from official university files and reflect graduation from CUNY colleges but not from institutions outside the university.

The file for the 1970 freshmen contains comparable data for a sample of

13,525 cases, or 38 percent of that class (35,515 students). Although it contains CUNY academic performance information for only five years (from fall 1970 through spring 1975), it includes official graduation data for the ten-year period ending in spring 1980, the same number of years for describing graduation that is available for the 1980 cohort. Although the 1970 cohort is one of the three (1970, 1971, 1972) included in the follow-up sample that we have used in the preceding analyses of this volume, the number of cases that represent this cohort in the follow-up, 2,020, is far smaller than the 13,525 in the original 1970 sample. Because of the much larger pool of respondents in the latter, and because graduation was measured in the same manner as for the 1980 cohort (through official university data), we have chosen to use the original file for comparison with the file for the 1980 cohort.[5]

In assessing the influence of policy changes at the university, we shall compare the cohorts in terms of a variety of outcomes. An important starting point is the level at which students begin college. Because community colleges have a net negative influence on ultimate educational attainment, initial level of college entry is an important aspect of educational opportunity. We shall consider this issue by examining whether there was a change in the proportion of students placed in CUNY's community colleges. Within the latter schools, curriculum is another influence on educational attainment: students in liberal arts programs are more likely than those in vocational tracks to transfer to four-year colleges and complete a B.A. degree. Whether there was a change in the proportion of entrants enrolled in the liberal arts curriculum is a second question that we shall address.

Might there have been changes in students' success in college, as measured by their grades and their progress in earning degree credits? Ultimately, what were the graduation chances of students in the 1980 cohort relative to those in the 1970? Of special importance is change in the proportions of students completing a B.A. degree, which is an economically more valuable credential than the A.A. We shall also consider whether, among B.A. recipients, there were cohort differences in the number of years required to complete degree requirements. Time to degree is a significant equity consideration, for it

[5]The graduation data for the original sample of the 1970 cohort do not contain the more extensive follow-up survey information on degrees earned at non-CUNY colleges or on graduate degrees. Because we have no such data for the 1980 cohort, we have compared the two cohorts using the official CUNY graduation records.

affects when individuals can begin to put their educational credentials to work for them in the labor market; additionally, it is the single most important influence on the likelihood of completing graduate school.

The assessments we shall be making are more complicated than they may seem. Policy changes at the university are only one among a number of possible explanations for differences in the academic success of the 1970 and 1980 cohorts. If B.A. completion rates have declined, for example, the difference could be due to modifications in CUNY's fiscal and academic policies that made college completion more difficult. But such a decline might instead be due to changes in the socioeconomic and educational backgrounds of the two cohorts. If 1980 entrants typically were less qualified academically than the 1970 group, their graduation rates would be expected to be lower. A third possibility is that policy change and cohort composition factors might be interwoven. Family income, for instance, might have influenced perseverance in college among 1980 entrants, but not those who started in 1970. It might be that the ability of low-income students to stay in school was diminished only after free tuition was abolished.

College completion might also be influenced by macroeconomic factors that are not included in our study—changes in unemployment rates, in types and availability of federal financial aid, and in relative economic returns to secondary and postsecondary education.[6]

[6]Even if we had included measures of such factors in our assessments, it is not clear whether they would contribute to the explanation of cohort differences in academic success. A rising rate of unemployment, for example, might reduce the "opportunity costs" of attending college, thus inducing more students to persist. On the other hand, unemployment might diminish disposable personal income, thus producing lower rates of college completion. At a public urban university like CUNY, the effect of reduced personal income is especially problematic, for in order to lower college costs many students undoubtedly enroll part-time rather than leaving school completely.

The rate of economic return to college graduates relative to high school graduates has been thought to influence college enrollment and persistence (Freeman 1976), but the direction of such an influence also seems unclear. When the difference in rate of return is widest in favor of college credentials, it would be expected to produce greater incentive to stay in college. The difference in rate of return narrowed in the 1970s (Freeman 1976) and widened in the 1980s (Fitzgerald undated), yet college persistence rates in the 1980s actually declined, not only at CUNY, but nationally (Grubb 1989).

Changes in the types and availability of federal financial aid in the 1980s—away from grants and toward loans—probably had a negative effect on students' ability to stay in school. On the other hand, need-based grants from New York State's Tuition Assistance Program were by far the most important source of aid for CUNY students. Overall then, there are no clear hypotheses that can be generated about the effects of economic factors upon students' academic careers.

In sum, differences in the academic success of the 1970 and 1980 cohorts could be a result of a variety of factors that cannot be completely disentangled: policy change, differences in the educational preparation and socioeconomic composition of the 1970 and 1980 cohorts, interactions between policy change and cohort characteristics, and unmeasured macroeconomic variables. In addition, unmeasured variables that pertain to cohort composition also could have an effect. English language proficiency undoubtedly affects academic attainments, for example, yet we have no measures of such proficiency that are comparable across cohorts. The proportion of students for whom English was not their native language was probably larger in the 1980 cohort than in the 1970.

Difficulty in unambiguously identifying policy effects is common in such assessments as we are making, and we should acknowledge at the outset that we cannot demonstrate unequivocally that policy changes at CUNY explain cohort differences in college outcomes. Nonetheless, this uncertainty does not preclude assessments of the sources of change in CUNY students' academic careers. Our data analyses will provide a clear idea of the changes that have occurred and a reasonable sense of the factors that seem to have played an influential role. We shall begin with a description of differences between 1970 and 1980 cohorts in a variety of academic outcomes. In the case of some but not all outcomes, we have carried out multivariate (regression) analyses that provide some insight into the processes that explain cohort differences.[7] Typically, we have conducted one analysis for each cohort in order to get an idea of the comparability of the academic process in each group. Then, to assess the determinants of cohort differences, we have done an analysis for both cohorts combined, in which a variable denoting cohort membership has been included.

Comparison of the 1970 and 1980 Cohorts
FRESHMAN ENROLLMENTS

We have not undertaken a systematic analysis of CUNY enrollment changes that were associated with its fiscal crisis. Nonetheless, it is helpful to provide at least an overview. With the fiscal crisis came a drastic decline in freshman

---

[7]To carry out analyses for each of the many outcome variables described would have produced an unwieldy volume of data. A full set of analyses would require another very lengthy manuscript.

enrollments. Between 1975, the last year before the crisis, and 1976, there was a drop of nearly 11,000 freshmen—a decrease of 30 percent (table 9.1). By 1980 there had been a small recovery, but the number of entrants was still well below the 1975 level. In fact it remained below the number of freshmen who had entered in 1970.

What caused the decline is not entirely clear, but the events of the fiscal crisis likely played some role. The exact nature of that role does not, however, correspond to what one might expect. One might think that with the imposition of tuition, the number of low-income students would have diminished. Because minority students had, as a group, far more meager resources than whites, this should be reflected in lower enrollments among blacks and Hispanics. CUNY's annual census data, however, show no such decline. The enrollment of black students fell off only slightly with the fiscal crisis, and that of Hispanics actually increased somewhat. Indeed, the CUNY freshman enrollment drop is accounted for almost entirely by a precipitous decline in the entry of white freshmen after 1975. We are not certain what was happening to them, but it seems likely that they decided to go elsewhere to college. A study by Lavin and Murtha (1984) showed that whites in the 1980 CUNY applicant pool disproportionately enrolled in Catholic colleges in the metropolitan area as well as in the colleges of the SUNY system. In effect then, it appears that students with more resources were the ones who went elsewhere after 1975. That the enrollment of minority students was little affected could be due partly to the availability of financial aid from New York State and partly to the possibility that in the post crisis era students tried to keep college costs down by enrolling part-time.

LEVEL OF ENTRY TO THE UNIVERSITY

In its original form, the open-admissions policy was baccalaureate oriented— designed to broaden the pathway to four-year colleges, especially among minority students who had been underrepresented in those institutions before 1970. As we have said, one result of the 1975–76 crisis was a change in admissions policy that made entry to senior colleges more difficult. A more stringent policy would be expected to shift a portion of freshmen enrollments away from CUNY's four-year colleges toward its two-year ones, and exactly such a shift occurred. When open admissions was inaugurated in 1970, well over half—57 percent—of the students in the first freshman class enrolled in CUNY's senior colleges (table 9.1). The proportion of freshmen entering

Table 9.1 Changes in the Proportion of Students Entering Senior Colleges, 1969–80

Freshman Cohort	% Entering Senior Colleges	Size of Cohort[a]
1969	57	17,645
1970	57	31,596
1975	53	36,606
1976	35	25,741
1980	33	26,936

Source: CUNY annual censuses.

[a]Figures in this table do not include students admitted to CUNY through its special admissions programs, SEEK and College Discovery, which are targeted mainly to minority students.

these B.A. institutions had remained stable over the program's first six years, and by 1975 a clear majority (53 percent) continued to enter them. Immediately after the change in admissions policy, the proportion of freshmen who entered senior colleges plummeted to 35 percent. This figure remained consistent thereafter, and in 1980 a third of entrants started at four-year schools.[8] In terms of freshman enrollments, then, CUNY was transformed into an institution centered around its community colleges.[9] Moreover, even though the minority presence in CUNY continued to grow after 1975, the proportion of black and Hispanic students entering four-year colleges declined more sharply than did the proportion of whites (table 9.2); among the latter there was a 23 percent drop in the proportions entering senior colleges, but among black entrants it was 35 percent and among Hispanics 45 percent.

To what extent was the changed admissions policy responsible for the dramatic shift in the distribution of freshmen across the tiers of CUNY? One

[8]Some CUNY colleges offer both A.A. and B.A. programs, so they cannot simply be classified as senior or community colleges. At these schools, only freshmen entering B.A. programs were classified as senior college entrants.

[9]Our analyses do not include students who entered CUNY through its special admissions programs (called SEEK in senior colleges and College Discovery in community colleges), which predate open admissions and that consist heavily of minority students. Inclusion of these students in the analyses would not alter the substance of our conclusion that there was a substantial shift of freshmen away from senior colleges and into community colleges.

Table 9.2 Freshman Placement in Senior and Community Colleges, 1970 and 1980, by Ethnicity

| | Percentages | | | |
| | 1970[a] | | 1980 | |
Ethnicity	Senior	Community	Senior	Community
White	60	40	46	54
Black	37	63	24	76
Hispanic	47	53	26	74
All students	57	43	33	67

Source: 1970 and 1980 cohort files.

[a]Placement percentages for this cohort have been weighted to correct for overrepresentation of senior college students.

way to approach this question is to identify the fractions of students in the 1970 and 1980 cohorts who would have been eligible for a senior college under the original and the revised admissions policies. Such an assessment makes it evident that the more stringent standard put in place in 1976 diminished the proportion who qualified for entry to four-year institutions. Among the 1970 freshmen, 63 percent were eligible for a senior college under the original policy; but had this contingent been subject to the new standard, only half would have been eligible. Among the 1980 entrants, 43 percent would have been eligible for a senior college under the original admissions criteria; 36 percent actually were eligible under the new criteria to which they were subject.

Although these figures leave no doubt about the effects of the changed admissions policy in diminishing eligibility for senior colleges, they suggest also that not all of the decline was due to tougher entry standards. The proportion of 1980 entrants who could have gotten into a B.A. school was lower under both the original and the new policies than the proportion of qualified entrants in the 1970 contingent, implying that changes in the academic background of the 1980 group also contributed to their diminished eligibility. The 1980 cohort contained new types of students who were hardly visible at all in 1970. One type was the student who had earned a high school general equivalency diploma, or GED—these students accounted for about 15 percent of the 1980 entrants (table 9.3). Typically, these individuals had dropped out of high school but later completed requirements by passing the GED examination. CUNY's central admissions office converted scores on this examination into high school average equivalents; based on these scores, hardly any of these applicants were eligible for a senior college and, overwhelmingly, they entered two-year schools.

Another kind of student present in the 1980 cohort was missing documentation about the high school record. Some of these students had graduated from foreign high schools or schools that used nontraditional grading systems; others were admitted directly by their CUNY college rather than through the university's central admissions office, which at that time did not have a mechanism for later collecting the high school record data. We think that most of these students were immigrants or the children of immigrants from a diverse array of Asian and Latin American countries, a source that represents a rising wave in the New York City populations. Such students constituted a negligible proportion of the 1970 cohort but 15 percent of the 1980 group. More than 90 percent of them enrolled in community colleges.

Taken together, these GEDs and students missing high school records made up 30 percent of the 1980 cohort, compared with less than 1 percent in 1970. The following contrast provides a sense of how their numbers affected the proportion of 1980 entrants eligible for CUNY's senior colleges: if we leave these students aside, 44 percent of that cohort qualified for four-year colleges (under the original 1970 admissions criteria, 52 percent would have qualified). When this new freshman element is added in, the proportion falls to the figure we mentioned earlier: 36 percent.

In effect, then, changes in both CUNY admissions policy and in cohort academic characteristics diminished the proportion of 1980 freshmen who were eligible for senior colleges, and thus the share of students who actually entered these institutions. Some of the decline in senior college placement, however, was probably due to factors other than the mechanics of changed admissions standards. Regression analyses suggest that the imposition of tuition might have affected students' level of college preference. These analyses show that income affected preferences in the 1980 cohort but not in 1970. Low-income students in 1980 were about 10 percent more likely to choose two-year schools than students who were comparable in other ways but were better off economically. Quite possibly, tuition triggered a change in student thinking about college choices in 1980. Under free tuition, low-income stu-

Table 9.3 Social and Academic Background of Students in the 1970 and 1980 Cohorts

Percentages, Except as Noted

	Senior College Entrants		Community College Entrants		All Entrants	
	1970	1980	1970	1980	1970[a]	1980
Ethnicity						
White	88	55	75	33	82	40
Black	5	24	15	37	9	33
Hispanic	7	21	11	30	8	27
Father's education						
Less than high school	35	37	42	52	38	47
High school graduate	35	28	36	29	35	29
Some college	17	15	13	10	15	12
College grad. or more	13	20	9	9	11	12
Mother's education						
Less than high school	29	36	37	49	33	45
High school graduate	51	39	49	35	50	36
Some college	12	14	9	10	11	11
College grad. or more	8	12	5	6	6	8
Family income						
$30,000 or higher[b]	20	12	17	4	19	6
Less than $7,500[b]	5	22	9	42	5	36
Female	45	61	48	60	46	60
Age 20 or older	2	14	8	48	5	37
Married	0.7	5	2	16	1	13
High school background						
Mean high school average	82.4	82.9	73.7	73.6	78.7	77.4
<70	3	3	26	27	13	17
70–74.9	9	6	34	34	20	23
75–79.9	23	18	27	24	25	21
80–84.9	30	37	10	10	21	21
85+	36	37	4	5	22	18

Table 9.3 *Continued*

Percentages, Except as Noted

	Senior College Entrants		Community College Entrants		All Entrants	
	1970	1980	1970	1980	1970[a]	1980
Top half of class	84	89	38	50	64	69
GED[c]	0	5	0.2	20	0.1	15
No data on high school average and rank[d]	0	4	1	20	0.4	15
College prep. courses	14.2	12.9	11.5	9.8	13.0	11.0
Degree aspirations						
A.A. or less	1	2	29	23	13	16
B.A.	33	34	34	38	34	36
Postgraduate degree	65	64	38	39	53	47

Source: 1970 and 1980 cohort files.

[a]Figures weighted to adjust for overrepresentation of senior college students in sample.

[b]Expressed in 1980 dollars.

[c]General equivalency diploma. For admissions purposes, scores on GED test are converted into high school averages by CUNY's admissions office.

[d]These data are unavailable because students graduated from foreign high schools or from schools that use nontraditional grading systems, or because students were admitted directly by their college rather than by CUNY's central admissions office.

dents who aspired to a B.A. could feel encouraged to enroll in a senior college, knowing that they might easily shift from full-time to part-time study if, for example, economic exigencies required them to take a full-time job. But when tuition was required such students might have faced a dilemma, for a shift to part-time study would risk a loss of financial aid. Consequently, economic considerations probably carried greater weight in 1980 for students' perceptions of their ability to persevere in college; low-income students may have been more likely to hedge their bets by taking the shortest and least expensive path to a degree of some kind. So the imposition of tuition may well have pushed such students toward two-year colleges.

In short, some of the decline in entry to senior colleges is due to the effect of changed admissions policy, some is due to cohort differences in academic characteristics, and some is probably due to ways in which policy is interwoven with the socioeconomic composition of the cohorts. But whatever the mix, students in the 1980s were much more likely to start college in two-year schools. As we have seen, community college entry constrains ultimate educational attainment, adds substantially to the time needed for completion of a B.A. degree, and produces less desirable outcomes in the labor market. In this light, educational opportunity clearly was not as great for 1980 entrants as it was in 1970. And because minority students were affected more than whites, opportunity was especially narrowed for them.

CURRICULUM PLACEMENT

Curriculum placement in the community college is a second important aspect of opportunity in higher education. As we have noted, the major distinction is between liberal arts transfer and career/vocational tracks. Both nationally (see Brint and Karabel 1989, chapter 4) and at CUNY, evidence indicates that placement in the career/vocational tracks diminishes the chances of transfer to a four-year college, reduces the likelihood of earning a B.A., and raises the chances of being employed in a low-status occupation. Notwithstanding this evidence, student perceptions about community colleges, and, in particular, their vocational programs, seemed to become increasingly favorable throughout the 1970s. During that period sensationalized media reports focused on B.A. recipients who were driving taxis or were otherwise underemployed.[10] Fueled perhaps in part by the media climate, the proportion of A.A. degrees awarded in occupational curricula rose from 43 to 63 percent between 1970 and 1980 (Brint and Karabel 1989, 117, table 4.1).[11]

CUNY results are consistent with this national trend: the proportion of community college students enrolled in vocational programs went from 56 percent in 1970 to more than 75 percent in 1980 (table 9.4). This change was

[10]While the returns to B.A. degrees declined somewhat, what the public discussion generally overlooked was that the job market prospects of those with less than a B.A. were even worse.

[11]Of course, more is involved than media reports. A fuller discussion can be seen in Brint and Karabel (1989, 116–20).

Table 9.4 Community College Entrants Placed in Career/Vocational Curricula, 1970 and 1980

	Percentages	
	1970	1980
White	50	76
Black	72	79
Hispanic	74	76
All students	56	77

Source: 1970 and 1980 cohort files.

produced almost entirely by a large shift in the proportion of whites who opted for these programs in 1980. Among minority students there was little change: about 75 percent from each cohort enrolled in vocational programs. As a result of the increased popularity of these tracks among whites, ethnic differences all but disappeared in 1980.

The process of curriculum selection seemed to change between 1970 and 1980. In 1970 older community college entrants from nonacademic high school tracks whose degree aspirations were relatively low (less than a B.A.) were much less likely than others to choose liberal arts.[12] In 1980 social and educational background characteristics did not significantly affect curriculum choice. Community college students, whatever their characteristics, were much more likely to enroll in a vocational course of study. Perhaps as a result of negative perceptions about the New York–area labor market and about the leverage of liberal arts in getting good jobs, these students opted overwhelmingly for vocational programs. Additionally, because tuition was required, they may have decided against the transfer-oriented liberal arts curriculum in favor of vocational programs, with their more apparent and immediate connection to jobs.

[12]For each cohort we regressed curriculum preference on a number of independent variables, including parents' education, income, ethnicity, age, gender, high school background, degree aspirations, marital status, and full-time employment. One equation was estimated for the 1970 cohort, one for the 1980, and one for a pooled data set consisting of both cohorts.

CREDITS, GRADES, AND DROPOUT

The level of placement in CUNY's colleges and curricula is only a starting point for describing cohort differences in college experience. Of equal importance is this question: How successful were students academically? A central consideration is their rate of progress, as indicated by the credits they earned toward graduation. By various measures it is evident that the students in the 1980 cohort progressed more slowly than did their 1970 counterparts (table 9.5). In their initial year of school, the 1980 entrants in CUNY's four- and two-year colleges earned about six fewer credits—the equivalent of two fewer courses—than the 1970 students. Although students in both cohorts typically lagged behind the standard of thirty credits that is traditionally associated with completion of the freshman year, the 1980 students were especially far behind. Indeed, community college students in 1980 who finished their first year, had, on average, only about one semester's worth of credits to show for it.

The immediate reason that 1980 entrants earned fewer credits in their first year is that they attempted fewer. Among senior college students the proportion who attempted fewer than twenty-four credits over the entire freshman year almost tripled, and among those in community colleges it almost doubled from an already high level. CUNY's remedial programs accounted for part of this decline in attempted credits. Under the new policy of university-wide skills testing, placement in remedial courses was supposed to be mandatory for those who failed the tests; indeed, 90 percent of 1980 entrants who failed one or more tests were so placed. Although students in the early 1970s also took academic skills tests before they entered CUNY, there was no university-wide policy that specified minimum passing scores, nor was there a uniform set of regulations to decree that the tests must be used for placement purposes. Complex placement criteria varied from college to college; of those who performed poorly on the 1970 tests, a smaller proportion were put into remedial classes.[13]

---

[13]In 1970 the university used specific scores on reading and math tests to designate students as needing "some" or "intensive" remediation. These were simply guidelines, however, and each campus had considerable autonomy in formulating criteria for placing students in remedial courses. For a more detailed discussion of CUNY's remedial programs in the original open admissions era, see Lavin et al. (1981, chapter 9). Different tests were used in 1970 and 1980. In 1970 they included a reading test and a numerical competence test selected from the Stanford achievement test battery (Stanford Achievement Test 1964, 1965). In 1980 three tests were administered to all entering freshmen: a writing test and a math test, both of which were locally developed, and a reading test developed by Educational Testing Service.

Overall, under the changed skills-testing policy, the percentage of freshmen taking remediation grew substantially: in senior colleges almost two-thirds of the 1980 freshmen were placed in remedial courses, compared with one-third in 1970, and in two-year schools, the proportion jumped from half in 1970 to well over 80 percent. Not only did the proportion placed in remediation grow, but so, too, did the number of courses they took. In effect, remedial courses occupied a larger portion of classroom time for the 1980 cohort than it did for the 1970 entrants.

The increase in remedial placement may have been due in part to a decline in entering students' academic skills. Because the skills tests used in 1970 were different from those used in 1980 and we have no way of converting them to a common metric, we are unable to specify how much of the increase might be a result of weaker academic preparation in the 1980 cohort. Some of it probably was due to a decline in preparedness, for our data (table 9.3) on high school background show that 1980 entrants took fewer college preparatory courses than those in 1970. Nonetheless, it seems unlikely that changes of the magnitude shown in table 9.5 could have occurred independently of modifications in testing and placement policy. Especially in CUNY's senior colleges, where very few students were found with GEDs or without high school background data, a doubling of the proportions taking remedial courses could hardly be attributed to a decline in the academic quality of students.[14] Because students had to take more tests in 1980 than were required in 1970 and because very specific placement rules were in effect, placement of a greater percentage of 1980 entrants in remediation was to be expected.

Remedial courses typically carry no academic credits toward graduation or carry fewer credits than regular courses for the class hours required.[15] Whatever might be their ultimate benefits, they create a drag on the number of credits attempted by freshmen. Although these courses are not the only

---

[14]A word is in order about the comparability of high school averages across the two cohorts. We addressed this issue by converting high school averages into Scholastic Aptitude Test (SAT) scores for those in each cohort who had such scores. The results indicated that high school averages in the 1970 and 1980 cohorts were comparable.

[15]Courses designated as "remedial," "compensatory," and "developmental" are included in our calculations of exposure to remedial instruction. In CUNY usage remedial courses carry no credit toward graduation. Compensatory and developmental courses provide some credit but require additional class hours.

Table 9.5 Academic Progress at Selected Time Periods for 1970 and 1980 Cohorts

Progress Indicator	Senior Colleges		Community Colleges	
	1970	1980	1970	1980
Remediation in freshman year				
% taking remediation	33	64	50	86
Mean number of courses	1.8	3.0	2.1	3.2
Credits attempted				
Mean in 1st semester	14	12	12	8
% <12 in 1st semester	12	32	43	72
Mean in 1st year	28	25	26	20
% <24 in 1st year	10	28	35	67
Mean in 2d year	29	28	27	25
% <24 in 2d year	10	12	33	38
Mean per semester in attendance[a]	13.6	12.5	11.9	9.7
For persisters	14.1	13.6	13.3	11.5
For dropouts	12.7	11.6	11.2	8.9
% part-time students[b]	17	29	45	67
Credits earned				
Mean in 1st semester	12	9	9	6
% <9 in 1st semester	16	38	47	73
Mean in 1st year	25	20	20	14
% <18 in 1st year	13	36	40	67
Mean in 2d year	26	22	22	19
% <18 in 2d year	14	26	32	45
Cumulative earned[c]	90	68	39	32
For persisters	117	109	65	65
For dropouts	47	29	23	16
Mean per semester[a]	11.4	9.2	8	6
For persisters	13.0	11.9	11.9	9.8
For dropouts	8.8	6.8	5.7	4.2
Ratio of credits earned/attempted				
1st year	.88	.79	.74	.70
2d year	.88	.79	.79	.74

Table 9.5 *Continued*

Progress Indicator	Senior Colleges		Community Colleges	
	1970	1980	1970	1980
Grade point average				
Mean in 1st year	2.5	2.4	2.2	2.1
% <2.0 in 1st year	21	23	37	35
Mean in 2d year	2.6	2.4	2.3	2.2
% <2.0 in 2d year	18	26	28	33
Cumulative[c]	2.5	2.3	1.9	1.8
For persisters	2.8	2.8	2.5	2.6
For dropouts	2.0	1.8	1.5	1.4
Dropout rate after freshman year[d]	10	18	20	31
Transfer rate from 2- to 4-year schools[c]	—	—	27	20

Source: 1970 and 1980 cohort files.

[a] Total after five years, divided by the number of semesters in attendance.

[b] Percent registered for an average of fewer than twelve credits per semester.

[c] After five years.

[d] Rate consists of individuals not present for the fall semester of the second year who had not reenrolled after ten semesters.

constraint on credit load in the first year—holding a full-time job is another—they are by far the most important.[16]

Cohort differences in rates of progress continued after the first year of college. On average, for each semester of enrollment, 1980 entrants both attempted and earned fewer credits than 1970 entrants; mostly because of full-time jobs and of remedial courses they were more likely to be part-time students (registered for fewer than twelve credits per term), especially in the community colleges. Students in the 1980 cohort also had more difficulty in completing courses successfully: they showed a decline in the proportion of

[16] This conclusion is suggested by analyses in which we regressed credits attempted in the freshman year on a number of determinants, including the number of remedial courses taken, full-time employment, ethnicity, age, gender, high school background, and family income.

credits that they earned relative to the number they attempted. Senior college entrants in the 1980 cohort earned 79 percent of the credits that they attempted, compared with 88 percent among the 1970 contingent. A decline is also evident for community college students, who in general had lower academic batting averages than their senior college peers.

Five years after starting college, the 1980 contingent lagged behind the 1970 students in total credits. Partly, this was because the 1980 group had more difficulty persisting in college, and when they dropped out, they did so earlier. Indeed, dropout after the freshman year almost doubled among senior college students and it increased by more than 50 percent among community college entrants. Credits earned in the freshman year are by far the most important determinant of return for a second year (Lavin et al. 1981, table 7.4, 172), and partly as a result of slower initial progress in earning degree credits, more 1980 entrants may have become discouraged. Because more of them left college earlier, the average number of credits earned in this cohort was diminished still further.

According to multivariate analyses that we carried out for both senior and community college entrants (results are not shown), the weaker performance of the 1980 cohort in earning credits is not entirely explained by academic and socioeconomic differences from the 1970 cohort.[17] Among senior college entrants, for example, less than half of the disparity between cohorts in the total number of credits earned is accounted for by differences in high school academic preparation and in social background. Even in community colleges, where credit differences were smaller, background factors explain only slightly more than half of the disparity.

Over the five-year period available for tracking students' academic records, the influence of remediation on credit accumulation waned, and other factors grew in importance. One such factor was employment: those who held full-time jobs earned fewer credits than others. The academic progress of working students probably was slower because they more often had to register as part-timers in order to balance the demands of school and work. Moreover,

[17]These analyses were done separately for senior and community colleges. We regressed total credits earned on a variety of independent variables, including ethnicity, parents' education, family income, age, gender, high school record, number of remedial courses taken, and full-time employment. We carried out one regression for the 1970 cohort, one for the 1980, and one for both cohorts combined. In the combined regressions we entered a dummy variable to represent cohort. This approach allowed us to assess how much of the difference between cohorts remained after controlling for composition variables.

some of them may have found themselves overextended academically and forced to drop courses as a result. The proportion of students holding full-time jobs was likely larger in the 1980 cohort.[18] Income also made a difference among the 1980 entrants: low-income students, whether they worked or not, accumulated fewer total credits. Among 1970 entrants, however, income was not related to credits. This difference between cohorts suggests that some 1980 entrants reduced the number of courses they took each term as a way of controlling college tuition costs.

Another likely contributor to slower progress in the 1980 cohort was a decline in the number of available course sections. Although we have no systematic data, discussions with students and administrators indicate that because of continuing fiscal constraints, fewer course sections were offered. As a result, students sometimes had to wait a semester or even more to enroll in courses needed to meet distribution or major requirements.

The academic picture for the 1980 cohort was a darker one in still other ways. The grades compiled by the 1980 entrants were lower than those of the 1970 contingent; by the end of their second year, 1980 senior college students had academic averages that were down by a fifth of a letter grade, and community college entrants were down by about a tenth of a grade. These are not dramatic differences, but they are associated with a decline after the second year of college in the proportions of students with satisfactory academic standing, that is, with a grade point average of at least 2.0, or C—the minimum required for graduation. Overall, at the end of five years, cumulative GPAs were modestly lower in the 1980 cohort, but only among dropouts. We suspect that relative to the context of the 1970s, the more stringent financial and academic requirements in place for the 1980 cohort made it more difficult for some students to protect their averages, so that more dropped out and had weaker records when they left.

For example, some students may have been affected by CUNY's more stringent policy on course withdrawals. Previously, those who were having academic trouble in one or more courses could withdraw fairly late in the semester. Subsequently, late withdrawal became more difficult. The new requirement for satisfactory academic standing—that students attain a 2.0 average by the time they had completed just twenty-five credits, may also have

[18]Full-time employment seems to have made a larger difference in 1980 than in the 1970 cohort, and we think that students in the latter more often held full-time jobs, but because of differences in the measurement of work in the two cohorts, we are not sure.

discouraged students who were having early difficulty. Perhaps these factors account in part for the higher early dropout rates in the 1980 cohort.

For community college entrants who aspire to a B.A. degree, transfer to a four-year institution is obviously a critical component of the educational attainment process. Rates of transfer (after five years) fell from 27 percent for the 1970 entrants to 20 percent among the 1980 cohort. Although we did not conduct any systematic multivariate analyses of transfer in these cohorts, it is worth sketching out some of the ways in which policy changes might help to account for diminished transfer rates. Under the university's new skills-assessment program, skills tests functioned as the gateway to the junior year of college, preventing students from going beyond sixty credits unless they had passed all of the tests. Among those who did not pass all of them on entry, some continued to fail on retest.[19] Although there is no limit on the number of times a student may retake these tests, a second failure would seem to be especially discouraging to community college students, for entry to the junior year generally requires a switch to a four-year institution.[20] In addition, some senior colleges set higher passing scores on the tests than the minimum required by the university, so some transfers who passed the tests at their original institutions would have been required to take additional remedial courses as they began their junior year in their new college. Furthermore, four-year schools no longer accepted automatically all of the credits that transfers brought with them from CUNY's two-year institutions. These changes may have discouraged some students from moving into B.A. programs. Moreover, because vocational curricula diminish the probability of transfer (Alba and Lavin 1981; Lavin et al. 1981, chapter 8), the substantial increase in the share of students found in those tracks probably contributed also to the 1980 cohort's lower rate of movement to four-year schools.

To summarize this review of academic progress, the 1980 cohort clearly enjoyed less academic success than did the 1970 group. Partly because of the presence of new kinds of students—GEDs and others with weak academic credentials—a smaller proportion of entrants was eligible to enter four-year

[19]CUNY had not established effective procedures in the 1980s for integrating retest information into its centralized data system. Although we know that students failed skills tests more than once, we do not know how often this happened.

[20]Two CUNY institutions are exceptions: John Jay College and the College of Staten Island are comprehensive colleges, offering extensive A.A. and B.A. programs, so A.A. students would not need to transfer to a new college if they continued on toward the B.A.

colleges. But the proportional increase in community college enrollments was also a consequence of the more selective admissions policy that was put in place after 1975. We suspect further that the introduction of tuition led some low-income applicants, who otherwise might have attended senior colleges, to think that they should opt for shorter and thus less expensive A.A. programs. At whatever level they started, the 1980 cohort lagged behind the 1970 in the pace of academic progress. The slowness of their progress in earning degree credits was in part a result of weaker academic preparation, but it was also a consequence of changes in CUNY's academic system that required remediation for more students. Whatever may have been the merits of remedial courses, they retarded credit accumulation, especially in the freshman year. Possibly because students were discouraged over the slowness of their start and because they completed a lower percentage of the courses they took, they were more likely to drop out of CUNY after their freshman year. Differences in rates of progress persisted after the first year. On average, for each semester they were enrolled, 1980 entrants earned fewer credits. For the credits they did accumulate, they earned lower grades. This pattern of slower progress undoubtedly was due in part to the difficulties faced by 1980 students in their efforts to juggle outside obligations, a full-time load of courses, and the need to remain eligible for financial aid.

GRADUATION

The weaker academic records compiled by students in the 1980 cohort translated into lower ten-year graduation rates. Judged by any measure of graduation—B.A. attainment among senior college students, A.A. attainment among community college entrants, or eventual receipt of the B.A. among two-year entrants—a smaller proportion of this contingent had, by 1990, succeeded in completing an undergraduate degree (table 9.6).[21] The cohort difference in A.A. attainment, 31 percent versus 24 percent, is not especially large, probably because the ten-year time period is ample for what is nominally a two-year

---

[21]Graduation figures shown in table 9.6 for the 1970 cohort are lower than those presented in Chapter 2. The two sets of results are not comparable for at least three reasons: (1) rates cited in Chapter 2 are based upon aggregate results for the 1970, 1971, and 1972 cohorts, whereas those in table 9.6 are based on results for the 1970 cohort only; (2) rates reported in Chapter 2 cover a period of fourteen years, compared with ten years in table 9.6; and (3) rates cited in Chapter 2 represent graduation from all institutions in the higher education system, whereas those in table 9.6 represent graduation from CUNY schools only.

Table 9.6 Ten-Year Graduation Rates in the 1970 and 1980 Cohorts, by Ethnicity

| | Percentages | | | | | | | |
| | 1970 | | | | 1980 | | | |
	W	B	H	Total	W	B	H	Total
A.A. among 2-yr. entrants	32	25	28	31	29	22	21	24
B.A. among 4-yr. entrants	54	41	38	52	46	28	26	37
B.A. among 2-yr. entrants	15	11	10	14	7	5	4	6
B.A. among all CUNY entrants[a]	38	22	23	36	24	10	9	16
Any degree (B.A. or A.A.) among all CUNY entrants[a]	46	32	34	44	39	25	24	31

Source: 1970 and 1980 cohort files.

Note: W = white, B = black, H = Hispanic.

[a]Figures for the 1970 cohort have been weighted to correct for overrepresentation of senior college students in the sample.

program. On the other hand, the decline in B.A. attainment among senior college entrants—15 percentage points—is substantial, and when all students are considered—both four-year and community college entrants—the 20 percent drop in university-wide B.A. rates seems especially steep.

The graduation chances of minority students diminished more than those of whites. Among senior college entrants, for example, the white graduation rate for the 1980 cohort was 85 percent of the 1970 rate, but for blacks and Hispanics it was only 68 percent; university-wide, including both senior and community college entrants, the B.A. rate for whites in the 1980 cohort was 63 percent of the 1970 rate, while for blacks it was only 45 percent and for Hispanics 39 percent.

What explains the graduation decline in the 1980 cohort? To what extent might it be accounted for by differences in cohort composition—in high school background, or in socioeconomic characteristics? To what degree might CUNY policy changes have influenced the downturn? To address these questions we conducted two sets of analyses of baccalaureate attainment, one for senior college entrants and one for all entrants, including those who started in community colleges.[22] For senior college entrants, a number of potential influences were looked at, including ethnicity, parents' educational attainments, family income on entry to CUNY, age, gender, high school background, degree intentions, number of remedial courses taken, curriculum, and full-time employment. We conducted one analysis for the 1970 cohort, one for the 1980, and a third for both cohorts combined, in which we added a variable representing cohort membership.[23]

Several variables help to explain the cohort difference among senior college entrants (table B.9).[24] One factor is the number of academic courses taken in high school: 1980 entrants took fewer such courses, and their more restricted exposure is part of the reason for their lower rate of B.A. attainment. Minority students—who formed a larger share of the 1980 cohort than the 1970 group—were less likely to graduate than whites (even after controlling for social background, high school record, and other factors). Older students (age twenty or more) were less likely earn a degree, and a higher percentage of 1980 entrants were older.

The influence of income on B.A. attainment seems best understood in the context of change in tuition policy. Although income did not affect graduation chances among 1970 entrants, it made a difference in the 1980 cohort; the lowest-income students were less likely to graduate than the "middle" income group ($7,500–29,999).[25] This finding suggests that tuition charges

[22]We focus on this degree because the original open-admissions policy emphasized the creation of opportunity for attainment of the B.A., the credential that is prerequisite for postgraduate study and that is more highly rewarded in the labor market than are lesser credentials.

[23]As in the case of our regression analyses of graduation in Chapter 2, we have opted to use ordinary least squares with a dichotomous dependent variable, rather than logistic regression, although it is arguable that the latter is more appropriate. We have taken this approach because the results are more accessible to many readers and because the format of presentation is consistent with other regression analyses in the book where the dependent variable is not dichotomous. As we noted in Chapter 2, where the split is not extreme, both techniques tend to produce similar estimates (Hanushek and Jackson 1977).

[24]Some variables—high school average and degree intentions, for example—had a strong influence on the graduation chances of senior college entrants, but because the cohorts differed little in these regards, they do not help to explain the cohort disparity in degree attainment. Also, women were more likely to graduate than men, but they formed a larger part of the 1980 cohort than the 1970 group.

[25]The highest income group (more than $30,000) appears to be no different in graduation chances from the lowest income group. Among the former, many "dropouts" left with respectable grade point averages, leading us to think that they were transferring to colleges outside the CUNY system.

jeopardized the ability of economically disadvantaged students to persist in college. As we said earlier, low-income students may have reduced the number of credits for which they enrolled as a way of controlling college costs, and some may have dropped out as they became discouraged by their slow progress. Because the 1980 entrants contained a larger proportion of low-income students, part of the cohort gap in graduation is accounted for by this economic disparity.

In both cohorts graduation chances were diminished by full-time employment. Because employment was measured differently in 1970 and 1980, however, and because the measures cannot be standardized across cohorts, we are unable to estimate directly the influence of work in explaining the cohort difference in graduation. We suspect, however, that because CUNY was more expensive in the 1980s, a larger share of 1980 entrants took full-time jobs to offset college expenses. Such a shift would explain part of the disparity in graduation rates.

Our analysis suggests that cohort differences in the academic background of senior college students explain only part of the disparity in B.A. attainment. Other cohort differences—in income and, most likely, in working full-time— became much more important because changes in fiscal and academic policies made it more difficult for low-income and working students to persist in college. Policy changes probably weighed more heavily on minority students than on whites because the former were more likely to come from low-income families, and they more often worked full-time.

CUNY's original open-admissions policy was designed to increase baccalaureate opportunities, both by using admissions criteria that created greater access to senior colleges and by guaranteeing transfer with full credit for all community college graduates. In light of this goal, the large drop in university-wide B.A. rates seen in table 9.6 requires further examination. To do so we carried out a set of analyses similar to those we conducted for senior college entrants, except that we added a measure of college entry level (senior or community) in order to estimate its influence on B.A. attainment.

This assessment (table B.10) identifies several factors that help to explain the downturn. Overall, the members of the 1980 cohort had weaker high school backgrounds and were somewhat less likely to aspire to postgraduate degrees, both of which explain part of their lower B.A. rates; a few other factors, like father's education and student's age at matriculation, play a minor role, and taking remedial courses has a very modest negative effect on graduation chances.[26] But clearly the single most important determinant of the cohort difference is level of entry to CUNY. In each cohort two-year entrants were almost 20 percent less likely to earn a B.A. than senior college entrants who were comparable to them in other ways (degree intentions, high school record, and socioeconomic background). Because 1980 entrants were far more likely than those in 1970 to start in two-year schools, their lower B.A. rate is explained by this cohort disparity more than anything else. Although not all of the great proportional increase in 1980 community college entry was due to more stringent criteria for admission to B.A. institutions, some of it resulted from this policy change, and so a part of the decline in CUNY-wide B.A. rates stems from this shift.[27] The large increase in the proportion of community college entrants in vocational curricula also depressed B.A. attainment in the 1980 cohort.

ACADEMIC TIMETABLES

As we have seen, the traditional notion that an undergraduate career spans four years does not correspond very closely with the realities of college-going among students who entered CUNY in the initial years of the open-admis-

---

[26]The role of CUNY's remedial effort deserves comment. On the face of it, remediation appears to have done nothing to enhance graduation chances. In the 1970 cohort those who took remedial courses were no more likely to graduate than comparable students who did not take them. For the 1980 entrants there is a very small negative association between graduation and the number of remedial courses taken. Policy change regarding remedial placement, however, makes this finding for the 1980 cohort ambiguous. In 1970 there was truly a group of students needing remediation, some of whom received it and some of whom did not. In effect, conditions for that cohort constituted a quasi-experimental situation. In the 1980 cohort, however, as a result of policy changes mandating remediation for those failing skills tests in reading, writing, and math, more than 90 percent of students defined as needing remediation received it. In the absence of a comparable "control" group as there was for the 1970 cohort, it is possible that benefits of remediation are obscured, for there are almost no "comparable" students who didn't take these courses. There is no way of knowing how much worse off remedial students might have been if they had not been enrolled in remedial courses.

[27]Some of the negative community college effect is a consequence of the lower rates of transfer from two-year to four-year colleges in the 1980 cohort. As we have said, CUNY's use of skills tests as a prerequisite for transfer, the diminished likelihood that senior colleges would accept all of the credits that community college students had earned, and the increased chances that transfers would be required to take additional remedial courses just as they began their junior year may have contributed to lower transfer rates and to higher rates of dropout after transfers had begun their senior college careers.

sions policy (see also Levin and Levin 1991; Orfield 1990). As one might expect from the preceding discussion, graduates in the 1980 cohort took even longer to cross the finish line (table 9.7). Among B.A. recipients who started in senior colleges, nearly a third needed six years or more to get through, compared with only 12 percent in the 1970 cohort. The especially lengthy careers of B.A. recipients who started in community colleges were even further extended among graduates in the 1980 cohort: 45 percent of that group took seven or more years, compared with less than 20 percent in the 1970 cohort.

The longer interval for degree completion characterized all groups in the 1980 cohort, but minority graduates were especially delayed. CUNY-wide, the time needed to complete the B.A. increased by a year among blacks and Hispanics, whereas among whites the increase was a half-year. As a result, minority graduates in the 1980 cohort lagged further behind whites than they did in the 1970 cohort.

In explaining the cohort difference in years needed to earn the B.A., the level at which graduates began college is of prime importance.[28] In each cohort starting in a community college delayed graduation by a half-year; about a quarter of B.A.'s in the 1980 cohort started in a two-year school, compared with only 10 percent of graduates from the 1970 cohort. Remediation added to the amount of time that graduates needed, and those in the 1980 group typically took more remedial courses. GEDs took longer to finish, and these students were a much larger share of graduates in the 1980 cohort. Low-income graduates were delayed relative to their more affluent peers, and those in the 1980 contingent were more delayed than those in the 1970. They were also more likely to have been part-time students than the 1970 group, suggesting that as a result of financial pressures stemming from tuition, low-income graduates in the 1980 cohort had registered for fewer credits per semester in attendance.

With these factors taken into account, much of the cohort gap in years to

---

[28]For the discussion to follow, we regressed the measure of years to B.A. upon indicators of social background (ethnicity, income, parents' educational attainment, gender, and age), educational background (high school average, rank in high school class, total college preparatory courses taken), degree aspirations, number of remedial courses taken, level of entry to the university, curriculum of enrollment (liberal arts versus vocational), and employment status. We conducted one regression for the 1970 cohort, one for the 1980, and one for both cohorts combined. In the combined regression we were unable to use an indicator of employment because the measures used in 1970 and 1980 were not comparable.

Table 9.7 Years to Degree Among Graduates in the 1970 and 1980 Cohorts

Percentages, Except as Noted

	1970				1980			
	W	B	H	Total	W	B	H	Total
	A.A. Holders Who Started in Community Colleges							
3 years or less	83	72	71	81	67	39	32	49
4 years	9	13	12	9	17	28	32	24
5 years or more	8	15	17	10	16	33	36	27
Mean years to A.A.	3.0	3.4	3.5	3.1	3.4	4.3	4.4	4.0
	B.A. Holders Who Started in Senior Colleges							
4 or 5 years	89	77	78	88	77	51	52	69
6 years	5	10	13	6	12	25	23	16
7 years or more	5	13	9	6	11	24	25	15
Mean years to B.A.	4.6	5.0	4.9	4.6	5.0	5.8	5.8	5.3
	B.A. Holders Who Started in Community Colleges							
4 or 5 years	70	45	57	66	42	22	14	30
6 years	16	15	11	16	28	22	23	25
7 years or more	14	40	32	18	30	56	63	45
Mean years to B.A.	5.2	6.3	6.0	5.4	6.1	6.9	7.2	6.6

Source: 1970 and 1980 cohort files.

Note: W = white, B = black, H = Hispanic.

B.A. is explained. Even more would be explained if we had been able to control for full-time employment while in college, for as our analyses in Chapter 2 clearly showed, this factor, more than any other, extends the time to degree completion. More graduates in the 1980 cohort probably held full-time jobs than in the 1970 group.

These considerations help us to understand why minority graduates in the 1980 cohort were more delayed relative to whites than they were in the 1970 contingent. Among graduates from the 1980 cohort there was a wider gap between minority and white students in the likelihood of having started in a community college, in the number of remedial courses taken, in the chances of being from a low-income family, and in having a GED.

All in all, policy changes at CUNY added to the time graduates in the 1980 cohort needed to complete their studies. The longer time it took them created further disadvantage, for it pushed back the point at which their educational credentials began to work for them in the labor market. Also, because time to B.A. is the single most important influence on attainment of postgraduate degrees, the members of the 1980 cohort were undoubtedly less likely to earn them.

The Era of Scarcity and Its Meaning for Open Admissions

In 1975 when New York's fiscal crisis hit, major changes occurred in the open-admissions program. Although the imposition of tuition could be seen as a response to that crisis, other changes—the narrowing of access to four-year colleges, more stringent requirements for satisfactory academic standing, mandatory skills testing and the use of these tests as a gateway to the junior year of college—were not governed mainly by fiscal considerations. Rather, they were changes in response to a perceived academic crisis at the university. They represented an expression of the belief among some CUNY administrators, trustees, and faculty, as well as among some in the media, that "educational excellence" had crumbled. Based on the academic records compiled by open-admissions students, there was little to support such a viewpoint. Nonetheless, this perception had real consequences in the policy modifications that flowed from it.

As we have seen in one instance after another, students who entered CUNY under the new policies achieved considerably less academic success than did the ones who had started a decade earlier. The members of the 1980 cohort were far more likely than their predecessors to begin college in a two-year institution, and, within those schools, in a vocational program. They took more noncredit or low-credit remedial courses; they attempted and earned fewer credits, and their grades were lower. They were more likely to drop out after their freshman year, and community college entrants were less likely to transfer to a four-year school. As of June 1990, ten years after this group started college, rates of B.A. attainment were down sharply. Among degree holders, the time needed to complete college exceeded even further the already lengthy periods observed for the 1970 cohort.

In part, the diminished academic success of the 1980 cohort was a consequence of changes in students' socioeconomic and educational background, especially among those who entered community colleges. Relative to the 1970 cohort, the 1980 group contained much larger proportions of entrants with high school equivalency diplomas; entrants also had taken fewer college preparatory courses in high school, and they were older. Students with these characteristics were academically less successful. Other differences in cohort composition became important because of policy changes. Income is the best example. After tuition was imposed—with attendant limitations on financial aid—low-income students found it more difficult to persist in college.

But even after taking account of disparities in cohort composition—the ones directly related to academic success in both cohorts, and one such as income that seems interwoven with policy change—significant outcome differences remain. To an important extent, we think that they are attributable to the changed academic context created by policy modifications. Stiffer entrance requirements for senior colleges and greater difficulty of transfer from two-year institutions contributed to the decline in university-wide rates of B.A. attainment. University-wide skills testing and mandatory placement in remedial courses lowered the number of credits students attempted and earned in their freshman year; as a result, some students, discouraged by the slowness of their progress, may have dropped out. Adding to higher dropout rates were stricter requirements for satisfactory academic standing; students whose averages were below a C after attempting twenty-five credits could be put on probation, possibly triggering a loss of financial aid.

Lower rates of B.A. attainment among 1980 entrants reduced the pool of those eligible for postgraduate study. This reduction probably has led to a decline in the proportions going on to earn advanced professional and academic degrees. Overall, as a consequence of lower educational attainments, one would expect that the members of this cohort are—in the aggregate— realizing smaller rewards in the labor market. In effect, then, life prospects in the 1980 cohort are less favorable than in the 1970 group. Even if the 1980 cohort were a clone of the 1970, policy changes undoubtedly would have diminished its overall academic success.

Although open admissions continues at CUNY in the sense that all New York City high school graduates still are guaranteed a seat, places in the university are less secure than they were in the early 1970s. In all the ways that we have recounted, educational opportunity has eroded and CUNY is a less hospitable place for students than it used to be. The new fiscal and academic hurdles seem especially high for economically and educationally disadvantaged students. CUNY's once distinctive open-access blueprint has given way to one that now looks more like other public higher education systems. The changes at the university seem consistent with the national trend: fiscal retrenchment and an emphasis on academic standards and on educational "excellence" coincident with more muted concern about educational opportunity.

The analyses in this book have implications for increasing educational attainment and the narrowing of ethnic inequalities—aims that appear to flow against the national currents. Consider first the issue of financial aid: substantial proportions of students attend college part-time, or they shift between full- and part-time enrollment. At CUNY in the 1970s, nearly 40 percent of minority students who earned B.A.'s took seven or more years to finish. Among students who entered in the 1980s, even higher percentages took that long. Although some federal aid is available for part-time students, it needs to be brought into better alignment with these time realities. Inadequate aid packages for long-term students undoubtedly extend even further already lengthy college careers. Time saved in completing undergraduate study not only increases the chances for graduate training but also hastens the point at which credentials begin to work for individuals in the labor market.

Our analyses have shown that high school curricula are important in influencing undergraduate degree chances: differential placement into non-academic or academically diluted high school curriculum tracks is a source of ethnic inequality in academic preparation. It is not beyond the reach of colleges—especially those in urban areas with high concentrations of minority youth—to influence the precollege course of study. Colleges should attempt to broaden exposure provided by high schools to the academic, college preparatory courses that contribute to better performance in college. (Efforts at change should reach even earlier into the primary level, where much of educational advantage and disadvantage is created.) Wider academic exposure in high school would give more students eligibility to apply to four-year colleges. It would also undoubtedly diminish the need for placement in college remedial courses, with their delaying effects on degree completion, and it would augment the number of B.A. recipients, enlarging the pool eligible for postgraduate study.

The community college and its role in educational opportunity is another important issue. Our findings, in line with those of others, indicate that both in the 1970s and the 1980s, community colleges had a net negative influence on educational attainment. Liberalized admissions policy for entry to four-year colleges and better financial aid packages for part-time students would likely direct more students toward these institutions and help counteract the trend toward lower graduation rates. But more fundamentally, attention should be focused on the ways in which the organizational boundaries of two- and four-year schools work against transfer and the academic success of community college students after transfer. As Dougherty (1991, 1994) has suggested, consideration should be given to making community colleges into lower-division branches of four-year institutions, and to merging the two kinds of colleges into single institutions. Providing A.A. and B.A. programs in the same institution would probably augment the transfer emphasis in two-year programs and would make credits earned in them more acceptable for the B.A. course of study. Students who do attend two-year schools, especially those in vocational curricula, would have better academic prospects after transfer if they received more exposure to core liberal arts courses that approximate those of four-year colleges in their requirements (such as writing assignments and the like).

These policy directions—more flexible financial aid packages, greater university influence on access to the high school academic curriculum, admissions policies that place more students in four-year colleges, better preparation of two-year students for senior college work, and structural integration of two- and four-year institutions—can increase educational attainments and narrow educational inequalities among groups.

One of the above policy considerations, university influence on the high school curriculum, has been the subject of a CUNY initiative that is intended to upgrade high school students' academic preparation. The aim of the College Preparatory Initiative (CPI), as it is called, is to phase in, during the 1990s, a gradually increasing set of high school academic requirements that applicants to CUNY would be expected to meet. According to the plan, by the year 2000 applicants should have completed a full complement of college preparatory courses in English, math, science (including laboratory science), social studies, foreign language, and performing and visual arts. In concert with this CUNY initiative, the chancellor of the New York City schools announced a new set of more stringent graduation requirements in math and science (Jones 1994). Although the CPI specifies that access to CUNY will be maintained for students who do not meet this standard, it adds a new selection criterion for admission to four-year colleges: by the end of the phase-in period no applicant with less than the complete set of high school academic courses would be eligible for a B.A. institution. Ineligible applicants would be placed in community colleges; whatever the level of placement, students, in order to graduate and/or to transfer to a B.A. program would be required to remove any high school deficiencies through course work or other measures—such as passing skills tests—designated by each CUNY college.

The high schools appear to face a daunting task, especially the heavily minority ones, where—according to analyses we have carried out—not more than 20 percent of graduates complete a full-fledged academic program. Obviously, such schools would need to expand tremendously the requisite course sections in math, biology, chemistry, English, and the like, in order to create access to the academic track for the thousands of students who would otherwise fail to meet the CPI guidelines. Such an expansion undoubtedly requires hiring substantial numbers of additional teachers with competence in the subject matter areas. Significant upgrading and expansion of laboratory science facilities will also be necessary. The nation's largest public school system has been hamstrung by severe budgetary constraints, providing strong grounds for skepticism that it can mount such a program successfully.

There are other grounds for concern about the public school effort. Undoubtedly, a substantial portion of academic inequality is created before high school—by tracking in primary and middle schools, for example. Moreover, large proportions of public school students, especially minority ones, are consigned to special education classes (for students labeled as learning disabled, retarded, and the like), which provide little in the way of college preparatory work; placement in these classes usually begins in elementary school, and movement back into academic course work is infrequent (Richardson 1994). Considering these processes by which educational inequalities are created, it does not take a great leap of imagination to think that many students would not be touched by interventions at the high school level unless those measures are preceded by considerable restructuring in the primary schools.

One can only speculate about the consequences for access to higher education if the schools are not able to make an academic curriculum available to larger proportions of students. Freshman enrollments may become even more heavily weighted toward community colleges than they are now, as even larger proportions of students are designated ineligible for B.A. programs. Potential college entrants, if not discouraged even from applying, will face the prospect of having to take numerous courses in two-year schools to remove high school deficiencies, while at the same time being placed in remedial courses after they fail CUNY skills tests. Such prospects might be so daunting to a large number of these students that they would not persist long in college.

Time will tell whether the collaboration between the colleges and high schools will create greater access to the high school academic curriculum. Whether admission to B.A. programs becomes more selective will depend, in part, on that outcome.

As this is published—more than twenty-five years after the beginning of open admissions—another fiscal crisis has engulfed public higher education in New York. Both New York City and New York State have proposed unprecedented budget cuts for CUNY and the State University of New York (SUNY). The cuts at CUNY were preceded by especially savage media attacks on the university.[29] In some respects they echo the themes heard at the inception of open admissions and during the New York fiscal crisis of 1975–76: that under the open-admissions policy CUNY abandoned entry standards and became a remediation mill, wasting inordinate resources in a vain effort to upgrade the basic academic skills of masses of incompetent and ineducable students, and that CUNY diplomas are of little value either in the job market or for admission to postgraduate studies. But in a departure from the earlier contention that the university would give away huge numbers of diplomas to undeserving students, the newer attacks took CUNY to task for low graduation rates. As some of the critics see it, grim budgetary prospects are really an opportunity for the salvation of the university; sharp cutbacks will force it to resurrect stringent admissions standards, finally shutting the door to the masses of students who never should have been in college to begin with. Through this process CUNY can regain academic respectability.

This depiction of CUNY flies in the face of the outcomes that this book has described. Current graduation rates from the university, though diminished relative to the 1970s, are comparable to national rates for public colleges.[30] Moreover, the most recent data from the National Research Council

[29]Illustrative of these media attacks are articles by MacDonald (1994) and McConnell (1995), and a book by Traub (1994).

[30]This conclusion is based upon a comparison of six-year graduation rates in the 1980 cohort with six-year rates that we calculated for college entrants in the High School and Beyond data set, a longitudinal survey of 1980 high school sophomores and seniors sponsored by the National Center for Education Statistics of the U.S. Department of Education.

(1994) show CUNY as a leader in the number of graduates who go on to get Ph.D.'s from American graduate schools.

Although the realities that we have described are not on the side of the critics, their assertions cannot easily be dismissed. Their arguments reflect, in microcosm, national efforts to reverse long-standing entitlements, including federal programs of financial aid in higher education. Times of scarcity intensify debates about how resources should be distributed. Those who are more privileged often seek to derogate those who have less as undeserving of support. In this perception CUNY's effort is treated as if it were a failed welfare entitlement program left over from the bureaucratically bloated days of the Great Society. Open admissions reflected the concept of higher education as a right for all who had completed earlier stages of education—just as for youngsters completing second grade, entry to the third grade is unanimously viewed as an entitlement.

In the late 1960s, people of color and ethnic minorities who had been largely disenfranchised from higher education successfully mobilized to help create a vast expansion of educational opportunity in New York. CUNY's experience with open admissions over more than two decades teaches us that the idea of higher education as a right is still not accepted. Forces of countermobilization continue a vigorous effort to demean and roll back those earlier gains.

Quality of the Follow-up Sample Data

When CUNY's seventeen senior and community colleges began the open-admissions policy in the fall of 1970, a longitudinal research effort was initiated to evaluate its results. Large samples of the 1970, 1971, and 1972 freshman classes were surveyed by questionnaire, generally at registration or in required freshman courses. The response rate for each class was as follows: 1970, 43 percent of 31,596 entrants; 1971, 24 percent of 35,639 entrants; 1972, 36 percent of 35,545 entrants. The survey data include information on race, ethnic group membership, gender, age, family income at the time of the student's entry to CUNY, parental educational attainments, educational aspirations, academic self-ratings, and other attitudinal factors. These survey data were integrated with two other official university data sources. The first consists of high school background information, including the number of college preparatory courses taken and the academic average compiled in these courses. The second contains collegiate records, including the level of placement in CUNY (senior or community college), academic performance (grades and credits, remedial course work), and graduation from the university through the spring semester of 1975.

To ascertain students' subsequent educational attainments (at CUNY and elsewhere), labor-market experiences, as well as other outcomes, we conducted a follow-up survey in 1984 of the 34,507 respondents who were members of the original 1970–72 cohort samples. Before mailing the survey questionnaire, we took steps to update the addresses in our files. For many respondents we were able to find more recent addresses. Overall, we found addresses (original or updated) for all but about 1,000 of the 34,507 cases.

After completing the updates, we sent a first-wave mailing (first class with postage-paid return envelopes) of the questionnaire to the pooled sample, using the most recent available addresses. This mailing yielded 3,204 respondents. The post office returned 11,171 questionnaires as undeliverable. A second-wave mailing went to the remaining 19,202 nonrespondents. It yielded an additional 1,159 respondents. The postal service returned 1,772 questionnaires from the second-wave mailing as undeliverable.

In a third mailing, certified return receipt letters (CRR) were sent on a selective basis. Because the representation of blacks and Hispanics in the original sample was far smaller than it was for whites (there were 23,495 whites, 4,868 blacks, and 3,190 Hispanics), we were concerned about obtaining enough minority respondents for reliable statistical analyses. Accordingly, we targeted the CRR mailing to the minority cases. This mailing produced an additional 475 respondents.

Our final data-collection step involved telephone interviews with minority nonrespondents to the CRR mailing. Using our address data and the information from the postal return receipt cards (the name of the person who signed for the letter), we tried to obtain telephone numbers by searching reverse telephone directories (sorted by address rather than by last name as in the standard telephone directory).[1] These procedures yielded interviews with 274 minority respondents.

The various procedures described above produced a total of 5,112 respondents to the survey questionnaire and 4,989 usable questionnaires. Almost 40 percent of the cases in the original sample were unlocatable. Hispanic respondents were the most difficult to locate—nearly 60 percent could not be found. Using locatable cases as the base, the overall response rate was 25 percent. Response rates for blacks and Hispanics were higher: 29 percent among the

---

[1] The procedures were complex. We recorded telephone numbers for the individual respondents where these were shown. In some cases no number was shown for the addressee, but one was shown for a person with a matching surname (presumably a relative or spouse). In other cases no number was available for anyone with the surname of the addressee, but one was available for the person who signed the CRR letter. In many cases no number was listed for anyone at the address with a surname matching that of the addressee, nor for the person who signed the CRR. In such cases we recorded phone numbers for all persons having a phone at the address in question. Where the building contained more than eight residents, we sampled eight telephone numbers. In some cases no phone was listed for any resident of a building. By these efforts we produced for each minority nonrespondent from our CRR mailing a list that included phone numbers for the person himself or herself, for others with identical surnames, for neighbors who signed for the CRR letter, and for other residents of the building.

When these procedures were completed, we began efforts to locate respondents via phone calls, using a staff of bilingual interviewers to assure that we could conduct all the conversations necessary to reach Hispanic respondents. We had expected that a delivered CRR letter ensured that we would be able to locate the respondent, but in the great majority of cases we could not. We were able to reach only about 15 percent of the cases for whom a CRR letter had been delivered. Almost without exception, if we reached a respondent by telephone, we were able to obtain a completed interview. In a few cases telephone calls produced an updated address for respondents. We then mailed a questionnaire to the newly obtained address.

former and 40 percent among the latter, compared with a white rate of 24 percent.

The data from the follow-up survey were merged with a single aggregated file containing the records for all respondents in the 1970–72 original samples, so the record for each follow-up respondent also contains information on high school background and academic performance at CUNY through spring 1975, as well as data on social origins and attitudes that were collected on entry to the university.

In using this merged data set to analyze a variety of educational, labor-market, and other outcomes of the open-admissions policy, we are generalizing from the follow-up sample of 4,989 cases to the population of entering freshmen for the years 1970–72. To assess the sample's representativeness, we have compared it with the aggregated original sample.

Our strategy in making this comparison is based partly upon earlier comparisons of the original samples with their respective populations. These assessments showed that although the samples contained greater proportions of students with strong high school records, and that the collegiate academic performance of these students was in some respects better than that of the populations, in almost all cases, the superiority of the samples was only slight. The overall pattern of the comparisons indicated that the original samples provided good representations of the populations. There was, in effect, little reason to suspect that response bias had led to invalid findings from the original samples. (A more detailed discussion of the variables, data quality, and the representativeness of the samples may be found in Lavin et al. 1981, chapter 3 and appendix A).

Our decision to compare the follow-up and original samples was guided also by the fact that the two have many more variables in common than does the follow-up sample with the population. The population, for example, lacks any data linked to individual records on variables that play an important role in our analyses—race and ethnicity, parents' education, and income on entry to CUNY. The larger number of variables common to the original and follow-up samples allowed us to make a more thorough assessment of nonresponse bias.

Comparisons of the original and follow-up samples are presented in table A.1. They are shown separately for those who originally entered CUNY senior colleges, for those who started in community colleges, and for both categories combined (in the columns under *All CUNY*). Comparisons have been made for three kinds of variables: (1) those referring to such demo-

Table A.1 Distribution and Means for Selected Variables: Comparison of Original Sample and Follow-up Sample

Percentages, Except as Noted

	Senior Colleges			Community Colleges			All CUNY		
	Original Sample	Follow-up Sample	Adjusted Follow-up Sample	Original Sample	Follow-up Sample	Adjusted Follow-up Sample	Original Sample[a]	Follow-up Sample	Adjusted Follow-up Sample
Age									
≤17	21.5	23.8	22.1	5.4	6.1	5.6	14.0	15.6	14.4
18	68.8	69.5	68.3	60.6	65.4	60.7	65.0	67.6	64.8
19	6.3	4.5	6.4	16.0	13.2	16.8	10.8	8.5	11.2
20+	3.5	2.2	3.3	18.0	15.3	17.0	10.2	8.2	9.6
Missing[b]	0.9	0.7	1.2	1.6	1.1	1.3	1.1	0.9	1.3
Gender									
Male	50.9	46.2	50.6	47.7	41.0	46.8	49.4	43.8	48.8
Female	49.1	53.8	49.4	52.3	59.0	53.2	50.6	56.2	51.2
Missing[b]	0.9	0.7	1.3	0.8	0.5	0.8	0.9	0.6	1.1
Race									
Black	7.1	9.0	7.2	20.6	23.7	20.6	13.4	15.8	13.4
White	83.1	82.1	83.1	64.1	60.3	64.1	74.3	72.1	74.3

Asian	2.2	1.6	2.2	1.5	1.2	1.5	1.9	1.4	1.9
Hispanic	6.6	6.6	6.4	12.0	13.7	12.4	9.1	9.9	9.2
Other	1.0	0.7	1.1	1.8	1.0	1.4	1.4	0.8	1.3
Missing[b]	2.4	2.3	3.0	3.5	2.6	3.2	2.9	2.4	3.1
Father's education									
Elementary or less	12.1	12.1	13.1	17.8	17.7	17.5	14.7	14.6	15.1
Some high school	22.6	21.0	21.5	29.1	28.8	29.0	25.6	24.5	24.9
High school grad.	34.6	33.6	33.4	32.5	31.1	31.1	33.6	32.5	32.3
Some college	16.4	16.7	15.9	12.3	13.3	13.2	14.5	15.2	14.7
College degree	9.8	10.9	10.6	6.2	6.3	6.4	8.1	8.8	8.7
Postgraduate degree	4.6	5.8	5.6	2.1	2.7	2.8	3.4	4.4	4.4
Missing[b]	5.0	3.9	4.3	9.0	8.2	7.8	6.9	5.9	5.9
Mother's education									
Elementary or less	10.3	10.4	11.5	16.0	15.7	15.4	12.9	12.8	13.3
Some high school	19.1	17.0	17.1	28.2	27.1	27.3	23.3	21.6	21.8
High school grad.	50.0	48.8	48.3	42.1	43.1	42.6	46.3	46.2	45.7
Some college	12.5	14.7	14.4	9.2	9.2	9.4	11.0	12.2	12.1
College degree	5.9	6.3	5.9	3.6	3.7	3.7	4.8	5.1	4.9
Postgraduate degree	2.1	2.8	2.9	0.9	1.3	1.5	1.5	2.1	2.3
Missing[b]	3.6	2.9	3.1	7.1	6.8	6.6	5.2	4.8	4.7

Table A.1 *Continued*

	Senior Colleges			Community Colleges			All CUNY		
	Original Sample	Follow-up Sample	Adjusted Follow-up Sample	Original Sample	Follow-up Sample	Adjusted Follow-up Sample	Original Sample[a]	Follow-up Sample	Adjusted Follow-up Sample
Income at entry									
<$4,000	4.9	3.7	5.2	10.1	7.9	9.7	7.3	5.6	7.2
$4,000–9,999	38.8	37.4	37.1	47.1	45.5	43.0	42.6	41.1	39.8
$10,000–14,999	36.2	37.1	36.0	28.9	32.5	32.1	32.8	35.0	34.2
$15,000–19,999	12.5	12.6	12.7	8.8	8.6	9.1	10.8	10.8	11.1
$20,000+	7.6	9.2	9.0	5.0	5.6	6.1	6.4	7.6	7.7
Missing[b]	14.0	12.9	12.7	16.9	17.1	16.7	15.3	14.8	14.5
High school average									
<70	3.1	2.5	3.2	31.2	26.1	31.2	16.1	13.2	15.7
70–74.9	8.7	7.3	8.8	31.7	28.9	31.5	19.4	17.1	19.0
75–79.9	23.2	19.7	23.5	23.7	26.7	24.0	23.4	22.9	23.7
80–84.9	28.8	28.7	27.4	9.6	12.9	9.7	19.9	21.6	19.4
85+	36.3	41.8	37.1	3.7	5.4	3.7	21.2	25.3	22.1
Missing[b]	1.6	1.0	1.4	7.8	5.0	7.2	4.5	2.9	4.1

	14.05	14.24	14.13	11.00	11.33	11.12	12.64	12.92	12.77
Mean total units of college prep. work in high school									
Number remedial courses taken									
None	60.4	63.6	61.5	50.7	52.1	49.7	55.9	58.3	56.1
1–2	27.7	25.6	26.5	34.3	35.4	36.5	30.8	30.2	31.2
3–4	8.0	7.2	8.1	11.1	9.8	10.5	9.4	8.4	9.2
>4	4.0	3.4	4.0	3.8	2.7	3.1	3.9	3.0	3.5
Cumulative GPA	2.51	2.70	2.56	2.06	2.31	2.13	2.30	2.53	2.37
Standard deviation	(.821)	(.720)	(.812)	(.908)	(.805)	(.887)	(.861)	(.783)	(.872)
Mean cumulative credits earned	80.96	90.93	82.95	43.44	55.00	46.45	63.57	74.29	66.02
Standard deviation	(43.05)	(38.32)	(42.18)	(33.28)	(32.57)	(33.26)	(38.52)	(40.00)	(42.41)
CUNY status as of June 1975									
Dropout	38.2	26.8	36.8	53.7	37.5	51.5	45.4	31.8	43.6
Persister	30.0	34.9	31.7	18.1	21.2	20.2	24.5	28.6	26.3
Graduate	31.8	38.3	31.4	28.2	41.2	28.4	30.1	39.7	30.0

Note: Percentages within each panel may not total 100 percent due to rounding.

[a]The figures for this column have been adjusted to reflect the proportions of senior and community college students in the population.

[b]For each panel of the table showing missing cases, percentages are calculated with the missing cases removed from the base.

graphic and social-origins variables as race and ethnicity, gender, age, parents' education, and income; (2) those referring to secondary school record (high school average, college preparatory courses taken); and (3) academic achievements in CUNY, such as grade point average, credits earned, and graduation status as of 1975.

With one exception, there is a close resemblance between the original and follow-up samples on the social origins variables. The exception concerns gender: the follow-up sample contains a higher proportion of females than does the original sample. To cite the largest discrepancy, among community college entrants women are 59 percent of the follow-up sample but were only 52 percent of the original sample. There is also a discrepancy regarding age: eighteen-year-olds who entered community colleges had greater representation in the follow-up survey (65.4 percent) than in the original sample (60.6 percent). Aside from these disparities, differences in social origins are quite small.

Overall, respondents with low averages in high school were somewhat underrepresented in the follow-up sample, whereas those with high averages were somewhat overrepresented. The samples were quite similar in the average number of college preparatory courses taken in high school.

Generally larger and more consistent differences are visible for the collegiate academic performance variables. Compared with the original sample, respondents in the follow-up sample were more likely to have graduated from CUNY by June 1975, they earned more total credits, and their cumulative grade point averages were higher. Most noteworthy are the differences in graduation: 38 percent of senior college entrants in the follow-up sample had graduated from CUNY by spring 1975, compared with 31.8 percent in the original sample. Among community college entrants, 41 percent in the follow-up sample were graduates, compared with 28 percent in the original group. Almost 40 percent of the total follow-up group had graduated by June 1975, but only 30 percent of those in the original sample had.

Overall, it appears that those who did better in college were more likely respondents to the follow-up survey, raising the possibility that our analyses might produce invalid findings because of response bias. For example, because those who earn a college degree generally receive greater benefits in their subsequent work careers than those who do not earn one, and because the follow-up sample overrepresents the graduates in the cohort, such response bias might well lead to overestimates of labor-market success.

To address such possibilities, we have used a weighting procedure based on a strategy suggested by Berk (1983). In essence, the procedure attempts to answer this question: among the respondents in the original sample, what are the odds that individuals with various characteristics will be in or not in the follow-up sample? To address this question, we used logistic regression in which the dependent variable is the odds that someone from the original sample would respond to the follow-up survey. We looked at the contribution of a number of sociodemographic and academic variables that we expected to affect the odds of being in the follow-up. These included race/ethnicity, age, gender, family income when the students entered CUNY, high school average, year of entry to CUNY (1970, 1971, or 1972), level of entry to CUNY (senior or community college), number of credits earned at CUNY, graduation from CUNY, and several indicators constructed to assess the effect of missing values.[2] After estimating the regression equation, we converted the log odds into probability levels and weighted individuals in the follow-up sample using the inverse of these probabilities.

The results of this procedure are shown in the columns of table A.1 labeled *Adjusted Follow-up Sample*. The results almost eliminate the difference between original and follow-up samples in gender, the background variable showing the largest disparity. For senior colleges, community colleges, and all of CUNY, initial differences of 4.7, 6.7, and 5.6 percentage points in the representation of females are reduced to 0.4, 0.1, and 0.6 points, respectively. Inspection of the table shows also that for high school background and collegiate academic performance measures, the weights closely align the follow-up distributions with those of the original sample. Graduation is an important example, because it is one of the major outcomes in our evaluation of open admissions and because we saw earlier that discrepancies between the original and follow-up samples are fairly large. In the original sample, 31.8 percent of senior college entrants had graduated by 1975, 28.2 percent of community college entrants had, and the total CUNY graduation rate was 30.1 percent. Among follow-up respondents the adjusted percentages almost match the corresponding figures in the original sample.

Overall, then, it appears that the logistic model was effective in adjusting

[2]For most variables included in the model, information was missing for some respondents. The percentage of respondents missing data on any variable was generally small. We wanted to know whether individuals with missing data were more likely to be in or not in the follow-up sample. Accordingly, for each variable with missing data, we constructed an additional variable in which respondents not missing data were scored as 0 and those who were missing were scored as 1. The resulting dummy variables were then included in the analyses.

the follow-up sample so that it provides a good representation of the original sample. Obviously, we do not have measures in the original sample for every variable measured in the follow-up, but as far as we have been able to compare the two, there seems little reason to suspect that findings from the follow-up survey are invalid. We do not find grounds for skepticism concerning the conclusions we draw from our analyses.

Selected Statistical Tables

Table B.1 Determinants of B.A. Attainment: Community College and Senior College Entrants

	Model 1[a]	Model 2[a]
Ethnicity[b]		
Black	−.04	−.03
Hispanic	−.10**	−.08*
H.S. grades	.011**	.004*
H.S. academic prep courses	.01**	.01*
Academic self-confidence	.07**	.05**
Degree aspirations[c]		
Not sure	−.15**	−.13**
A.A. only	−.23**	−.22**
B.A. only	−.08**	−.07**
Began at a community college	−.17**	−.19**
Liberal arts curriculum	.08**	.07**
Worked full-time in college	−.05*	−.04
First-year GPA		.13**
Constant	−.49	−.11
R^2 (adjusted)	.29	.33
N (unweighted)	4,418	4,418

Source: Follow-up survey.

Note: Only significant coefficients are presented.

[a]Unstandardized coefficients.

[b]The reference category is whites.

[c]The reference category is postgraduate degree.

*P <0.01

**P <0.001

Table B.2 Determinants of Time to B.A.

	Unstandardized	Standardized
Ethnicity[a]		.07*
Black	.41	
Hispanic	.48	
College preparatory courses	−.07	−.07*
Entered a community college	.81	.16**
Worked full-time in college	2.37	.33**
Number of remedial courses taken	.17	.09**
GPA	−.99	−.28**
Constant	6.96	
R^2 (adjusted)	.355	
N (unweighted)	2,255	

Source: Follow-up survey.

Note: Only significant coefficients are presented.

[a]The reference category is whites.

*p < 0.01

**p < 0.001

Table B.3 Determinants of Changes in Occupational Status and Earnings Between 1978 and 1984: Males

	Change in Occupational Status Scores				Earnings Change (Dollars)[a]			
	Model 1		Model 2		Model 1		Model 2	
	Unstandard-ized	Standard-ized	Unstandard-ized	Standard-ized	Unstandard-ized	Standard-ized	Unstandard-ized	Standard-ized
Ethnicity[b]		-.126**		-.099**		-.157***		-.085*
Black	-5.87		-4.03		-4,107		-1,657	
Hispanic	-5.38		-4.01		-4,575		-2,990	
Father's ed. (some college or more)			2.80	.063*			2,026	.076*
Mother's ed. (some college or more)			-.02	-.000			567	.019
Parents' income[c]				.072				.072
<$10,000			2.73				-1,476	
$10,000–14,999			3.16				-1,975	
Educational attainment[d]				.141**				.273***
Some college			2.83				931	
A.A.			1.74				1,705	
B.A.			6.63				6,790	
Work exp. before high-est degree			.15	.013			28	.004

Table B.3 *Continued*

| | Change in Occupational Status Scores | | | | Earnings Change (Dollars)[a] | | | |
| | Model 1 | | Model 2 | | Model 1 | | Model 2 | |
	Unstandardized	Standardized	Unstandardized	Standardized	Unstandardized	Standardized	Unstandardized	Standardized
Work exp. after highest degree			.01	.002			406	.078
Public sector job in 1978			−3.53	−.081**			−3,623	−.138***
Status score for 1st full-time job			.05	.046			62	.094**
Score for 1978 job[e]	−.43	−.44***	−.50	−.522***	−.26	−.22***	−0.27	−.233***
Constant	27.70		23.31		12,039		6,001	
R² (adjusted)	.205		.228		.062		.153	
N (unweighted)	899				840			

[a] 1978 earnings were converted to 1984 dollars in computing earnings change.

[b] The reference category is whites.

[c] The reference category is $15,000 or more.

[d] The reference category is high school diploma.

[e] SEI score in the case of job status; dollar amounts in the case of earnings.

*p <0.05

**p <0.01

***p <0.001

Table B.4 Determinants of Changes in Occupational Status and Earnings Between 1978 and 1984: Females

| | Change in Occupational Status Scores | | | | Earnings Change (Dollars)[a] | | | |
| | Model 1 | | Model 2 | | Model 1 | | Model 2 | |
	Unstandardized	Standardized	Unstandardized	Standardized	Unstandardized	Standardized	Unstandardized	Standardized
Ethnicity[b]		−.210***		−.146***		−.157**		−.101*
Black	−7.19		−4.94				−1,952	
Hispanic	−7.21		−5.06				−2,397	
Father's ed. (some college or more)			3.92	.112			2,154	.101**
Mother's ed. (some college or more)			−1.13	−.028			1,382	.056
Parents' income[c]				.131*				.074
<$10,000			4.78				1,351	
$10,000–14,999			3.74				−188	
Educational attainment[d]				.230***				.107*
Some college			3.20				1,552	
A.A.			2.96				38	
B.A.			9.53				2,382	
Work exp. before highest degree			−.07	−.007			−193	−.036

Table B.4 Continued

	Change in Occupational Status Scores				Earnings Change (Dollars)[a]			
	Model 1		Model 2		Model 1		Model 2	
	Unstandard-ized	Standard-ized	Unstandard-ized	Standard-ized	Unstandard-ized	Standard-ized	Unstandard-ized	Standard-ized
Work exp. after highest degree			1.08	.133*			−173	−.035
Public sector job in 1978			−1.31	−.028			−1,653	−.059
Status score for 1st full-time job			.15	.117**			62	.078*
Score for 1978 job[e]	−.58	−.509***	−.67	−.588***	−.59	−.534***	−0.61	−.546***
Constant	37.44		19.89		15,843		11,006	
R² (adjusted)	.269		.316		.295		.332	
N (unweighted)	773				671			

[a]1978 earnings were converted to 1984 dollars in computing earnings change.
[b]The reference category is whites.
[c]The reference category is $15,000 or more.
[d]The reference category is high school diploma.
[e]SEI score in the case of job status; dollar amounts in the case of earnings.

*p <0.05
**p <0.01
***p <0.001

Table B.5 Determinants of Work Complexity

	Model 1		Model 2	
	Unstandard- ized	Standard- ized	Unstandard- ized	Standard- ized
Ethnicity[a]		−.209***		−.084***
Black	−.550		−.240	
Hispanic	−.392		−.093	
Female			−.016	−.008
Educational attainment[b]				.584***
Some college			.197	
A.A.			.308	
B.A.			.730	
M.A.			1.484	
Advanced			2.038	
Work exp. before highest degree			.005	.017
Work exp. after highest degree			.020	.076*
Public sector job			−.165	−.073***
Constant	.124		.741	
R^2 (adjusted)	.043		.308	
N (unweighted)	3,392			

Source: Follow-up survey.

Note: The analysis is for the full range of the work complexity variable, which is described in Chapter 5.

[a]The reference category is whites.

[b]The reference category is high school diploma.

*p <0.05

**p <0.01

***p <0.001

Table B.6 Determinants of Work Complexity for Public- and Private-Sector Workers

	Public Sector				Private Sector			
	Model 1		Model 2		Model 1		Model 2	
	Unstandard-ized	Standard-ized	Unstandard-ized	Standard-ized	Unstandard-ized	Standard-ized	Unstandard-ized	Standard-ized
Ethnicity[a]		−.150***		−.039		−.221***		−.125***
Black	−.407		−.112		−.586		−.354	
Hispanic	−.275		.004		−.380		−.147	
Female			.287	.127***			−.118	−.064**
Educational attainment[b]				.671***				.481***
Some college			.170				.195	
A.A.			.371				.242	

	(1)		(2)	
B.A.	.844		.601	
M.A.	1.834		1.038	
Advanced	2.346		1.827	
Work exp. before highest degree	.013	.042	.003	.009
Work exp. after highest degree	.024	.084	.013	.050
Constant	−1.247	.440	.494	.246
R^2 (adjusted)	.132	.048	.069	.020
N (unweighted)	2,063		897	

Source: Follow-up survey.

[a] The reference category is whites.

[b] The reference category is high school diploma.

*p < 0.05

**p < 0.01

***p < 0.001

Table B.7 Determinants of Job Authority

	Model 1		Model 2	
	Unstandard-ized	Standard-ized	Unstandard-ized	Standard-ized
Ethnicity[a]		−.189***		−.110***
Black	−.499		−.271	
Hispanic	−.414		−.272	
Female			−.072	−.035*
Educational attainment[b]				.158***
Some college			.153	
A.A.			.180	
B.A.			.347	
M.A.			.355	
Advanced			.708	
Work exp. before highest degree			.029	.097***
Work exp. after highest degree			.044	.160***
Public sector job			−.251	−.107***
Union member			−.655	−.298***
Constant	1.532		1.122	
R^2 (adjusted)	.035		.178	
N (unweighted)	3,114			

Source: Follow-up survey.

Note: The analysis is for the full range of the job authority variable, which is described in Chapter 5.

[a]The reference category is whites.

[b]The reference category is high school diploma.

*p <0.05

**p <0.01

***p <0.001

Table B.8 Determinants of Job Authority for Public- and Private-Sector Workers

	Public Sector				Private Sector			
	Model 1		Model 2		Model 1		Model 2	
	Unstandard-ized	Standard-ized	Unstandard-ized	Standard-ized	Unstandard-ized	Standard-ized	Unstandard-ized	Standard-ized
Ethnicity[a]		−.138***		−.085		−.197***		−.141***
Black	−.318		−.197		−.568		−.399	
Hispanic	−.201		.118		−.447		−.334	
Female			.013	.007			−.132	−.063*
Educational attainment[b]				.087				.228***
Some college			−.096				.236	
A.A.			−.040				.270	
B.A.			.061				.461	
M.A.			−.138				.555	
Advanced			−.002				1.066	
Work exp. before high-est degree			.004	.016			.039	.118***

Table B.8 *Continued*

	Public Sector				Private Sector			
	Model 1		Model 2		Model 1		Model 2	
	Unstandardized	Standardized	Unstandardized	Standardized	Unstandardized	Standardized	Unstandardized	Standardized
Work exp. after highest degree			−.010	−.044			.072	.249***
Union member			−.658	−.328***			−.703	−.245***
Constant	1.066		−1.602		1.726		.797	
R^2 (adjusted)	.017		.130		.038		.124	
N (unweighted)	828				1,881			

Source: Follow-up survey.

[a]The reference category is whites.

[b]The reference category is high school diploma.

*p <0.05

**p <0.01

***p <0.001

Table B.9 Determinants of B.A. Attainment for 1970 and 1980 Entrants to Four-year Colleges

	1970	1980	Both Cohorts
Cohort (1980 = 1)	—	—	−.09
Ethnicity[a]			
Black	.00	−.07	−.05
Hispanic	−.09	−.10	−.09
High school average	.01	.01	.01
High school rank	.001	.003	.002
No record on rank	—	−.05	—
H.S. academic courses	.02	.01	.01
Father's education[b]			
College grad. or more	.01	.10	.04
Some college	.05	.00	.05
H.S. graduate	.03	.02	.03
Family income[c]			
$7,500–29,999	—	.08	.05
$30,000+	—	.03	.04
Age (20+ = 1)	—	—	−.07
Gender (female = 1)	.04	.05	.05
Degree intentions[d]			
Not sure	.10	—	.08
B.A.	.09	—	.08
M.A. or higher	.15	—	.13
Number of remedial courses	—	—	—
Full-time work[e]	−.10	−.16	—
Constant	−.91	−.92	−.93
Adj. R^2	.08	.11	.10
N	8,235	2,638	11,123

Source: 1970 and 1980 cohort files.

Note: Significant unstandardized coefficients are displayed.

[a]The reference category is whites.

[b]The reference category is less than high school.

[c]The reference category is less than $7,500.

[d]The reference category is A.A. degree or less.

[e]Measures of employment are not comparable across cohorts and are omitted from the combined equation.

Table B.10 Determinants of B.A. Attainment for 1970 and 1980 Entrants to Four- and Two-Year Colleges

	1970	1980	Both Cohorts
Cohort (1980 = 1)	—	—	−.07
Ethnicity[a]			
Black	−.02	−.04	−.03
Hispanic	−.07	−.05	−.06
High school average	.01	.005	.007
High school rank	.001	.001	.001
No record on rank	—	−.03	—
H.S. academic courses	.01	.01	.01
No record of courses	—	—	−.04
Father's education[b]			
College grad. or more	.00	.06	.03
Some college	.05	.01	.03
H.S. graduate	.02	.00	.01
Gender (female = 1)	.03	.02	.02
Age	—	—	−.02
Degree intentions[c]			
Not sure	.06	.01	.04
B.A.	.08	.03	.06
M.A. or higher	.14	.07	.12
Number of remedial courses	—	−.006	−.004
Began in community college	−.19	−.18	−.19
Vocational curriculum	−.04	−.04	−.04
Full-time work[d]	−.08	−.05	—
Constant	−.86	−.44	−.69
R^2 (adjusted)	.20	.21	.25
N	12,022	8,358	21,031

Source: 1970 and 1980 cohort files.

Note: Significant unstandardized coefficients are displayed.

[a]The reference category is whites.

[b]The reference category is less than high school.

[c]The reference category is A.A. degree or less.

[d]Measures of employment are not comparable across cohorts and are omitted from the combined equation.

REFERENCES

Ackerman, Tom. 1969. The South Campus Seizure. *Alumnus Magazine,* no. 1, p. 16.

Adler, Paul. 1986. Technology and Us. *Socialist Review* 16: 67–96.

Agnew, Spiro. 1971. Quoted in *Time,* April 26, p. 81.

Alba, Richard D. 1990. *Ethnic Identity.* New Haven: Yale University Press.

Alba, Richard D., and David E. Lavin. 1981. Community Colleges and Tracking in Higher Education. *Sociology of Education* 54: 223–47.

Alexander, Karl L., Scott Holupka, and Aaron M. Pallas. 1987. Social Background and Academic Determinants of Two-Year Versus Four-Year College Attendance: Evidence from Two Cohorts a Decade Apart. *American Journal of Education* 96: 56–80.

Allen, Walter R., and Reynolds Farley. 1986. The Shifting Social and Economic Tides of Black America, 1950–1980. *Annual Review of Sociology* 12: 277–306.

Allison, Paul D. 1990. Change Scores as Dependent Variables in Regression Analysis. In *Sociological Methodology,* American Sociological Association, 93–113.

Alwin, Duane F., Ronald Cohen, and Theodore M. Newcomb. 1992. *Political Attitudes Over the Life Span: The Bennington Women After Fifty Years.* Madison: University of Wisconsin Press.

Anderson, Kristine. 1981. Post–High School Experiences and College Attrition. *Sociology of Education* 54: 1–15.

Angle, John, and David A. Wissman. 1981. Gender, College Major, and Earnings. *Sociology of Education* 54: 25–33.

Aronowitz, Stanley. 1973. *False Promises: The Shaping of American Working Class Consciousness.* New York: McGraw-Hill.

Aronowitz, Stanley, and Henry A. Giroux. 1988. Schooling, Culture and Literacy in the Age of Broken Dreams: A Review of Bloom and Hirsch. *Harvard Educational Review* 58: 172–94.

Astin, Alexander W. 1977. *Four Critical Years.* San Francisco: Jossey-Bass.

———. 1993. *What Matters in College? Four Critical Years Revisited.* San Francisco: Jossey-Bass.

Astin, Alexander W., Helen S. Astin, Kenneth C. Green, Laura Kent, Patricia McNamara, and Melanie Reeves Williams. 1982. *Minorities in American Higher Education.* San Francisco: Jossey-Bass.

Astin, Alexander W., Kenneth C. Green, and William S. Korn. 1987. *The American Freshman: Twenty Year Trends, 1966–1985.* Los Angeles: Cooperative Institutional Research Program, American Council on Education–University of California.

Astone, Nan Marie, and Sara S. McLanahan. 1991. Family Structure, Parental Practices, and High School Completion. *American Sociological Review* 56: 309–20.

Attewell, Paul. 1990. Information Technology and the Productivity Paradox. Ph.D. program in sociology. Graduate School of the City University of New York.

Augustyniak, Sue, Greg J. Duncan, and Jeffrey K. Liker. 1985. Income Dynamics and Self Conceptions: Linking Theory and Method in Models of Change. In *Life Course Dynamics: Trajectories and Transitions, 1968–1980,* ed. Glenn H. Elder. Ithaca: Cornell University Press.

Bailey, Thomas, and Roger Waldinger. 1991. The Changing Ethnic/Racial Division of Labor. In

Dual City: Restructuring New York, ed. John H. Mollenkopf and Manuel Castells. New York: Russell Sage Foundation.

Baron, James N. 1984. Organizational Perspectives on Stratification. *Annual Review of Sociology* 10: 37–69.

Becker, Howard S., Blanche Geer, Everett C. Hughes, and Anselm Strauss. 1961. *Boys in White: Student Culture in Medical School.* Chicago: University of Chicago Press.

Bell, Daniel. 1973. *The Coming of Post-Industrial Society.* New York: Basic.

Bennett, William J. 1984. *To Reclaim a Legacy.* Washington, D.C.: National Endowment for the Humanities.

Berk, Richard. 1983. An Introduction to Sample Selection Bias in Sociological Data. *American Sociological Review* 48: 386–98.

Bernstein, Basil. 1973. Social Class, Language and Socialisation. In Karabel and Halsey 1977a.

———. 1977. *Class, Codes and Control.* Vol. 3, *Towards a Theory of Educational Transmission.* London: Routledge.

Berube, Maurice, and Marilyn Gittel. 1969. *Confrontation at Ocean-Hill Brownsville.* New York: Praeger.

Bianchi, Suzanne M. 1981. *Household Composition and Racial Inequality.* New Brunswick, N.J.: Rutgers University Press.

Bielby, Denise V. 1978. Career Sex–Atypicality and Career Involvement of College-Educated Women: Baseline Evidence From the 1960s. *Sociology of Education* 51: 7–28.

Bielby, William T. 1981. Models of Status Attainment. In *Research in Social Stratification and Mobility,* ed. Donald J. Treiman and Robert V. Robinson, vol. 1. Greenwich, Conn.: JAI.

Bills, David B. 1988. Educational Credentials and Promotions: Does Schooling Do More Than Get You in the Door? *Sociology of Education* 61: 52–60.

Birnbaum, Robert, and Joseph Goldman. 1971. *The Graduates: A Follow-up Study of New York City High School Graduates of 1970.* New York: Office for Research in Higher Education, City University of New York.

Blalock, Hurbert M. 1979. *Social Statistics.* Rev. 2d ed. New York: McGraw-Hill.

Blau, Peter, and Otis Dudley Duncan. 1967. *The American Occupational Structure.* New York: Free Press.

Bloom, Allan. 1987. *The Closing of the American Mind.* New York: Simon and Schuster.

Board of Higher Education. 1968. *Master Plan for the City University of New York, 1968.* New York: City University of New York.

———. 1969a. Minutes of Meeting. June 30, attachment F.

———. 1969b. Scratch notes from executive session. June 16.

———. 1969c. Statement of Policy. July 9, item 4.

———. 1969d. Summary of Public Hearings Before the Board of Higher Education on the Report of the Commission on Admissions. October 22, November 5.

———. 1969e. Statement of Admissions Policy Adopted by the BHE. November 10.

Bourdieu, Pierre. 1973. Cultural Reproduction and Social Reproduction. In *Knowledge, Education and Cultural Change,* ed. Richard Brown. London: Tavistock.

———. 1977. Cultural Reproduction and Social Reproduction. In Karabel and Halsey 1977a.

———. 1984. *Distinction: A Social Critique of the Judgment of Taste.* Cambridge: Harvard University Press.

Bourdieu, Pierre, and Jean-Claude Passeron. 1977. *Reproduction*. Beverly Hills: Sage.

Bowen, Howard R. 1977. *Investment In Learning: The Individual and Social Value of Higher Education*. San Francisco: Jossey-Bass.

Bowles, Samuel, and Herbert Gintis. 1976. *Schooling in Capitalist America*. New York: Basic.

Braverman, Harry. 1974. *Labor and Monopoly Capital*. New York: Monthly Review Press.

Brint, Steven, and Jerome Karabel. 1989. *The Diverted Dream: Community Colleges and the Promise of Equal Opportunity in America, 1900–1985*. New York: Oxford University Press.

Cain, Pamela S., and Donald J. Treiman. 1981. The "Dictionary of Occupational Titles" As A Source of Occupational Data. *American Sociological Review* 46: 253–78.

California Postsecondary Education Commission. 1987. Time Required to Earn the Bachelor's Degree. Sacramento: California Postsecondary Education Commission report 87–14.

California State Colleges. 1969. Those Who Made It: Selected Characteristics of the June 1967 California State College Graduates. Long Beach: Division of Institutional Research, Office of the Chancellor.

Campbell, Richard T. 1980. The Freshman Class of the University of Wisconsin, 1964. In Kerckhoff 1980.

Campus. 1969. (CCNY student newspaper.) Article on events preceding student strike, April 22.

Caplow, Theodore. 1983. *Managing an Organization*. New York: Holt, Rinehart, and Winston.

Carnoy, Martin, and Henry M. Levin. 1985. *Schooling and Work in the Democratic State*. Stanford: Stanford University Press.

Catsambis, Sophia. 1994. The Path of Math: Gender and Racial-Ethnic Differences in Mathematics Participation from Middle School to High School. *Sociology of Education* 67: 199–215.

City University of New York, Office of the Vice Chancellor for the Executive Office. 1968–70. Undergraduate Ethnic Census.

Clark, Burton. 1960. The "Cooling Out" Function in Higher Education. *American Journal of Sociology* 65: 569–766.

———. 1961. *Educating the Expert Society*. San Francisco: Chandler.

Cleary, Paul D., and Ronald Angel. 1984. The Analysis of Relationships Involving Dichotomous Dependent Variables. *Journal of Health and Social Behavior* 25: 334–48.

Cohen, Arthur M. 1990. The Case for the Community College. *American Journal of Education* 98: 426–42.

Cohen, Arthur, and Florence B. Brawer. 1982. *The American Community College*. San Francisco: Jossey-Bass.

Cohen, Jacob, and Patricia Cohen. 1983. *Applied Multiple Regression / Correlation Analysis for the Behavioral Sciences*. Hillsdale, N.J.: Lawrence Erlbaum Associates.

College Board. 1985. *Equity and Excellence: The Educational Status of Black Americans*. New York: College Entrance Examination Board.

Collins, Randall. 1979. *The Credential Society*. New York: Academic Press.

Collins, Sharon. 1983. The Making of the Black Middle Class. *Social Problems* 30: 369–81.

Cose, Ellis. 1993. *The Rage of a Privileged Class*. New York: HarperCollins.

Crook, David. 1989. *Women at the University: Their Academic Progress, Achievement and Choice of Curriculum*. New York: City University of New York Office of Institutional Research and Analysis.

Daymont, Thomas, and Paul Andrisani. 1984. Job Preferences, College Major, and the Gender Gap in Earnings. *Journal of Human Resources* 19: 408–28.

DeCamp, Suzanne. 1992. *Selected New York City Public School Data 1990–1991.* New York: Community Service Society.

DiMaggio, Paul. 1982. Cultural Capital and School Success: The Impact of Status Culture Participation on the Grades of U.S. High School Students. *American Sociological Review* 47: 189–201.

DiMaggio, Paul, and John Mohr. 1985. Cultural Capital, Educational Attainment, and Marital Selection. *American Journal of Sociology* 90: 1231–61.

DiPrete, Thomas A. 1987. The Professionalization of Administration and Equal Employment Opportunity in the U.S. Federal Government. *American Journal of Sociology* 93: 119–40.

Dougherty, Kevin. 1987. The Effects of Community Colleges: Aid or Hindrance to Socioeconomic Attainment. *Sociology of Education* 60: 86–103.

———. 1991. The Community College at the Crossroads: The Need for Structural Reform. *Harvard Educational Review.* 64: 311–36.

———. 1992. Community Colleges and Baccalaureate Attainment. *Journal of Higher Education* 63, no. 2, pp. 188–214.

———. 1994. *The Contradictory College: The Conflicting Origins, Impacts, and Futures of the Community College.* Albany: State University of New York Press.

Dougherty, Kevin, and Floyd M. Hammack. 1990a. *Education and Society: A Reader.* San Diego: Harcourt Brace Jovanovich.

———. 1990b. The Other Side of College: The Nonacademic Effects of Higher Education. In Dougherty and Hammack 1990a.

Duncan, Greg J. 1984. *Years of Poverty, Years of Plenty.* Ann Arbor: Institute for Social Research, University of Michigan.

Duncan, Otis Dudley. 1961. A Socioeconomic Index for All Occupations. In Reiss 1961.

Eckland, Bruce K. 1964. College Dropouts Who Came Back. *Harvard Educational Review* 34: 402–20.

Educational Testing Service. 1978. *Descriptive Tests of Language Skills.* Princeton: Educational Testing Service.

England, Paula. 1979. Women and Occupational Prestige: A Case of Vacuous Sex Equality. *Signs* 5, Winter, pp. 252–65.

England, Paula, and Lori McCreary. 1987. Gender Inequality in Paid Employment. In *Analyzing Gender,* ed. Myra Marx Ferree and Beth B. Hess. Beverly Hills: Sage.

Faculty Senate. 1969. Text of the Negotiated Agreement on Admissions Policy as Revised by the City College Faculty Senate. June, point 1, p. 1.

Farkas, George, Robert P. Grobe, Daniel Sheehan, and Yuan Shuan. 1990. Cultural Resources and School Success: Gender, Ethnicity, and Poverty Groups Within an Urban District. *American Sociological Review* 55: 127–42.

Farley, Reynolds. 1984. *Blacks and Whites: Narrowing the Gap?* Cambridge: Harvard University Press.

Featherman, David L., and Robert M. Hauser. 1978. *Opportunity and Change.* New York: Academic Press.

Feldman, Kenneth A., and Theodore M. Newcomb. 1969. *The Impact of College on Students.* San Francisco: Jossey-Bass.

Fitzgerald, Robert. Undated. Attrition from Postsecondary Education: Change Across Two Cohorts. Diss. prospectus, University of California, Berkeley.

Fox, Sylvan. 1969a. Candidates Score Dual Admissions for City College. *New York Times,* May 26.

———. 1969b. Faculty Rejects CCNY Dual Plan. *New York Times,* May 30.

———. 1969c. 400 from Slums Urged for CCNY. *New York Times,* June 2.

Freeman, Richard B. 1976. *The Overeducated American.* New York: Academic Press.

Freeman, Richard B., and James L. Medoff. 1984. *What Do Unions Do?* New York: Basic.

Furstenberg, Frank F., Jr. 1976. *Unplanned Parenthood: The Social Consequences of Teenage Childbearing.* New York: Free Press.

Furstenberg, Frank F., Jr., J. Brooks-Gunn, and S. Philip Morgan. 1987. *Adolescent Mothers in Later Life.* Cambridge: Cambridge University Press.

Gamoran, Adam. 1992. The Variable Effects of High School Tracking. *American Sociological Review* 57: 812–28.

Gamoran, Adam, and Mark Berends. 1987. The Effects of Stratification in Secondary Schools: Synthesis of Survey and Ethnographic Research. *Review of Educational Research* 57: 415–35.

Gamoran, Adam, and Robert D. Mare. 1989. Secondary School Tracking and Educational Inequality: Compensation, Reinforcement, or Neutrality. *American Journal of Sociology* 94: 1146–83.

Glazer, Nathan, and Daniel P. Moynihan. 1970. *Beyond the Melting Pot.* 2d ed. Cambridge: MIT Press.

Gordon, Sheila C. 1975. The Transformation of the City University of New York, 1945–1970. Ph.D. diss., Columbia University.

Gorelick, Sherry. 1981. *City College and the Jewish Poor: Education in New York, 1880–1924.* New Brunswick, N.J.: Rutgers University Press.

Granovetter, Mark. 1974. *Getting a Job: A Study of Contacts and Careers.* Cambridge: Harvard University Press.

Grant, W. Vance, and Leo J. Eiden. 1982. *Digest of Education Statistics, 1982.* Washington, D.C.: National Center for Education Statistics.

Greenspan, Arthur. 1969. CCNY's in the Campaign Now. *New York Post,* May 26.

Griffin, Larry J. 1978. On Estimating the Economic Value of Schooling and Experience. *Sociological Methods and Research* 6: 309–35.

Grimm, James W., and Robert N. Stern. 1974. Sex Roles and Internal Labor Market Structures: The "Female" Semi-Professions. *Social Problems* 21: 690–705.

Grubb, W. Norton. 1989. Dropouts, Spells of Time, and Credits in Postsecondary Education: Evidence from Longitudinal Surveys. *Economics of Education Review* 8: 49–67.

———. 1992a. The Economic Returns to Baccalaureate Degrees: New Evidence from the Class of 1972. *Review of Higher Education* 15: 213–31.

———. 1992b. Postsecondary Vocational Education and the Sub-Baccalaureate Labor Market: New Evidence on Economic Returns. *Economics of Education Review* 11: 225–48.

———. 1992c. Correcting Conventional Wisdom: Community College Impact on Students' Jobs and Salaries. *Community, Technical, and Junior College Journal* 62, June–July, pp. 11–14.

Hall, Richard H. 1975. *Occupations and the Social Structure.* 2d ed. Englewood, N.J.: Prentice Hall.
———. 1986. *Dimensions of Work.* Beverly Hills: Sage.

Hammack, Floyd M. 1985. Review of *Liberating Education,* by Zelda Gamson et al. *American Journal of Education* 94: 128–34.

Hanushek, Eric A., and John E. Jackson. 1977. *Statistical Methods for Social Scientists.* New York: Academic Press.

Hauser, Robert M. 1988. *Declining Black College Entry: How Did It Happen?* Madison: Center for Demography and Ecology, University of Wisconsin.

Hauser, Robert M., and David L. Featherman. 1977. *The Process of Stratification.* New York: Academic Press.

Heise, David R. 1972. Employing Nominal Variables, Induced Variables, and Block Variables in Path Analyses. *Sociological Methods and Research* 1: 147–73.

Hill, Martha S. 1981. Some Dynamic Aspects of Poverty. In *Five Thousand American Families: Patterns of Economic Progress,* ed. Martha S. Hill, D. H. Hill, and J. N. Morgan, vol. 9. Ann Arbor: University of Michigan Press.

Hill, R., and F. Stafford. 1980. Parental Care of Children: Time Diary Estimates of Quantity, Predictability, and Variety. *Journal of Human Resources* 15: 219–39.

Hirsch, E. D. 1987. *Cultural Literacy: What Every American Needs to Know.* Boston: Houghton Mifflin.

Hirschhorn, Larry. 1984. *Beyond Mechanization: Work and Technology in a Postindustrial Age.* Cambridge: MIT Press.

Hofferth, Sandra A. 1984. Kin Networks, Race, and Family Structure. *Journal of Marriage and the Family* 46: 791–805.

Holy, Thomas C. 1962. *A Long Range Plan for the City University of New York, 1961–1975.* New York: Board of Higher Education.

Hout, Michael. 1984a. Status, Autonomy, and Training in Occupational Mobility. *American Journal of Sociology* 89: 1379–1409.
———. 1984b. Occupational Mobility of Black Men, 1962 to 1973. *American Sociological Review* 49: 308–22.
———. 1988. More Universalism, Less Structural Mobility: The American Occupational Structure in the 1980s. *American Journal of Sociology* 93: 1358–1400.

Hurn, Christopher. 1993. *The Limits and Possibilities of Schooling: An Introduction to the Sociology of Education.* Boston: Allyn and Bacon.

Hyllegard, David, and David E. Lavin. 1992. Higher Education and Challenging Work: Open Admissions and Ethnic and Gender Differences in Job Complexity. *Sociological Forum* 7: 239–60.

Hyman, Herbert H., Charles R. Wright, and John Shelton Reed. 1975. *The Enduring Effects of Education.* Chicago: University of Chicago Press.

Jackman, Mary R., and Michael J. Muha. 1984. Education and Intergroup Attitudes. *American Sociological Review* 49: 751–69.

Jacobs, Jerry A. 1989. *Revolving Doors: Sex Segregation and Women's Careers.* Stanford: Stanford University Press.

Jacoby, Sanford M. 1985. *Employing Bureaucracy: Managers, Unions, and the Transformation of Work in American Industry, 1900–1945.* New York: Columbia University Press.

Jaffe, A. J., and Walter Adams. 1971. Two Models of Open Enrollment. In *Universal Higher Education: Costs and Benefits,* 143–68. Washington, D.C.: American Council on Education.

Jaynes, Gerald David, and Robin M. Williams Jr., eds. 1989. *A Common Destiny: Blacks and American Society.* Washington, D.C.: National Academy Press.

Jencks, Christopher, Susan Bartlett, Mary Corcoran, James Crouse, David Eaglesfield, Gregory Jackson, Kent McClelland, Peter Mueser, Michael Olneck, Joseph Schwartz, Sherry Ward, and Jill Williams. 1979. *Who Gets Ahead?* New York: Basic.

Jencks, Christopher, Lauri Perman, and Lee Rainwater. 1988. What Is A Good Job? A New Measure of Labor Market Success. *American Journal of Sociology* 93: 1322–57.

Jencks, Christopher, and Paul E. Peterson, eds. 1991. *The Urban Underclass.* Washington, D.C.: Brookings Institution.

Jencks, Christopher, Marshall Smith, Henry Acland, Mary Jo Bane, David Cohen, Herbert Gintis, Barbara Heyns, Stephan Michelson. 1972. *Inequality: A Reassessment of the Effect of Family and Schooling in America.* New York: Basic Books.

Jones, Charisse. 1994. New York City to Stiffen Rules for Graduating. *New York Times,* May 2.

Kalmijn, Matthijs. 1991. Shifting Boundaries: Trends in Religious and Educational Homogamy. *American Sociological Review* 56: 786–800.

Kanter, Rosabeth Moss. 1977. *Men and Women of the Corporation.* New York: Basic.

——. 1978. Work in a New America. *Daedalus* 107: 47–78.

Karabel, Jerome. 1972. Community Colleges and Social Stratification. *Harvard Educational Review* 42: 521–62.

Karabel, Jerome, and A. H. Halsey, eds. 1977a. *Power and Ideology in Education.* New York: Oxford University Press.

——. 1977b. Educational Research: A Review and Interpretation. In Karabel and Halsey 1977a.

Karabel, Jerome, and Katherine McClelland. 1987. Occupational Advantage and the Impact of College Rank on Labor Market Outcomes. *Sociological Inquiry* 57: 323–47.

Karen, David. 1990. Access to Higher Education in the United States, 1900 to the Present. In Dougherty and Hammack 1990a.

——. 1991. "Achievement" and "Ascription" in Admission to an Elite College: A Political-Organizational Analysis. *Sociological Forum* 6: 349–80.

Kasarda, John D. 1983. Entry-Level Jobs, Mobility, and Urban Minority Unemployment. *Urban Affairs Quarterly* 19: 21–40.

Kaufman, Robert L. 1986. The Impact of Industrial and Occupational Structure on Black-White Employment Allocation. *American Sociological Review* 51: 310–23.

Kaufman, Robert L., and Thomas N. Daymont. 1981. Racial Discrimination and the Social Organization of Industries. *Social Science Research* 10: 225–55.

Kerckhoff, Alan C. 1980. *Research in Sociology of Education and Socialization: Longitudinal Perspectives on Educational Attainment.* Greenwich, Conn.: JAI.

Kessler, Ronald C., and David F. Greenberg. 1981. The Algebra of Change. In *Linear Panel Analysis.* New York: Academic Press.

Kirschenman, Joleen, and Kathryn M. Neckerman. 1991. "We'd Love to Hire Them, But . . .": The Meaning of Race for Employers. In Jencks and Peterson 1991.

Kluegel, James R. 1978. The Causes and Cost of Racial Exclusion From Job Authority. *American Sociological Review* 43: 285–301.

Kluegel, James R., and Eliot R. Smith. 1986. *Beliefs About Inequality: Americans' Views of What Is and What Ought To Be.* New York: de Gruyter.

Kohn, Melvin L., and Carmi Schooler. 1983. *Work And Personality: An Inquiry into the Impact of Social Stratification.* Norwood, N.J.: Ablex.

Kramer, Rena, Barry Kaufman, and Lawrence Podell. 1974. *Distribution of Grades, 1972.* New York: Office of Program and Policy Research, City University of New York.

Kusterer, Kenneth C. 1978. *Know-How on the Job: The Important Working Knowledge of "Unskilled" Workers.* Boulder, Colo.: Westview.

Labov, William. 1972. *Language in the Inner City: Studies in the Black English Vernacular.* Philadelphia: University of Pennsylvania Press.

Lareau, Annette. 1989. *Home Advantage: Social Class and Parental Intervention in Elementary Education.* Philadelphia: Falmer.

Lavin, David E. 1965. *The Prediction of Academic Performance: A Theoretical Analysis and Review of Research.* New York: Russell Sage Foundation.

Lavin, David E., and Richard D. Alba. 1981. Mass Higher Education in an Era of Scarcity: Open Admissions and Changing Educational Opportunities at the City University of New York. Proposal to the National Institute of Education, Program on Educational Policy and Organization, Washington, D.C.

Lavin, David E., Richard D. Alba, and Richard A. Silberstein. 1979. Open Admissions and Equal Access: A Study of Ethnic Groups in the City University of New York. *Harvard Educational Review* 49: 53–92.

——. 1981. *Right Versus Privilege: The Open Admissions Experiment at the City University of New York.* New York: Free Press.

Lavin, David E., and David B. Crook. 1990. Open Admissions and Its Outcomes: Ethnic Differences in Long-Term Educational Attainment. *American Journal of Education* 98: 389–425.

Lavin, David E., and James Murtha. 1984. *Who Goes Where to College: The Position of the City University of New York in the Student Market.* New York: Office of Institutional Research and Analysis, City University of New York.

Lee, Valerie E., and Kenneth A. Frank. 1990. Students' Characteristics that Facilitate Transfer from Two-Year to Four-Year Colleges. *Sociology of Education* 63: 178–94.

Lee, Valerie E., Christopher Mackie-Lewis, and Helen M. Marks. 1993. Persistence to the Baccalaureate Degree for Students Who Transfer from Community College. *American Journal of Education* 102: 80–114.

Levin, Jack, and William C. Levin. 1991. Sociology of Educational Late Blooming. *Sociological Forum* 6: 661–71.

Lichter, Daniel T., Felicia B. LeClere, and Diane K. McLaughlin. 1991. Local Marriage Markets and the Marital Behavior of Black and White Women. *American Journal of Sociology* 96: 843–67.

London, Howard. 1978. *The Culture of a Community College.* New York: Praeger.

MacDonald, Heather. 1994. Downward Mobility: The Failure of Open Admissions at City University. *City Journal,* Summer, pp. 10–20.

Mare, Robert D. 1991. Five Decades of Assortative Mating. *American Sociological Review* 56: 15–32.

Mare, Robert D., and Christopher Winship. 1991. Socioeconomic Change and the Decline of Marriage for Blacks and Whites. In Jencks and Peterson 1991.

Mayer, Martin. 1973. Higher Education for All? The Case of Open Admissions. *Commentary*, February, pp. 37–47.

McConnell, Scott. 1995. Can Pataki Budget Cuts Actually Save CUNY? *New York Post*, March 15.

McLanahan, Sara. 1985. Family Structure and the Reproduction of Poverty. *American Journal of Sociology* 90: 873–901.

McLanahan, Sara, and Gary Sandefur. 1994. *Growing Up With a Single Parent: What Hurts, What Helps.* Cambridge: Harvard University Press.

McNamara, Joseph. 1969. Proc Blasts CCNY Pact, Will Fight It in the Courts. *New York Daily News*, May 26.

Mechanic, David. 1962. *Students Under Stress.* New York: Free Press.

Mehan, Hugh. 1992. Understanding Inequality in Schools: The Contribution of Interpretive Studies. *Sociology of Education* 65: 1–20.

Merton, Robert K., George G. Reader, and Patricia L. Kendall, eds. 1957. *The Student Physician.* Cambridge: Harvard University Press.

Miller, Ann R., Donald J. Treiman, Pamela S. Cain, and Patricia A. Roos. 1980. *Work, Jobs, and Occupations: A Critical Review of the "Dictionary of Occupational Titles."* Washington, D.C.: National Academy Press.

Mincer, Jacob. 1974. *Schooling, Experience, and Earnings.* New York: Columbia University Press.

———. 1989. Human Capital and the Labor Market: A Review of Current Research. *Educational Researcher* 18: 27–34.

Mollenkopf, John Hull. 1988. The Postindustrial Transformation of the Political Order in New York City. In *Power, Culture and Place: Essays on New York City,* ed. John Hull Mollenkopf. New York: Russell Sage Foundation.

Monk-Turner, Elizabeth. 1985. Sex Differences in Type of First College Entered and Occupational Status: Changes Over Time. *Social Science Journal* 22: 89–97.

———. 1990. The Occupational Achievements of Community and Four-Year College Entrants. *American Sociological Review* 55: 719–25.

Mueller, Charles W., and Toby L. Parcel. 1986. Ascription, Dimensions of Authority, and Earnings: The Case of Supervisors. In *Research in Social Stratification and Mobility,* ed. Robert V. Robinson. Greenwich, Conn.: JAI.

Mulkey, Lynn M., Robert C. Crain, and Alexander J. C. Harrington. 1992. One-Parent Households and Achievement: Economic and Behavioral Explanation of a Small Effect. *Sociology of Education* 65: 48–65.

Murphy, Kevin, and Finis Welch. 1989. Wage Premiums for College Graduates: Recent Growth and Possible Explanations. *Educational Researcher,* 18: 17–26.

National Center for Educational Statistics. 1982. *Digest of Educational Statistics.* Washington, D.C.: U.S. Government Printing Office.

———. 1990. *The Condition of Education 1990.* Vols. 1, 2. Washington, D.C.: U.S. Department of Education.

National Commission on Excellence in Education. 1983. *A Nation at Risk.* Washington, D.C.: U.S. Government Printing Office.

National Research Council. 1994. *Survey of Earned Doctorates*. Washington, D.C.: National Research Council.

Newcomb, Theodore M. 1943. *Personality and Social Change*. New York: Holt.

Newcomb, Theodore M., Katherine E. Koenig, Richard Flacks, and Donald P. Warwick. 1967. *Persistence and Change: Bennington College and Its Students After 25 Years*. New York: Wiley.

New York Times. 1969. Article on violence in student strike, May 8.

——. 1994. At Stanford, a Rebellion on Grades. May 31.

Oakes, Jeannie. 1985. *Keeping Track: How Schools Structure Inequality*. New Haven: Yale University Press.

Observation Post. 1969. (CCNY student newspaper.) Article on negotiations surrounding student strike, February 7.

Orfield, Gary. 1990. Public Policy and College Opportunity. *American Journal of Education* 98: 317–50.

Pallas, Aaron M., Doris Entwisle, Karl Alexander, and Doris Cadigan. 1987. Children Who Do Exceptionally Well in First Grade. *Sociology of Education* 60: 257–71.

Parcel, Toby L., and Charles W. Mueller. 1983. Occupational Differentiation, Prestige, and Socioeconomic Status. *Work and Occupations* 10: 49–80.

Parsons, Talcott. 1959. The School Class as a Social System: Some of Its Functions in American Society. *Harvard Educational Review* 29: 297–318.

Pascarella, Ernest T., and Patrick T. Terenzini. 1991. *How College Affects Students*. San Francisco: Jossey-Bass.

Penzer, Jonathan. 1969. BPR Seize Building after Seeing BGG. *Observation Post,* February 14.

Pincus, Fred L. 1980. The False Promises of Community Colleges: Class Conflict and Vocational Education. *Harvard Educational Review* 50: 332–61.

——. 1986. Vocational Education: More False Promises. In *The Community College and Its Critics,* ed. L. Steven Zwerling. San Francisco: Jossey-Bass.

Piore, Michael J. 1974. Upward Mobility, Job Monotony, and Labor Market Structure. In *Work and the Quality of Life: Resource Papers for "Work In America,"* ed. James O'Toole. Cambridge: MIT Press.

Reiss, Albert J. 1961. *Occupations and Social Status*. New York: Free Press.

Reskin, Barbara F., and Heidi I. Hartmann. 1986. *Women's Work, Men's Work: Sex Segregation on the Job*. Washington, D.C.: National Academy Press.

Richardson, Lynda. 1994. Minority Students Languish in Special Education System. *New York Times,* April 6.

Ronco, William, and Lisa Peattie. 1988. Making Work: A Perspective from Social Science. In *On Work: Historical, Comparative and Theoretical Approaches,* ed. R. E. Pahl. New York: Basil Blackwell.

Rosenbaum, James E. 1979. Organizational Career Mobility: Promotion Chances in a Corporation During Periods of Growth and Contraction. *American Journal of Sociology* 85: 21–48.

Rosenfeld, Rachel A. 1992. Job Mobility and Career Processes. In *Annual Review of Sociology,* ed. Judith Blake and John Hagen, vol. 18. Palo Alto: Annual Reviews.

Rouche, John E., and Jerry J. Snow. 1977. *Overcoming Learning Problems*. San Francisco: Jossey-Bass.

Rudy, S. Willis. 1949. *The College of the City of New York: A History, 1847–1947*. New York: City College Press.

Ruggles, Steven. 1994. The Origins of African-American Family Structure. *American Sociological Review* 59: 136–51.

Rumberger, Russell. 1981. The Changing Skill Requirements of Jobs in the U.S. Economy. *Industrial and Labor Relations Review* 34: 578–90.

Schoen, Robert, and James R. Kluegel. 1988. The Widening Gap in Black and White Marriage Rates: The Impact of Population Composition and Differential Marriage Propensities. *American Sociological Review* 53: 895–907.

Sewell, William H., and Robert M. Hauser. 1975. *Education, Occupation, and Earnings: Achievement in the Early Career*. New York: Academic Press.

Sibley, Elbridge. 1963. *The Education of Sociologists in the United States*. New York: Russell Sage Foundation.

Singlemann, Joachim. 1978. *From Agriculture to Services: The Transformation of Industrial Employment*. Beverly Hills: Sage.

Sokoloff, Natalie J. 1980. *Between Money and Love: The Dialectics of Women's Home and Market Work*. New York: Praeger.

Spaeth, Joe L. 1979. Vertical Differentiation Among Occupations. *American Sociological Review* 44: 746–62.

———. 1984. Structural Contexts and the Stratification of Work. In *Research in Social Stratification and Mobility*, ed. Donald J. Treiman and Robert V. Robinson. Greenwich, Conn.: JAI.

Spenner, Kenneth I. 1983. Deciphering Prometheus: Temporal Change in the Skill Level of Work. *American Sociological Review* 48: 824–37.

———. 1985. The Upgrading and Downgrading of Occupations: Issues, Evidence, and Implications for Education. *Review of Educational Research* 55: 125–54.

Spilerman, Seymour. 1977. Careers, Labor Market Structure, and Socioeconomic Achievement. *American Journal of Sociology* 83: 551–93.

Spitze, Glenna, and Joe L. Spaeth. 1979. Employment Among Married Female College Graduates. *Social Science Research* 8: 184–99.

Stanford Achievement Tests. 1964. *High School Reading Test, Form W*. New York: Harcourt.

———. 1965. *Advanced Arithmetic Tests, Form X*. New York: Harcourt.

Stedman, Lawrence C., and Marshall S. Smith. 1983. Recent Reform Proposals for American Education. In Dougherty and Hammack 1990a.

Steinberg, Stephen. 1974. *The Academic Melting Pot*. New York: McGraw-Hill.

Strober, Myra. 1984. Toward a General Theory of Occupational Sex Segregation: The Case of Public School Teaching. In *Sex Segregation in the Workplace*, ed. Barbara F. Reskin. Washington, D.C.: National Academy Press.

Strumpel, Burkhard. 1971. Higher Education and Economic Behavior. In *A Degree and What Else?* ed. Stephen B. Withey. New York: McGraw-Hill.

Swartz, David. 1990. Pierre Bourdieu. In Dougherty and Hammack 1990a.

Swidler, Ann. 1986. Culture in Action: Symbols and Strategies. *American Sociological Review* 51: 273–86.

Thomas, Gail E. 1981. Student and Institutional Characteristics as Determinants of the Prompt and Subsequent Four-Year College Graduation of Race and Sex Groups. *Sociological Quarterly* 22: 327–45.

——. 1987. Black Students in U.S. Graduate and Professional Schools in the 1980s: A National and Institutional Assessment. *Harvard Educational Review* 57: 261–82.

Traub, James. 1994. *City on a Hill: Testing the American Dream at City College.* Reading, Mass.: Addison-Wesley.

Treiman, Donald. 1970. Industrialization and Social Stratification. *Sociological Inquiry* 40: 207–34.

University Commission on Admissions. 1969. *Report and Recommendations to the Board of Higher Education.* New York: Board of Higher Education.

U.S. Bureau of the Census. 1975. *Historical Statistics of the United States, Colonial Times to 1970.* Part 1. Washington, D.C.: U.S. Government Printing Office.

——. 1983a. *Statistical Abstract of the United States, 1984.* Washington, D.C.: U.S. Government Printing Office.

——. 1983b. *1980 Census of Population: Detailed Population Characteristics, New York.* Washington, D.C.: U.S. Government Printing Office.

——. 1984a. *1980 Census of the Population.* Vol. 1, chapter D. Washington, D.C.: U.S. Government Printing Office.

——. 1984b. *1980 Census of Population: Detailed Population Characteristics, U.S. Summary.* Washington, D.C.: U.S. Government Printing Office.

——. 1985. Marital Status and Living Arrangements, March 1984. *Current Population Reports.* Series P-20, no. 399. Washington, D.C.: U.S. Government Printing Office.

——. 1986. *Statistical Abstract of the United States, 1987.* Washington, D.C.: U.S. Government Printing Office.

——. 1987a. *Statistical Abstract of the United States, 1988.* Washington, D.C.: U.S. Government Printing Office.

——. 1987b. Male-Female Differences in Work Experience, Occupation and Earnings, 1984. *Current Population Reports.* P-70, no. 10. Washington, D.C.: U.S. Government Printing Office.

——. 1991a. *Statistical Abstract of the United States, 1991.* 11th ed. Washington, D.C.: U.S. Government Printing Office.

——. 1991b. Marital Status and Living Arrangements, March 1990. *Current Population Reports.* Series P-20, no. 450. Washington, D.C.: U.S. Government Printing Office.

——. 1992. *Statistical Abstract of the United States, 1992.* Washington, D.C.: U.S. Government Printing Office.

U.S. Department of Education. 1990. *The Condition of Education, 1990.* Vol. 2, *Postsecondary Education.* Washington, D.C.: National Center for Education Statistics.

U.S. Department of Labor. 1977. Dictionary of Occupational Titles. 4th ed. Machine readable data file available from Inter-University Consortium for Political and Social Research, University of Michigan, Ann Arbor.

——. 1988. *The New York Transformation: Dimensions of the Knowledge Economy.* New York: Bureau of Labor Statistics.

Useem, Michael, and Jerome Karabel. 1986. Pathways to Top Corporate Management. *American Sociological Review* 51: 184–200.

Velez, William. 1985. Finishing College: The Effects of College Type. *Sociology of Education* 58: 191–200.

Vesey, Lawrence. 1965. *The Emergence of the American University.* Chicago: University of Chicago Press.

Waldinger, Roger. 1986–87. Changing Ladders and Musical Chairs: Ethnicity and Opportunity in Post-Industrial New York. *Politics and Society* 4: 369–401.

Wechsler, Harold S. 1977. *The Qualified Student: A History of Selective College Admissions in America.* New York: Wiley.

Weiss, Robert S. 1984. The Impact of Marital Dissolution on Income and Consumption in Single-Parent Households. *Journal of Marriage and the Family* 46: 115–27.

Wilson, William J. 1980. *The Declining Significance of Race: Blacks and Changing American Institutions.* 2d ed. Chicago: University of Chicago Press.

——. 1987. *The Truly Disadvantaged: The Inner City, the Underclass and Public Policy.* Chicago: University of Chicago Press.

Wright, Erik Olin, and Donmoon Cho. 1992. The Relative Permeability of Class Boundaries to Cross-Class Friendships. *American Sociological Review* 57: 85–102.

Zuboff, Shoshana. 1988. *In the Age of the Smart Machine: The Future of Work and Power.* New York: Basic.

INDEX

NOTE: Page numbers in italics refer to tables.

Admission standards: California, 15, 16, 196; class rank, 9, 15, 250; community colleges, 14–15, 33; for CUNY generally, 6–7; national policy shifts, 2; remedial courses, 6–7, 15, 212, 230; senior colleges, 14–16, 21, 33, 210, 217–19, 230, 235, 242. *See also* Open-admissions policy; Quality, educational

Age, student: degree attainment and, 233; distribution, *38,* 40–41, *220;* postgraduate education and, 63; time to degree and, 56, 63. *See also* Time to degree

Agnew, Spiro, 17

Asian-Americans, 18n

Aspiration, educational, *39,* 43–44, 49 and n, 54, *221,* 223. *See also* Intentions for college

Associate's degree (A.A.): attainment levels, 45, 48–49, *49–50,* 55, *66, 68;* career development and, 135; children and, 168–70, *169, 171;* civic interest and, *181;* cohort comparisons, 231–32, *232, 237;* earnings and, *127–28,* 133; economic value of, 89–90, *95,* 96–97, *99,* 100–102 and nn, *105,* 106; job authority, *149,* 150, 152; majors, 104, *105,* 106; marriage and income, 165, 166; occupational status and, *127–28,* 130, 132, 133, 168n; reinforcement of inequalities, 120; student intentions, *39,* 44, *221;* time to degree, *237;* vocational curricula, 222; work complexity and, 143, *144,* 145. *See also* Attainment, educational; Community colleges, CUNY

Attainment, educational: academic standards and, 205; age and, 233; career development and, 119, *127–28,* 129–33, 134–37; civic interest, 180–83, *181;* cohort comparisons, 231–35 and nn, *232, 267–68;* cognitive skills and, 185–86; earnings and, *87,* 89–

90, 96, 102, *127;* ethnicity and, 45–48, *46,* 51, 64–65, *66,* 90, *169, 171,* 170, *232,* 232; gender and, 54, 64; health and, 188; high school preparation and, 65–66, 233; homogamy, 163, 165–67, 170n; job authority and, *149,* 149–50, 151, 152, 153; level of entry and, 235; occupational status and, *86,* 89–90, 102, *127–28,* 168n; open-admissions students, 45–46, 51, 55, 64–67, *68–69,* 70; policy effects, 3, 46, 63–64, 67, 70; postgraduate, 61–64, *66, 69;* some college, *127–28. See also* Associate's degree; Bachelor's degree; Master's degree; Postgraduate education

Attitude and values, 165

Authority, job: defined, 139, 148 and n, *264;* educational attainment and, *149,* 149–50, 151, 152, 153; ethnic differences, 148–49, *149,* 151, 152–53; gender differences, *149,* 149–53; private vs. public sector, 141, 150–53, *265–66. See also* White-collar employment

Bachelor's degree (B.A.): attainment levels, 45–48 and n, *46,* 51, 52–55, *53, 66,* 67, *69,* 231–35, *232;* career development and, 119, *127–28,* 129–33, 134–37; children of, 168–70, *169, 171;* civic interest and, *181;* cohort comparisons, 214n, 222 and n, 231–35, *232, 237;* community college and, 30–31, 51, 52–53, *53,* 54–55, 231–35, *232;* cultural participation, 183, *184,* 185; defined, 30n; earnings and, 73, 89–90, *95,* 96, 97, *99,* 100, *105, 127–28,* 129, 130, 132–33, 134; earnings forgone, 56; factors influencing attainment, 31, 35–36, 51n, 52, 53–55, 59, 232–33, *255, 267–68;* importance for open admissions,